HR HOW-TO

Workplace Safety

Everything you need to know to ensure a safe and healthy workplace ...

by Lisa A. Milam-Perez, J.D.

CCHKnowledgePoint®

Essential HR Solutions

D0939456

Publisher: Catherine Wolfe
Editorial Director: Jeanne Statts
Portfolio Managing Editor: Mike Bacidore
Contributing Editors: Jan Gerstein, J.D.
                       Joy Waltemath, J.D.
Production Coordinator: Rebekah J. Bonnell
Cover Design: Craig Arritola, Laila Gaidulis
Interior Design: Laila Gaidulis
Layout: Publications Design

This publication is designed to provide accurate and authoritative information in regard to the subject matter covered. It is sold with the understanding that the publisher is not engaged in rendering legal, accounting, or other professional service. If legal advice or other expert assistance is required, the services of a competent professional person should be sought.

ISBN 0-8080-0942-7
©2003 **CCH** Incorporated
4025 W. Peterson Ave.
Chicago, IL 60646-6085
1 800 248 3248
hr.cch.com

Acknowledgements

I want to acknowledge several of my coworkers for their contributions and support: Jan Gerstein, my Managing Editor, gave me this opportunity and graciously freed up my time so I could devote my efforts to writing it, while my colleagues David Stephanides and Ron Miller willingly covered for me. Jan also edited several chapters and offered guidance along the way. Joy Waltemath was a masterful editor and indexer, and provided enthusiastic feedback at every turn.

Laila Gaidulis turned lifeless pages into visual art, and exercised extraordinary patience while doing so. Craig Arritola's striking cover design wrapped the book in brilliant color. Rebekah Bonnell spotted and fixed my errors throughout the production process.

Steve Avadek, our resident OSHA expert, told me to call upon him as needed—and generously shared his expertise when I did. Zrinka Allen, CCH's Manager of Employee Relations, gave hours of her time offering professional insights and HR war stories.

I also want to thank my husband Sam (my old-school grammarian) and son Antonio, and to express my gratitude to Mom and Dad, as well as Bito and Bita, for their support. And to Simone, who lives on in my heart.

Lisa Milam-Perez
February, 2003

Contents

Introduction to workplace safety

Julia was excited to be starting her first day at work at your company, a large insurance agency. During orientation, she pored over the paperwork with enthusiasm, until she got to the new employee training schedule. She looked confused as she glanced at the required session on Employee Safety. "Why do we need to take a safety course?," she demanded to know. "We're not doing factory work."

Not just hard hats

To many employees, "workplace safety" evokes images of assembly lines, hard hats and safety goggles, chemical hazards and spills. And back in the days of the "personnel office," HR directors defined safety management solely as controlling workers' compensation costs. Of course, all of these are a part of workplace safety. But "safety" also has come to mean much more in today's workplace.

Increasing employer liability, research in ergonomics, and the shock and devastation of 9/11 have compelled HR professionals to think in broader terms about how to keep employees safe and secure while they are at work. And as the human resources department expands its role as a strategic partner in your organization, you're no doubt thinking more about how safety issues impact productivity and the bottom line. Safety issues affect every employer, and an unsafe workplace can jeopardize the health of your employees and your organization.

Workplace safety and the law

An employee sued his employer after he was injured when a hatchet fell on him. The hatchet had been hanging on a rack that stood next to his workspace. When the rack was installed about a year earlier, the long-term employee expressed his concern about its safety, telling his employer that the pegs on the new rack were easily loosened and that it wasn't safe. When he complained, he was told that he could quit if it concerned him, but he would have to use the rack or leave.

The court was unsympathetic to the employee's plight. By the employee's own admission, it said, "He appreciated the danger more than anyone, but he stayed and took the risk." The employee willingly assumed the risk of having a hatchet fall on him, the court decided, so he could not recover for his injury.

(Lamson vs. American Axe and Tool Company).

That case was decided by the Supreme Judicial Court of Massachusetts on October 2, 1900. You probably don't need to be told that the law has changed a great deal since this unfortunate employee suffered his fate. Courts gradually shifted away from the view that workers assumed the risk of any dangers that befell them on the job. And with the passage of the Occupational Safety and Health Act (OSHA) in 1970 and the emergence of workers' compensation systems in the states, government formally recognized that employers owed a legal duty to ensure the safety of their employees in the workplace.

Before OSHA, workplace injuries and illnesses happened far more often in the United States. The reduction in injuries that followed was partly a result of the shift from a manufacturing, heavy-lifting economy to the service oriented, light-duty workplace of today. But federal enforcement of safety standards was a significant factor as well. (Sure, many states had occupational safety laws, but depending on the state, these were poorly or selectively enforced.) OSHA focused attention on the safety of the American workforce and made sure employers did so, too.

Of course, the most enlightened organizations already knew the value of their workforce and took great pains to ensure employee safety and security. They understood the connection between their people and their profit margin. After OSHA, though, workplace safety was not merely a "best practice," it became a compliance issue for all employers.

If OSHA applies to you (and it almost certainly does), then under the law, your organization has "a general duty to provide a workplace that is free from 'recognized hazards' that are likely to cause death or severe physical harm." This is OSHA's "general duty clause," and it applies to all covered workplaces.

OSHA administers more specific safety standards in particular work environments, since some worksites or jobs are inherently more hazardous than others.

As mentioned, most states have their own occupational safety laws that employers also must follow. You'll need to comply with both the federal and state safety standards applicable to your workplace. If a state's regulations impose higher standards than OSHA's provisions, your organization will be expected to comply with the more stringent requirements. Don't assume OSHA compliance is enough!

Workplace safety concerns differ in each organization, depending on such factors as company size and location, but safety needs will be determined most by the nature of the work performed or service provided. For example, a manufacturing industry, warehouse, or construction site can pose risks not faced by employees in an office setting. Organizations that serve the public such as hospitals, universities, and even retail stores have enhanced security concerns.

When assessing your own organization's particular vulnerabilities, also consider various segments of your workforce that might pose different safety challenges. For example, do you have a large sales force that spends a great deal of time on the road, away from home? This raises unique safety issues as well.

The politics of workplace safety

Business and organized labor continually battle it out in Washington—and within state legislatures too—over issues affecting the safety of workers. As industry strives to reduce its regulatory burden and unions seek to impose safety standards to protect their members, individual employers are left trying to keep score and to stay compliant with changing legal requirements.

The battle will rage on. In the meantime, whether safety standards are voluntary or compulsory, you still want to keep your employees safe, and to adopt cost-effective measures that reduce the potential for employee injury.

Consider the many highly emotional issues of the day that touch on workplace safety: the gun control debate, tort reform initiatives, and of course, the ramifications of the terrorist attacks of 9/11 not only on a global scale, but right at the office. However these issues may play out in the political spectrum, they will impact how you address workplace violence, liability for workplace injuries, and emergency preparedness. You can't afford to wait and see how the political winds will turn, though. You'll want to adopt the best practices available now, and ensure compliance later with whatever laws and regulations emerge from the rubble.

Your employees' most basic need

Did you take a college social science course? No doubt you encountered a theory about the "hierarchy of human needs." It says that people have various human needs that must be met to attain optimal happiness and well-being, and that these needs must be satisfied in order of basic importance. For starters, people must have physical safety and security. It's the most essential human desire.

This theory holds true at work too, as numerous surveys have confirmed. Aon Consulting's Loyalty Institute, in partnership with the American Society for Healthcare Human Resources Administration (ASHHRA), undertook a study on retention. It focused in particular on the "workforce needs" that impact employee decisions whether to leave or stay put.

Aon developed a "Performance Pyramid" to illustrate its findings on what those needs were. After reviewing more than 60,000 responses, "safety and security" was found to be the most foundational need, the base of the pyramid. That is, employees' safety and security needs must be met first, the study concluded, before moving up the pyramid to higher-level needs like compensation or self-actualization. (Source: "In Our Hands: How Hospital Leaders Can Build A Thriving Workforce," AHA Commission on Workforce for Hospitals and Health Systems, April 2002).

Employees want to be fairly compensated and to do meaningful work. But more importantly, they want to feel safe and secure at their jobs. In the Aon study, safety and security were framed as a larger concept that encompassed basic job security, and the psychological comfort of knowing you could go to work without facing fear, intimidation, or threatening behavior. Painted in these broader strokes, it's clear that issues such as harassment, while less obviously related to safety and security, must be factored into your organization's workplace safety philosophy and strategies.

How well your organization can satisfy your employees' most basic need will directly impact retention rates, productivity, and consequently, your bottom line.

How to keep employees safe? Consider the many ways to enhance employees' sense of security while at work:

♦ Careful recruiting and background checks

♦ Aggressive safety training

♦ Strict adherence to workplace security policies and procedures

♦ An understanding of the factors that undermine the ability of employees to work safely

♦ A safety check of your workplace that identifies potential hazards, and the resources and authority to eliminate them

♦ A well-designed emergency preparedness plan

♦ Well-lit, well-ordered, and ergonomically designed workspaces

♦ Sanitary bathrooms, cafeterias, and breakrooms

♦ Work-life benefits that ease employee stress

♦ Wellness programs and other healthcare benefits that enhance employee well-being

♦ A culture that values and rewards safety

Workplace safety challenges come in various shapes and sizes, but this means there are many different opportunities to enhance employee security and well being. Inroads can be made through many avenues: benefits, policies and procedures, and attention to your organization's physical environment. Within your organization, consider which functional units are best situated to seize these safety opportunities.

Who plays a role in workplace safety?

In short: every member of your organization. When safety is a mission-critical goal, employees will come to understand the integral role they each play in keeping themselves and their coworkers safe, secure, and healthy.

DON'T miss this

A safety mind-frame should be nurtured during new employee orientation, reinforced in your employee handbook, and given continued voice in communications from the top brass.

But who is most directly involved in safety? How are the various safety roles allocated? For certain employees, like your organization's safety manager and security professionals, safety *is* their job.

Other employees such as your facilities office and maintenance staff play a heightened role by virtue of how critical their efforts are to a healthy workplace. And HR professionals have an enhanced safety role to play as well.

- ◆ **Executive office.** You can't make safety an integral part of the organization without the direct involvement of upper management. These are the individuals who can convey the importance of safety to the larger mission, who can shape a culture that acknowledges and rewards safe practices, and who control the resources necessary to implement health and safety measures.

- ◆ **Safety professional.** Does your organization have a safety officer? When you consider the many factors affecting health and safety in the workplace, it's quite a big job. The safety professional sets policies for controlling workplace hazards and reporting accidents, implements security measures, and devises evacuation procedures, among other big-picture duties. But safety is in the details, too. For example, the law requires that worksites maintain equipment and tools like fire extinguishers and alarms in case something goes wrong. It also requires employers to keep basic first aid necessities at the worksite and to provide reasonably close access to medical assistance. Does your safety officer claim ownership of these functions? If not, who does?

- ◆ **Security officers.** Sometimes security can be a thankless job. When things are humming along safely, employees and visitors can be put off by the minor inconvenience of adhering to even minimal security procedures. And your security staff is called upon to act with eternal vigilance in the face of it. But when there's trouble, they're on the spot in an instant, putting themselves on the line for the safety of your employees and the organization. Do you reward them accordingly? Are your guards employees of your company or of an outside agency? Consider the safety ramifications of the answers to these questions.

- ◆ **Facilities maintenance.** Honor thy maintenance staff! OSHA imposes basic requirements that all employers must follow when it comes to keeping the workplace safe and clean. Sometimes we take these functions for granted, but probably only when they're being done right. Though unheralded they may be, the law *requires* that these duties be carried out to ensure basic workplace comfort.

Clean and numerous restrooms, sanitary waste receptacles, ample drinking water—all of these impact employee health and safety. Federal law dictates that employees are also expected to enjoy the benefits of ample lighting, freedom from excess noise, a comfortable temperature, and clean air. These standards are meant to make sure that all employees are working in conditions that maximize comfort and well being. On a daily basis, your building maintenance staff and cleaning crew have the most profound impact on employee health and safety.

◆ **Safety committee.** A safety committee can be composed of leaders from the various units with safety functions, or whose operations raise particular safety concerns. Many organizations include workers below the management level as well, and for good reason.

A safety committee with representatives from throughout the ranks goes a long way toward educating all employees about workplace safety and achieving buy-in across the organization. It's also the best way to include the experts in identifying safety needs and setting appropriate policies: those who work each day on the front lines. What's more, here's where employees can play a tangible policy role and participate in employee governance.

Also, the safety committee is one arena where unions and management can work cooperatively, not as adversaries, in striving for shared safety goals. A safety committee advances your health and safety goals and builds positive employee relations at the same time.

◆ **Human resources.** Because workplace safety is so interrelated to recruitment, productivity, employee wellness, and other human resources concerns, HR professionals must develop a thorough understanding of workplace safety issues. In addition, particularly in smaller companies, HR may take on the safety officer role. So many human resources functions touch upon safety, it's clear that HR's operations are safety-mission critical.

HR's critical role

HR professionals play an invaluable role in meeting employees' safety needs. Health and safety are not just the province of security and building offices. That's because safety is more than just a physical plant issue. Human resources must implement safety training, set policies and procedures, and forge strategic initiatives to maximize the health of an organization and its employees.

Think about the many ways HR contributes. Here are just some of the human resources functions that impact workplace safety:

◆ **Recruiting.** Careful selection and screening of applicants to ensure that an employee isn't hired who has a troubled past and potentially dangerous future.

◆ **Retention.** Longevity increases safety in the workplace. Studies show that veteran employees are the safest workers, and are less likely to have workplace accidents. And the converse is true, too —employees are more likely to stick around if they feel safe and secure.

◆ **Training.** Orienting new employees to the safety goals and mindset of your organization is a key element of gaining buy-in and thus building a safer workplace.

◆ **Termination.** An HR professional's expertise in handling delicate discharge situations helps alleviate potential conflicts or violence.

◆ **Benefits.** Designing a benefits package that offers innovative wellness programs and services, work-life policies that alleviate employee stress, and rewards and incentives for safe work and healthy personal habits enhance employee well being and reduce accidents as well.

◆ **Expert knowledge.** You know your employees, their needs, and their work habits. This expertise is a critical resource in shaping safety policies. You also have the strongest grasp on workplace policies and practices. Do you offer flextime? Do you have second-shift workers? You can see, for example, the importance of ensuring your parking lot is well lit and that the outside lighting system maximizes the safety of your night owls.

◆ **Culture.** Save for perhaps the executive team, no other unit shapes the culture of your organization more than human resources. The way you communicate the importance of workplace safety as a mission-critical goal can make or break your employees' sense of ownership and responsibility for a safe, secure workplace. Workplace safety requires a well-devised strategy and a strong commitment across the organization. As an HR professional, you're uniquely situated to make those things happen.

◆ **Orientation.** Remember Julia, your new employee? You'll be the first to orient her, right there on her first day of work, into the safety culture so highly valued within your organization.

✔ ✔ Checklist

Reality check: Do you have a safety culture?

"Safety first." Is that the motto in your organization? Ask yourself the following yes or no questions posed by OSHA to gauge whether your workplace has a health and safety culture:

1. Safety and health are an integral part of our operations.
   ☐ YES ☐ NO ☐ DON'T KNOW

2. Teamwork is apparent in all parts of the organization.
   ☐ YES ☐ NO ☐ DON'T KNOW

3. Managers and supervisors are out on the floor frequently and always observe the company safety and health rules.
   ☐ YES ☐ NO ☐ DON'T KNOW

4. Employees are encouraged to identify safety and health hazards and correct them on their own.
   ☐ YES ☐ NO ☐ DON'T KNOW

5. Employees have full and open access to all the tools and equipment they need to do their job safely.
   ☐ YES ☐ NO ☐ DON'T KNOW

Did you answer "Yes" to these questions? Congratulations; your organization is well on its way. If there were some "no's," there's room for improvement. Time to put on the hard hat and get to work!

Accidents will happen

There's no way around it; your organization will encounter a workplace accident or incident despite the best-laid security plans and safety procedures. As an HR professional you'll play a crucial role in minimizing the effects on the employees involved, their coworkers, and the organization itself. Your grace under pressure will be invaluable—and it won't go unnoticed.

Dealing with the aftermath of an accident, altercation, or other workplace incident will require you to draw upon both the hard and soft skills you've honed as an HR professional. Depending on what actually happened, there will be recordkeeping requirements. Your workers' compensation expertise may come into play. If employee negligence or sabotage was a contributing factor, you'll need to impose discipline with particular care and effectiveness.

Just as importantly, your employees will look to you to restore some semblance of normalcy after an incident takes place. You'll be soothing jangled nerves through one-on-one counseling and reminding workers of the EAP or other work-life benefits that were wisely included in the benefits package. You might be giving line managers a refresher course in performance management to get productivity back on track.

Safety and HR strategy

Workplace safety and OSHA are important factors in many business decisions, from buying a new business or building a new plant to drafting the smallest details of employee work rules. Workplace injuries and illnesses cost U.S. employers billions of dollars each year. Liberty Mutual Insurance, which devises safety programs for businesses, estimates that injuries and disabilities can account for 5% of an organization's costs. Employee days off due to disability, workers' compensation claims, operating time lost due to accidents—all of these impact operational costs in measurable ways.

But here's the good news: according to OSHA, employers can reap solid financial benefits from implementing an effective safety and health program. A safety program designed by human resources with clear metrics that reflect its payoff has the added benefit of displaying the critical role HR can play as a profit center within the organization.

DON'T miss this

"$AFETY PAYS" is an interactive software program designed by OSHA to help organizations measure the impact of occupational injuries and illness on their profitability. The program projects the amount of sales a company would need to generate to cover the average costs of an injury or illness, using an organization's profit margin and an indirect cost multiplier. The program also compiles a report on the findings. Download this tool from the agency's website, www.dol.gov. You'll find it in the "Safety & Health Management Systems" etools section.

Human resources fulfills its larger strategic role as it carries out its safety-related functions. In addition to the goal of keeping your employees safe, attention to safety issues is an important part of controlling operating costs. A well-designed safety program can show a marked improvement in the bottom line and enhance the value of human resources within the organization.

The Quiz

1. Human resources has an important role to play in shaping a workplace culture of safety. ❑ True   ❑ False

2. OSHA regulations apply only to manufacturing plants and construction sites, not service-based employers. ❑ True   ❑ False

3. Requiring employees to get involved with safety issues will just distract them from their work and productivity will suffer. ❑ True   ❑ False

4. Workplace safety is one of your employees' most basic employment needs. ❑ True   ❑ False

5. Employers can reap financial benefits by investing in safety. ❑ True   ❑ False

Answer key: 1 T, 2 F, 3 F, 4 T, 5 T

Recruiting for safety

> *Raul, a recruiter, hired three customer service reps and got them on board just in time for them to attend the next training session. He'd been pressured to get these positions filled, and was confident that Kim, the hiring manager, made the right choices. Then Jason, one of the reps, was a no-show on the first day of training. His new colleagues were understandably concerned, Raul and Kim were puzzled as well. Where could he be? Finally, Kim got a phone call: Jason had been arrested on an outstanding warrant for violating an order of protection. His estranged wife had blown everything out of proportion, Jason insisted. This left Raul and Kim fairly skeptical about Jason's judgment—not to mention concerned about his potential for violence. It also left Raul wondering what he should have done differently.*

Recruiting with safety in mind

Think about the way your recruiting practices can further the goal of workplace safety. No doubt you've considered whether to implement pre-hire background checks given growing concerns over violence in the workplace. But you shouldn't stop there. In auditing your recruiting policies with the goal of workplace safety in mind, consider the following:

- ◆ **Applicant experience.** Can you afford to hire entry-level workers, given the safety demands of the job, or do you need experienced professionals? Do your training resources (or lack thereof) decide for you?

- ◆ **Recruiting sources.** Job seekers find work through networking and personal connections more frequently than newspaper job ads or online services. There's probably a good reason for that, from the employer's perspective: the individual is a known commodity. Recruiting someone you know is good for business for many reasons—not the least of which is workplace safety.

  What about other recruiting options? When you're recruiting for a particular skilled trade and need to ensure that your applicants have specific safety qualifications and certification, the best source can be the trade school or training program that provides the education and certification that a qualified candidate needs. Even if you're not looking to hire "fresh out," these organizations might be able to recommend more experienced alumni. If you regularly hire workers for this position, a strong rapport with the school's placement professionals can be invaluable.

- ◆ **Diversity.** Some organizations use employee referral programs to recruit job applicants. This can be a useful tool to promote safety. While striving to hire employees that someone can vouch for, though, make sure that you're not undermining your diversity goals. Is your workforce composed predominantly of white males? People tend to fraternize with—and refer—people like themselves. So if your workplace isn't already sufficiently diverse, then an employee referral program might have discriminatory results.

- ◆ **Respect.** Treat every applicant with courtesy and respect. Rejected applicants who felt mistreated during the consideration process are more likely to provoke conflict. What's more, you're modeling for those applicants you *do* hire that your organization insists its people treat each other with dignity.

◆ **Employer of choice.** As a recruiter, you are the human face of your organization to outside job applicants. You have a unique opportunity to shape the image of an employer that takes its employees' safety and well being seriously. Now think about how that image can enhance your recruiting efforts!

Let's look in greater detail at some of the strategies you use to help guide your organization's hiring decisions. We'll observe them with an eye to workplace safety in particular. A combination of your seasoned recruiting skills and these selection tools can help to identify and avoid problem employees—unsafe ones.

Job descriptions

Well-crafted job descriptions are a crucial element of a recruiting strategy geared to safety. Joseph A. Kleinkort of WorkSTEPS, Inc, speaking at the SHRM 54th Annual Conference and Exposition in Philadelphia says that 10 percent of the workforce is incapable of performing the essential functions of their jobs, leading to 75 percent of all injured workers. That's why a functional job analysis and accurate and thorough job descriptions are so critical.

Most job descriptions identify the skills and experience needed to perform in a position competently, and list the major duties and responsibilities the job entails. But standard job descriptions often overlook the important safety component. What credentials are required to do the job *safely*? What are the conditions in which an applicant will be working if hired? To integrate safety goals into job specifications, here's what they should include:

◆ A description of the knowledge and competencies required to safely perform essential functions;

◆ Identification of any duties that relate specifically to safety, such as housekeeping, security checks, or lockout/tagout;

◆ Analysis of the physical demands of the position, such as heavy lifting, etc.;

◆ A list of any dangerous machinery that the employee must use;

◆ Information about the existence of specific hazards involved, such as high levels of electricity;

◆ An overview of the work environment, including particular conditions such as excessive noise or temperature extremes.

Including this information enables job applicants to better understand the requirements of the position and helps the hiring manager select the best candidate based on these important, itemized criteria.

WHAT you need to know

Job conditions of "white collar" positions should also be considered. Don't make the false assumption that office-based employees are never subjected to adverse working conditions. Office noise and factors like a poorly designed work area should also be conveyed to applicants (if they can't be eliminated altogether).

Consent and release

Maybe you already require job applicants to complete an employment application in addition to the resume they provide. Great! It's an ideal way of getting the candidate's information in the format *you* need. And you can also use the form to secure a signature from the applicant that acknowledges:

◆ The information the applicant provided is truthful and accurate.

◆ The applicant understands that inaccurate or incomplete information will eliminate him or her from consideration.

◆ If the applicant receives an offer of employment, the discovery of falsified information on the employee's application can result in immediate discharge at any time.

◆ You will carefully verify the information the applicant provided (or *failed* to provide).

◆ You will check employment references and other sources.

◆ The applicant consents to your checking these references.

◆ The applicant waives liability for information released or obtained as a result of such inquiries.

DON'T miss this

RED FLAG: *Resume trouble spots: an employment application or resume that includes gaps in years of employment experience. It could simply mean an unfortunate break in employment. Or it could mean a prior prison stay! You won't know until you check further.*

Show potential hires that you take the accuracy of resumes and job applications seriously. They will be less likely to falsify or withhold information.

Worst case scenario

Problem: Verifying an applicant's driving record.

Terrell, a recruiter for a courier company, required applicants for driver's jobs to list all traffic convictions from the past five years. The company's job application form stated, in small print, that "Information furnished by applicants is subject to verification." Still, he found that applicants would often omit some or all of their citations or convictions.

Verifying traffic convictions took a long time, especially for applicants who had lived previously in other states. On a few occasions, Terrell hired applicants based on clean records from police departments where the applicants admitted they lived; but later, he uncovered information on convictions elsewhere that the applicant had omitted. The organization had to discharge one employee after discovering a particularly serious driving conviction in his past.

Solution. Terrell changed the application form and the interview protocol. He highlighted the warning statement on the application, posting it in larger print, and revising it to read:

"All the information you furnish on this form will be checked (except that present employers will not be contacted if you specifically request it). Driving records will be thoroughly investigated with local and state police departments. Other conviction information will also be verified and considered in evaluating your application, if it is related to the job for which you are applying. Your failure to include important information may bar you from employment."

Terrell went one step further: he told his interviewers to relay the message verbally to applicants as well. And he outlined the following steps:

◆ Tell applicants that false information could bar them from getting hired.

◆ Tell applicants that false information, if uncovered after they are employed, can be a basis for termination.

◆ Invite applicants to review their application to be sure they didn't omit information.

After implementing this solution, Terrell found that the applications he received had far fewer errors, inaccuracies, and omissions. It sped up the hiring process, reduced aggravation, and eliminated unpleasant surprises.

Interviewing

Interviewing serves numerous functions, as you know. With respect to workplace safety, an interview can screen out potential problem employees or those lacking the safety qualifications and experience you need. But the employment interview also sets the tone for incoming employees that you choose to hire. It's here that attitudes towards job safety and work-related injuries can first be shaped. Tell them at the interview how important safety is in your organization. When you outline those safety expectations during the interview, applicants will know what will be expected of them and have a chance to opt out *now* if they are unwilling to comply.

WHAT you need to know

Coach your line managers, when interviewing job applicants, to never tell candidates that they'll have "a job for life here," or words to that effect. It can set your organization up for a lifelong employment contract. And from a safety point of view, it can enrage an employee, whose expectations were dashed by rejection or a discharge down the line, causing a potentially volatile response.

Questioning the applicant

As you assess an applicant's qualifications during an interview, you're also looking for signs that indicate certain characteristics or behaviors that are deemed positive in the workplace—and looking out for indicators of less desirable traits. Which of those behaviors also demonstrate a potentially "safe" employee? What questions do you use to identify "unsafe" employees? Here are some important character traits, as well as queries to spot behaviors that may suggest a propensity for violence:

Tolerance for stress:

- ◆ "What were the most intense work-related pressure situations you have been under in recent years? Tell me about some of them. How did you deal with them?"
- ◆ "When was the last time something at work made you angry? What were the circumstances? What was the outcome?"

Teamwork:

- ◆ "We've all had to work with someone who is very difficult to get along with. Give me some examples of when this happened to you."
- ◆ "Why was that person difficult? How did you handle that person?"
- ◆ "How important is it to build strong relationships with coworkers?"

Communication:

- ◆ "We've all had occasion when we misinterpreted something someone told us. Give me an example of when this happened to you and why you think it happened."
- ◆ "Tell me about an instance in which you said something at work that you wish you could have taken back."

Be aware that the applicant might provide information you don't want to hear. For example, the job candidate might respond that he reported his former employer to the EEOC for discrimination. Then you might end up sitting across from a potential retaliation claim!

DON'T miss this

You probably learned quickly when performing recruiting functions that direct questions seldom elicit useful information. Consider the question: *"Have you ever behaved in a violent manner while on the job?"* It's pretty unlikely that an applicant will say "yes" and then proceed to explain his or her conduct in detail. Indirect questions always work best: *"When you had a problem with your previous employer, how did you handle it?"*

So you've asked the questions aimed to spot an applicant with potentially violent tendencies. But what about the employee who is an accident waiting to happen? Remember that these individuals can be just as dangerous—especially when they are applying for jobs that are particularly hazardous or safety-sensitive. Some hazardous work tasks require excruciating attention to detail if they are to be done safely, for example. You'll want to be extra certain that a potential employee will take the necessary care to carry out functions safely. It's also important to ensure the candidate has the technical knowledge to perform tasks in accordance with safe procedures.

Gauge the enthusiasm and detail with which the applicant responds to the following:

Safety experience:
◆ "Did your former employer have a safety program in place?"
◆ "Have you received training in accident avoidance or safe practices?"

Careful work habits:
◆ "We've all had occasions when we were working on something that just 'slipped through the cracks.' Can you give me some examples of when this happened to you? Why did it happen? What was the result?"
◆ "Describe your system for controlling errors in your work."

Job-specific questions:
◆ "Where did you receive your hazardous materials training?"
◆ "Do you have your forklift certification?"

WHAT you need to know

Beware! Avoid asking questions about the applicant's workers' compensation history; it's unlawful to discriminate against an applicant who has a claim in his or her record. While you can't ask for this information at the interview stage, it is permissible to review an applicant's workers' compensation history *after* extending a job offer.

Interviewing and ADA compliance. Remember, the Americans with Disabilities Act (ADA) prohibits you from asking about an applicant's medical condition, or requesting a medical exam, until you make an offer to the candidate. After you've extended a job offer, though, you can ask questions about the candidate's health and request that a medical test be taken to confirm that the applicant would be able to perform the functions of the job for which he is being hired.

This is particularly important for jobs that may require heavy lifting or other physical skills that, if lacking, could endanger the employee as well as his or her coworkers.

Keep in mind, though, that you can't single out a particular job applicant for a medical exam merely because you suspect that the applicant has a disability. All new hires in that same position must also be required to take the exam.

Obtaining a release

We talked about the importance of telling candidates you'll be checking their background and seeking a release for this purpose. Now is the time to do it. When they know what you'll be asking—and they've signed that waiver on the job application—they'll be more likely to let you in on unfavorable information themselves. This is especially true if you inform them that inconsistencies between what they tell you and what a former employer says can delay or even bar them from employment at your organization.

Even if the applicant already signed the release on the completed application before you conducted the interview, it's important to review what he or she has signed off on. Spend a few minutes acknowledging the applicant's signature and reminding him or her of what that signature means. Document this conversation in your interview notes.

Should you interview walk-ins? In some fields, it has always been standard practice to interview applicants who come in off the street. In others, the practice is a relatively new development. For example, in response to the crisis-level shortage of registered nurses across the industry, one hospital HR professional adopted the following policy: a qualified nurse does not walk through the door without getting an on-spot interview. Faced with such acute staffing issues, this is clearly a best practice for healthcare organizations. But it's important to recognize the safety implications of such a policy.

When considering whether to interview walk-in candidates, safety is a critical factor to weigh. Evaluate the following:

◆ What is your business need? Do your staffing issues require an open-door policy of this sort?

◆ Will you have ample time to prepare for an interview with just a few short moments to review a resume? Will you be ready to quickly identify red flags on the employment application, and to ask the candidate about them?

◆ Is your reception area secure enough and sufficiently staffed to accommodate walk-ins? Who will escort unexpected applicants from the building entrance to the human resources office and back?

◆ Are your security personnel located near your human resources office and available to be at arm's length during an interview, if necessary?

Verifying applicant information

In addition to using interview questions geared specifically toward gauging safety or violence concerns, other preemployment precautions can help you screen out potential problems at the recruiting stage. Reference and criminal background checks are the most common measures.

We verify applicant information to ensure that prospective hires actually hold the credentials they say they have. But there are additional safety reasons for such inquiries as well. Along with confirming work-related qualifications, HR professionals can check for evidence of behaviors or attitudes in an applicant's record that raise cause for alarm.

WHAT you need to know

Reference and background checking can have great potential for abuse. An applicant's right to privacy must be balanced against an employer's need to know. For this reason, both federal and state law may restrict the collection and/or use of certain types of information. Always comply with the applicable law in this area to avoid liability.

Why conduct reference and background checks on prospective hires?

◆ To verify that applicants really are who they say. (Identity theft is a growth industry, after all.)

◆ To verify that applicants haven't lied about their qualifications, training, or experience. Did the applicant really receive training in handling hazardous materials? Does your new driver have a valid commercial driver's license? Can you confirm the warehouse applicant's forklift certification?

◆ To learn about applicants' past work habits and whether they behaved safely and responsibly on the job. What was the applicant's safety record? How many accidents were they involved in? Did the employee wear required protective equipment? Did he or she engage in dangerous horseplay?

◆ To identify any indicators of a violent predisposition or past criminal activity. Did the job candidate have altercations with former coworkers? Was there any other antisocial behavior such as harassment? Is there an assault and battery conviction on the record?

◆ To deter applicants with unsavory backgrounds from seeking work at your organization.

◆ To reduce liability for negligent hiring.

RED FLAG: *If an applicant says he or she has been living in the area for a long time, but has no local references, you're right to be suspicious.*

Consider not hiring a candidate if there is insufficient verification of past work history and credentials.

Checking employment references

Do you check employment references? Some experts advise that it's the single most important step in recruiting and selection—if done well.

There's an old adage among journalists about the importance of verifying sources: "If your mother says she loves you, check it out." Their profession demands a high level of accuracy and certainty that the information they're receiving is legitimate. You should treat employment references with no less care.

Does a former employer say that an applicant is "careless" or "reckless"? If so, ask for factual examples. Did the employee refuse to wear safety gear? Neglect lockout-tagout requirements? Leave tools laying around that coworkers could trip on? Similarly, if an applicant is described as "a hothead," elicit more specifics about when and where this trait emerged. Don't settle for generalizations, even if they are positive ones. Then confirm your findings with a different source, such as another former employer. If the impressions you get from each source are dramatically different, probe further.

DON'T miss this

Just as you can't question applicants about workers' compensation filings, such queries are also off-limits for former employers. Don't inquire about workers' compensation claims until after a conditional offer of employment has been made. The same holds true for requesting a medical examination.

Getting former employers to respond

Past employers can alert you to whether an applicant has engaged in misconduct or reckless behavior while on the job. But you may run into resistance checking former references. You know that former employers are simply trying to avoid liability for providing information that might be damaging to the applicant. That's why a release signed by the applicant can encourage full and frank disclosure by former employers.

The following steps can help elicit more detailed information about job applicants from former employers:

◆ Put the request in writing.
◆ Include a copy of that release form the applicant signed.
◆ Limit requests for information to those subjects relevant to the employment decision.

If the employer still won't cooperate, be sure to carefully document your attempts to get information, as well as the employer's refusal to provide it. Include in your records the date and time of the call and the name of the person who refused to comply. This record will help show that you made a good-faith attempt to obtain these references.

Providing references

You know the difficulty of checking references when employers worry about disclosing information that can lead to defamation claims. You face the same concern. But you know how important workplace safety is and want to alert other employers if there is potential danger. Here's how to ensure that, when giving a reference, you can provide information without incurring liability because of a former employee:

◆ You may not have a legal duty to disclose prior violent or abusive acts by the former employee. But you cannot misrepresent the facts to his or her benefit, either. You may sympathize with a former employee's struggle with alcohol, for example, but you can't sugarcoat the unpredictable workplace behaviors that it caused.

◆ Stick to verifiable and objective facts. Remember, the truth is always a defense to a defamation claim. So tell a recruiter that "employee Smith punched his supervisor" instead of making a subjective statement like "employee Smith is violent."

◆ When you must discharge an employee, consider asking at that time for the employee's authorization to respond to reference requests. Most likely, the employee will not give you authorization. Then when potential employers call, you can tell them the truth: the employee refused to give authorization for a reference. That should tip off most recruiters.

Criminal background checks

Organizations are using background checks more frequently these days due to growing concerns about workplace violence. Many HR professionals adopt them with considerable discomfort, though. They can be burdensome, costly, and delay hiring. Some fear that it sets a bad tone for new employees. Others insist that their organization is progressive, and they are hesitant to intrude on employee privacy. Still others think it's just unfair to penalize potential employees into infinity for irresponsible or unlawful actions committed in the past.

These are all legitimate reservations. If you share them, however, consider whether you need to set them aside for the well being of your employees and your organization. This is especially true if you perform HR functions for an organization engaged in dangerous or security-sensitive services.

Coach your line supervisors that background checks are not their domain! It's easy these days for managers to go online and access all sorts of confidential information about a job prospect. It's almost certain they won't have obtained a release before doing so, though. That means they're setting your organization up for liabilities stemming from violations of the Fair Credit Reporting Act or other laws. Only human resources should be authorized to conduct background checks. Remind hiring managers of this policy every time you send them resumes you've screened for consideration.

Required checks. Certain types of employers will be *required* by federal or state law to check criminal records. Healthcare employers, financial services firms, law enforcement and security agencies, and day care or educational institutions may have industry-specific background checking requirements. But those aren't the only employers who need to be on heightened alert:

◆ Organizations in industries with high turnover rates (such as retail or telemarketing employers) can attract greater numbers of "vagrant" workers, who fluctuate between short-lived employment and criminal activity.

◆ Employers who send their workers out into the field to see customers, especially to customers' homes, are endangering the public at large, not just their own employees, if no criminal check is done.

◆ Following the terrorist attacks of 9/11, many other organizations have come to be seen as vulnerable. Water treatment plants, biomedical research firms, ground transportation services, nuclear power plants—all of these industries are potential targets.

Policy checklist. Will you use criminal background checks to screen your potential new employees? If you're one of the employers above, it's hard to argue against such a policy. But *all* employers should evaluate whether to adopt a policy of background checks. Before you do, though, keep the following points in mind:

◆ Carefully review the applicable federal and state laws on the subject, as well as relevant privacy provisions, to ensure full compliance with them.

- Create a written policy that outlines precisely when you will conduct a criminal background check of an applicant. Decide whether you will do background checks for all new hires or just certain openings. If you conduct background checks on a selective basis, be sure you make choices about background screening based on the nature of the position you're hiring for, and not based on particular applicants.
- Don't use criminal background checks to screen out prospects. Use them only after you've made a verbal offer to an applicant.
- Advise applicants that you will be verifying their criminal history information through law enforcement authorities and records. (Many state laws *require* such notification.)
- Do not consider an applicant's prior arrests in your evaluation of the candidate. Only use actual convictions to make decisions whether to hire. Some state laws and federal agency guidelines prohibit employers from using information that did not result in a conviction.

According to the EEOC, excluding applicants solely on the basis of arrests, without a job-related correlation, may be discriminatory. The agency has recognized that in some areas, minorities are more likely to be arrested and questioned, so asking about arrest records might unfairly burden minority applicants.

Your state may disallow the use of criminal records that have been ordered expunged, sealed, or impounded. Some court records, such as records of juvenile offenses, may be unavailable because they are sealed.

A number of companies provide verification services that include checking job experience, work performance, attendance, training and education, criminal convictions, motor vehicle driving records, and social security reports. In addition to verifying information, these companies also conduct pre-employment searches of applicants' backgrounds and provide comprehensive reports. These searches may include workers' compensation claims, credit bureau records, bankruptcy filings, and interviews with coworkers and neighbors to determine an applicant's reputation in areas such as honesty and alcohol or drug abuse. Most firms will investigate the previous five years of an applicant's history. The fee for these services depends upon how much investigation is done.

Keep in mind, if you choose to hire such an agency, that not all the information uncovered can be validly considered in making hiring decisions. (A workers' compensation record is one such example.) Other items, such as credit and financial information, might be more prejudicial than truly indicative of how well an applicant will do the job. Moreover, these background search services are subject to the Fair Credit Reporting Act.

WHAT you need to know

> ### *Criminal background checks: some caveats.*
> ◆ Criminal records can be incorrect! Instances of mistaken identity and court records that have not updated the disposition of a criminal case are commonplace. Police records, for example, often show arrests without indicating whether the defendant was convicted or found not guilty.
> ◆ Only two percent of employees who commit violent acts in the workplace have any criminal history! Be very clear: you cannot screen out all potential violence through this mechanism. Background checks will enable you to screen out *some* potential offenders, though. And they can help to rebut a negligent hiring claim in case an incident does occur.

DON'T miss this

Do you screen the backgrounds of all of your employees? Perhaps you only think you do. If you've failed to do background checks on your part-timers, your temporary or contingent workforce, your consultants and independent contractors—even your vendors—you're not as safe as you might think.

So, would you hire an ex-con?

Remember Jason, our once-promising sales rep? Is there anything Raul could have done to avoid hiring what he now fears could be a problem employee? What might a criminal background check have uncovered? Perhaps there are numerous arrests on his record for domestic battery. What if there are no convictions?

Well, he might think, *I know I'm not supposed to consider those arrests. But there's that order of protection. Why would she get an order of protection against him unless he was violent? On the other hand, maybe he's just violent towards his wife, not at work. But do we want someone working for us who hits his wife? But what if his wife is just making this up? It's been known to happen in contentious divorces. But why didn't Jason tell us about this when he applied? Well, I guess it is pretty embarrassing; I wouldn't want to volunteer that sort of information either...*

What if there *is* a conviction on Jason's record? Let's say Jason attended domestic violence counseling and anger management classes as part of his sentencing. Does this mean he's rehabilitated? That he no longer poses a threat? Is Raul qualified to make that call?

Raul's quandary is a particularly thorny one. But it demonstrates the difficulties that can arise when using criminal background checks of potential employees. The law might restrict you from using information that you've uncovered. But now you know the information and you're suspicious anyhow. And as an HR professional—not a criminologist or psychologist—you just might not feel equipped to make judgments about whether a convict is likely to repeat the crime.

Zrinka Allen, manager of employee relations at CCH Incorporated, simplifies the matter with the following question: "Does the type of behavior the applicant was convicted for put us at risk?"

You should also consider:

- ◆ the nature of the offense;
- ◆ the time elapsed since it was committed;
- ◆ the nature of the job in question;
- ◆ tangible evidence of the applicant's rehabilitation.

A conviction for marijuana possession 20 years ago, with no further criminal history, may not be a reason to reject an applicant. On the other hand, a recent theft conviction may well be.

If you do decide to hire an applicant with a criminal history, guard the employee's conviction information closely. It should be disclosed only to persons with a clear, job-related need to know. Also keep in mind that, if you've decided the applicant is employable and poses no danger to your workplace, he or she deserves the same respect, dignity, and due diligence that you afford each of your employees.

Driving record

For potential employees whose work will require them to drive for your organization, a review of their driving record is critical. Some states have special licensing requirements for chauffeuring duties and driving trucks over a certain tonnage. Does the applicant have the required license? What about a commercial driver's license? Check the record for reckless driving convictions, driving under the influence of alcohol, and speeding tickets. A thorough investigation will include a review of department of motor vehicles records, law enforcement information, and court records in some cases.

Don't overlook this important duty: background verifications examined in 2001 by ADP Screening and Selection Services revealed that over 40 percent of applicants had one or more moving violations, a DUI or DWI, or a suspended driver's license.

When recruiting for a job that requires driving, consult with applicants' former employers as well. Question references about any preventable on-the-job vehicle accidents involving the applicant, evidence of safe driving awards, years of driving experience, the types of vehicles driven, and the completion of driver training courses.

To keep the hiring process moving along while waiting for information about applicant driving records, have applicants take part in driving tests and vision screenings in the meantime.

Drug testing

You may want to conduct drug tests on all your applicants, or just those in particular jobs. If you're hiring a driver, these applicants definitely should undergo drug screening. The same goes for those applying for positions in which they'll operate dangerous machinery. In many cases, your insurance carrier will require it.

You probably know the drill by now: Don't use drug tests to screen applicants, only test those you've extended job offers to. Obtain the applicant's consent and a release before conducting a drug screen. If regular drug testing is a condition of ongoing employment, tell the potential employee now, so he or she can decide before taking the job.

Are you conducting drug testing on a selective basis? If so, be sure that you decide whether to test based on the position at hand, not on the individual applying for the job. Not only would the latter policy be unlawful discrimination, it would be inaccurate and therefore useless. Don't presume individuals of a certain age, race, ethnicity or gender are more or less likely to be drug users!

WHAT you need to know

Will you be conducting some other kind of pre-employment test? It might be necessary when the position you are filling requires demonstrated skill to safely perform a certain function. Consider the following factors to determine whether the test is necessary:

DON'T miss this

◆ Is the test cost-justified? Has its cost been quantified and budgeted? What is the expense of not doing the test—such as the likelihood of accidents caused by an unqualified employee?

◆ Is the test closely aligned to specific job requirements and safety goals? Make sure the test measures a function or skill that is truly necessary to carry out the functions of the job in a safe manner.

◆ Are procedures in place to ensure that the test is administered appropriately?

◆ If an applicant reveals that he or she has a disability, can you provide an accommodation that will allow the applicant to complete the test?

What not to do...

Some pre-hire measures don't serve a useful safety purpose, and some uses can even be illegal. Reconsider your need to use the following devices:

- **Medical examinations.** The ADA expressly prohibits preemployment medical exams. A medical exam can be conducted after a provisional job offer has been made, though, as long as you require a medical exam of all persons employed in that same position. (Note that physical agility or fitness tests to evaluate job-essential physical skills are *not* considered medical examinations.)

- **Financial information.** Is it really critical to know whether an employee has a bad credit rating, or even a bankruptcy in his or her past? When recruiting for openings in accounts receivable or banking services, the answer may be "yes," for purposes of loss prevention. However, most positions don't require a background check of applicants' financial data in order to ensure workplace safety and security.

- **Polygraph tests.** Both federal and state laws control the use of polygraph ("lie detector") tests by private employers. The federal law, the Employee Polygraph Protection Act of 1988, only allows certain employers to administer polygraph tests. Polygraph testing of applicants for jobs at security firms or positions doing security work, and for applicants with manufacturers, distributors, or dispensers of controlled substances, is allowed under federal law if the applicant will have direct access to such substances.

  Even then, an employer can only *request* that job applicants take the test, and employers must inform them that they cannot be required to take the test as a condition of employment. Neither a job applicant's refusal to take a polygraph test, nor the analysis of test results, can be the sole basis for denying employment.

Under some conditions, other employers can ask employees to take a lie detector test in the course of an ongoing investigation following a theft or other economic loss. The only employees that can be asked to take a test are those who had access to the property that is the subject of the investigation. The results of the test, without additional supporting evidence, cannot be used as the basis for discipline or discharge.

Fingerprinting: Some states prohibit employers from requiring fingerprinting of job applicants as a condition of employment. However, a number of states require fingerprinting of employees in certain fields, such as law enforcement, child care, private security, detective agencies, or state gambling agencies.

Rejecting an applicant

Ying hated this part of the job—calling applicants to tell them they didn't get the job. And when Brenda, a finalist for a programming job, answered the phone, Ying cringed upon hearing the excitement in her voice. But Brenda's tone changed quickly after hearing the bad news. "I should have gotten that job. You're going to regret this, you bitch!" Brenda yelled over the phone. "You haven't seen the last of me," she added angrily before hanging up on Ying.

You can be diligent in your recruiting efforts to avoid employees with the potential for violence or who raise other safety concerns. But you also have to be prepared for threats posed by these applicants after they are *not* given offers of employment.

✓
✓ **Checklist**

Here are some tips for recruiters to reduce the risk of conflict—and to respond to it when faced with an incident like the one Ying encountered:

☐ Provide periodic training to ensure that interviewers can identify building anger or overreaction by an applicant and can respond appropriately. Train all managers who have hiring and rejection authority in how to comply with the law and in the best practices for interviewing and rejecting applicants.

☐ Don't raise false hopes in the process of being warm and friendly. Anger can quickly follow dashed expectations when the applicant believes the recruiter encouraged and therefore misled him or her. Never lie to a candidate, no matter how much a "little white" lie can temporarily ease discomfort.

☐ Carefully document the reasons for rejecting an applicant. This is important for a number of reasons, such as fending off liability. Moreover, having the specific, objective reasons for rejection on hand when fielding a call from a rejected applicant will go far to ease the volatility of the situation.

☐ Notify unsuccessful candidates as soon as possible after they are no longer being considered.

☐ Stay in control, no matter how offensive a rejected candidate may be. Do not allow her anger to cause you to do or say something that you and the organization might regret. Don't tolerate abuse, however; it will more than likely just escalate. Tell the candidate that abusive behavior is unacceptable and end the conversation. Carefully document the circumstances of such an encounter, and make note of this in the applicant's file to alert recruiters who might unknowingly consider this applicant when another position comes available.

☐ Take all threats seriously. Notify the hiring manager—who may also have cause for concern—and your organization's security team. Contact local law enforcement.

While applicant rejection is not a prominent cause of violence in the workplace, sensible precautions must still be taken.

Retention is a safety issue, too!

Remember that "hierarchy of human needs"—the theory that employees first want safety and security above all else? It should be a clear indicator that to retain employees, you have to keep them safe. Safety issues impact employee satisfaction. Simply put, you can't be an employer of choice if your employees are working in danger, discomfort or fear. A safe workplace can help ensure greater retention and longevity.

Here's something that's equally interesting: Employee longevity breeds safety. Statistics show that long-term employees are safer workers. So the more successful your retention efforts, the safer your organization and its employees will be.

Best Practices

The Oklahoma Department of Labor, in July 2002, initiated a public/private partnership to enhance workplace safety through employee retention.

Data gathered by that state's Department of Labor showed that employees with less than one year on the job comprised more than 37 percent of all injuries resulting in days away from work in 2000. Employees with less than one year on the job were more than twice as likely to be injured as employees with an excess of five years working for the same company. Employees with less than five years on the job accounted for 70 percent of all workplace injuries involving days away from work. The statistics show a stable workforce translates into fewer workplace injuries and lower workers' compensation costs.

Negligent hiring

There can be serious, even tragic, consequences of negligent hiring. A job applicant may pose a risk to self, coworkers, or the public if:

- ◆ he or she is not qualified for the job; or
- ◆ he or she has done something in the past that would have significant consequences if it happened again.

Worst case scenario

A manager of an apartment complex hired an applicant to work in its maintenance department. The employee murdered a tenant of the complex, whose parents then sued the apartment owners for negligent hiring. It seems the manager had neglected to conduct a background check on the employee and failed to uncover the individual's violent personality, as shown by prior convictions for assault as well as probation violations.

The owners will very likely be found negligent. Since its employees gain access to client residences, the apartment complex should take enhanced safety precautions, including criminal background checks, when hiring. Had the manager conducted an investigation, he would have quickly seen that this individual was trouble waiting to happen.

HR professionals have a duty to act in a "reasonably safe" manner in their recruitment efforts. You're expected to avoid hiring a person that you know, *or should know*, is so unsuitable for a job that he or she poses a threat of harm to coworkers, customers, or property. So you'll be expected to have conducted a reasonable investigation into a prospective employee's fitness.

What's reasonable will depend upon the nature of the position, the cost and difficulty of obtaining information, and the customary practices in your industry. Do you recruit for one of the security-sensitive employers that we discussed above? Then there is a heightened duty to investigate more thoroughly, a higher standard of what is "reasonable."

When considering an applicant, ask yourself: "Would a reasonably safe manager in my industry investigate this potential problem about an applicant before hiring him or her?"

DON'T miss this

Here's an important reminder: Workplace violence is foremost on HR professional's minds. But violence is not the only workplace danger that your organization needs to screen out. You're also expected to avoid hiring employees that you should know are negligent or incompetent—particularly for jobs that entail hazardous or safety-sensitive work. These individuals can also cause serious injury to self or others if they are unqualified to perform the functions expected of them.

Remember, you have a crucial role to play in protecting not just your employees, but your organization's bottom line. Using safe and proper hiring methods can go a long way in reducing potential liability.

The Quiz

1. The best job descriptions for furthering your safety goals should include a list of any dangerous machinery required to do the job. ❑ True ❑ False

2. Criminal background checks through court records provide ironclad information about an applicant's prior criminal history. ❑ True ❑ False

3. Your organization can't be held liable for a violent employee's actions if it didn't know about his violent tendencies. ❑ True ❑ False

4. Ideally, your hiring managers will take ownership of the background check process for their applicants. ❑ True ❑ False

5. The job interview is a good opportunity for you to convey your organization's commitment to health and safety. ❑ True ❑ False

1. T 2. F 3. F 4. F 5. T

A safe workforce

Ruben has been working on your loading dock for longer than anyone can remember. Even though he's the department manager in shipping and receiving, he's not afraid of doing the "grunt work," and when a delivery goes out, he's right there with his workers, pulling merchandise and loading the truck—usually at a faster pace then the younger guys.

Ever since he started on the dock, Ruben has been jumping on and off the trucks without benefit of a ladder or other equipment. Your safety officer spoke to him about this once, but he shrugged it off. "I load faster this way. I've been doing it like this for twenty years," he replied.

Yesterday Ruben slipped off the truck as he was getting down. He wasn't injured or even sore. But it made you wonder about how many close calls he's escaped over the years. He's in his forties now—is he as agile as when he started? What if he does injure himself? Ruben is one of your most valued and knowledgeable employees, and shipping operations would really suffer without him, even temporarily.

What's more, Ruben's recklessness is setting a bad example for his team, too.

Introduction

So you've recruited the employees you need, and now you're taking steps to ensure they work safely for their own benefit and the well being of their coworkers and the organization. You're restructuring the new hire orientation to include a discussion of the company's safety mission and education about health and safety in your workplace.

What will you tell them?

Well, there's the obligatory rundown of general safety rules, emergency and evacuation procedures, and the other information that applies to employees across the organization. Then you'll explain that individual supervisors will provide in-depth safety training relevant to their particular jobs—and that they should contact human resources if they don't feel they are receiving adequate training and preparation for their duties.

DON'T miss this

Perhaps even more than these crucial messages, your orientation must convey the importance of adopting a safety mindset, a work attitude that takes health and safety seriously.

You also know that an orientation session won't be enough. You'll have to get your front-line supervisors and current employees on board with the organization's new safety initiatives if they are going to have a lasting impact and really show results. This means you're going to have to face the "Ruben problem" head-on.

As an HR professional grappling with health and safety in the workplace, there are several other relevant human resources-related safety issues you'll need to ponder. First, you already know to pay special attention to your new employees and their safety needs, but there are other workers at heightened risk as well. These include shift workers, non-English speakers, and other segments of your workforce.

It's also important for you to know the rights and responsibilities of your employees as they relate to safety in the workplace. This knowledge is essential so that you can properly navigate performance issues or conflicts that arise when a safety concern emerges. And you'll need to train your managers on how to respond in such instances as well.

A safety mindset

Let's look at the figures that are commonly cited:

20% of injuries are caused by unsafe conditions.

80% of injuries are caused by unsafe acts.

Are these numbers to be believed? What do they show?

You can ensure that every square foot of your worksite is as safe as possible. It's the human behavior that's harder to control.

ToolBoxTopics.com is a workplace safety website that provides safety information and offers sample safety meetings. One of its sample meetings conveys the following message to workers: "Your employer has a responsibility to provide you with a safe workplace. But the rest of the responsibility for safety lies with you... You have an even greater role to play than the organization does."

An employee's bad attitude about safety can be dangerous. Complaints about having to comply with precautions and safety rules, refusing to use safety devices or wear personal protective equipment, or even a general lax or reckless attitude—these can impact workplace safety as much as the physical hazards in the workplace.

How can you tell when an employee's failure to follow safety rules and procedures is the result of a bad attitude? First, poor motivation is usually the culprit if the employee *can* perform the task in accordance with safety procedures, but does not do so. This means that the employee knows the proper method, but is simply unmotivated to use it.

✓ Checklist

General safety pointers

The following checklist contains important safety messages to convey to your employees:

☐ Safety is everyone's job. That means you!

☐ Follow required safety procedures each and every time.

☐ Don't work angry. Get enough sleep. Make sure nothing is distracting you from doing your job safety.

☐ Pay attention to known safety hazards and be on the lookout for unknown ones.

☐ Report unsafe conditions immediately. Don't overlook defective equipment or unsafe conditions when you spot them. And don't assume it's someone else's job to report them.

☐ Report accidents or injuries immediately. Report near misses, too. A near miss is a warning!

☐ If you're injured, get first aid immediately, even if the injury appears to be "just a scratch." It may be more serious than it looks.

☐ Give special aid and attention to your newer coworkers.

☐ Don't assume you're accident-immune just because you've been doing the job awhile.

(Source: ToolboxTopics.com)

The supervisors' role

Before you can even begin to work on your employees, though, you need to make sure that your supervisors are on the safety bandwagon. Don't assume that your line managers are ready to take up the safety cause, especially if their departments have been incident-free lately.

WHAT you need to know

Your line managers have several safety roles to play. They need to:

◆ Train employees in their units on how to do their specific jobs safely.

◆ Manage safety attitudes and performance and motivate their employees to fend off carelessness.

◆ Model safe work behaviors.

Your supervisors might already be doing a solid job of training their charges. They see the direct payoff in productivity. But the performance management issues are always tougher for managers, aren't they? And that's what the second role entails. Managing safety attitudes and motivating a safety mindset are the very kinds of performance management functions they turn to you for help with.

The third role will be a tough sell to the Rubens on your team: the need to model safe behavior themselves. Here's where some of your veteran managers may roll their eyes. Let's look at Ruben, for example. Ruben sounds like a great worker with a bad safety attitude. He's been at the job for so long, and he's stayed out of harm's way the whole time—he's sure he'll never be the victim of a workplace accident. Ruben knows what he's doing. He's hustling to get the job done. He's never filed a workers' comp claim. So what's the problem?

For starters: Ruben's luck may soon be running out. He's tempting fate. Perhaps Ruben isn't deterred by the prospect of a broken ankle—or worse—but the organization needs to avoid an extended absence or workers' compensation costs. You'll need to confront him on this issue. He might be a valued employee, but his continued refusal to comply with safety rules is a disciplinary matter that should be treated as such.

What's more—Ruben's not just an employee, he's a supervisor.

And he needs to understand how he impacts the safety culture. In fact, because he rose up through the ranks to become the boss, in the mind of his employees, the company condones Ruben's work, safety lapses and all.

Ruben is modeling reckless behavior to his employees, and sending the tacit message that it's OK to thwart the safety precautions in place. He's also implicitly telling his staff that there's no danger in the work that they do. Each of these subtle messages detracts from your efforts to instill a safety mindset.

Meet with Ruben and the rest of your organization's line managers. Do it before you overhaul your new employee orientation—this task is more important. Explain that you've been researching safety issues, and assessing the potential impact of accidents and injuries on productivity and their financial costs to the organization. Tell them you'll be partnering with them to treat safety as a high priority. (Ideally, you'll have convinced upper management to tie supervisor performance evaluations in part to desired safety outcomes as well.)

Then schedule training sessions with your line management team in which you'll instruct supervisors on:

◆ the organization's safety goals and its place in the larger mission;

◆ general safety information and an overview of the organization's safety rules and procedures;

◆ the importance of safety training at the worksite;

◆ the importance of modeling safe behaviors;

◆ motivating and performance management tools to encourage safe behaviors;

◆ how safe behaviors are to be evaluated and rewarded; and

◆ human resources policies and programs available to assist them and their employees in enhancing workplace safety.

WHAT you need to know

A message to managers: What comes after training?

Once you ensure that all employees are properly trained in how to do their jobs safely, then the next step is reinforcing the safety mindset. Remind employees of their responsibility for safety—it's a regular drill, and it must be carried out on a consistent basis.

Behavior-based safety

Employers who want to enhance workplace safety and health should consider *why* their employees behave in an unsafe manner. That's the recommendation of Donald Theune, vice president of the Topf Organization, a consulting firm specializing in behavior-based safety programs. Theune spoke at a session of the American Society of Safety Engineers' 37th Annual Professional Development Conference and Exposition in Seattle.

Employees often take calculated risks and shortcuts, or choose comfort and convenience over safety, in part because of the common misconception that serious consequences "won't happen to me." That myth needs to be shattered. Theune recommends the following cognitive exercise: when your employees are about to face a safety risk at work, have them imagine their sons or daughters performing the task, and encourage them to carry out the duty as they would have their children do.

Jack L. Stirzaker, another conference speaker, discussed what he referred to as "The ABC's of BBS (Behavior-Based Safety)":

◆ An **A**ntecedent triggers a behavior.

◆ A **B**ehavior is an observable act.

◆ A **C**onsequence is anything that directly follows from a behavior.

For example, if safety goggles don't fit properly or are in poor condition (*antecedents*), then employees won't wear them (*behavior*). By not wearing the goggles, employees will experience more comfort and better vision (*consequence 1*). But they will also expose themselves to a higher risk of injury (*consequence 2*).

What are the telling differences between the possible consequences? Not wearing goggles results in a consequence that is soon, certain, and positive (the increased comfort and improved vision, consequence 1). Not wearing the goggles *might* result in a bad consequence (an eye injury, consequence 2). But this consequence is remote and uncertain—and the more immediate outcome of this behavior is negative (discomfort and reduced vision).

According to the behavior-based approach, the strongest influences on human behavior are the most immediate consequences of that behavior. The trick, then, is to make the immediate consequences of goggle-wearing more favorable to your employees. Or to make the immediate consequences of *not* wearing goggles more tangibly negative.

Employers use many antecedents in the workplace to encourage employees to work in a safe way. They might be in the form of positive reinforcements such as rewards or bonuses, or negative reinforcements like reprimands or fines. Under the behavior-based safety theory, these measures will reduce accidents if they minimize the risky actions taken by employees as they go about their daily duties.

Taking this approach, your first step would be to take a "critical behavior inventory" in your workplace. What are the behaviors that are causing accidents in a workplace? By analyzing accident data and seeking employee input, an employer can determine what behaviors result in occupational accidents. Then you can try to devise antecedent measures to alter those behaviors.

WHAT you need to know

When can discipline be used as an effective behavioral tool?

◆ *When safety and health rules are stated in writing.*

◆ *When discipline is administered promptly after a safety deficiency arises.*

◆ *When the discipline meted out is fair and appropriate to the deficiency.*

◆ *When rewards are used far more frequently than punishment.*

Is something wrong with this picture?

Think about those safety goggles from the behavior-based safety example. What about the fact that, according to our scenario, they "didn't fit properly" and were in poor condition? Clearly the employer did not supply adequate protective equipment to its employees. Yet we're looking at why the employee wouldn't wear the equipment!

Are we unfairly blaming the victim, and dismissing the unsafe conditions that cause injuries and illness? That's what some critics of the behavior-based safety approach believe.

In an article entitled "Blame the Worker: The Rise of Behavioral-Based Safety Programs," the authors discuss the origins of those numbers we shared earlier: 80% accidents from unsafe acts/20% from unsafe conditions. Those figures are largely based on research conducted by an insurance investigator in the 1930s. The 80-20 conclusion was based on reviews of supervisor's accident reports, which "naturally blame workers for accidents and injuries."

Consider the example of a manufacturer who had a behavior-based safety program in place. A worker slipped on the ice while using the parking-lot sidewalk. The official accident report stated "Worker's eyes not on path" as the cause of the employee's injury. As the article notes: "The report did not mention the need to have ice and snow removed from the parking lot. It did not mention that the sidewalk had not been cleared of snow and ice for several weeks, even though workers were required to use the sidewalk periodically." (Source: "Blame the Worker: The Rise of Behavioral-Based Safety Programs," by James Frederick and Nancy Lessin. *Multinational Monitor,* November 2000, Volume 21, Number 11.)

Here's the moral of the story: Let's not place *too* great an onus on the employee for ensuring safety in the workplace. The fact is, there are real hazards in the workplace—not just hazardous workers. It's important to train employees and orient them to the safety mindset, but we shouldn't use this approach to unfairly place blame or avert our safety responsibilities as employers.

Safety and your new employees

A meatpacking company worker was overcome by toxic gases released from decomposing blood and solid organic material while attempting to clean the top of a blood storage tank that had just been drained of six-day-old blood.

The employee had only been working at the company for two weeks. He was not working under the direction of a supervisor. He was not told about toxic fumes released from decomposing organic material. He was not given or required to wear a respirator.

Two coworkers near the storage tank were also overcome by fumes when they went to his rescue. But their attempts to save him were to no avail. The employee was killed.

New employees are the most vulnerable members of your workforce. Statistics suggest that up to 60% of all job injuries occur to new employees with less than six months on the job. That doesn't just mean the brand-new hire; those who are new to a particular job, though they're veterans in your organization, are at greater risk as well. Your employees face heightened danger each time they change positions or switch to new work environments.

Why are these workers so vulnerable? One major factor is that they haven't yet received the proper training. Also, they're simply not accustomed to performing the tasks at hand, and can't work with the skill and confidence of a seasoned veteran. Yet at this particular stage in their employment, they're eager to please and to show they can perform the work. It's a tough situation to be in.

Here's how effective HR policies can help:

◆ Conduct a general safety orientation.

◆ Appoint a mentor within the same work team; the employee might find it less intimidating to ask questions of a colleague than of the boss. And an employee who is involved in the job day-to-day is probably more equipped to train than the supervisor who is once removed.

◆ Allow for "ramp-in" to especially difficult jobs. Don't expect your new workers to work at the same capacity right from the start as your long-term employees. Increase productivity expectations gradually, as the worker's experience, dexterity, and comfort level builds. One ramp-in approach is to rotate new workers into more difficult jobs for two hours at a time until they can work up to capacity.

◆ After 30 days, meet with the new employee to discuss general safety concerns, ergonomic problems or discomforts, understanding of tools, machinery, and procedures, knowledge of emergency procedures, etc.

New-hire training doesn't end when the employees leave the training room. Most would say it's just beginning, in fact. On-the-job training is the real knowledge builder. And it encompasses more than the step-by-step "how-to" instructions. New employees also receive on-the-job training in workplace culture: what the boss will tolerate, what the company frowns upon, how to take shortcuts, whether workers are mocked for not taking them, and many other lessons—not all of them good ones.

That's why it's important that current employees buy into the safety mindset. They play a critical role in training newcomers and building a safe workforce. Convey this message forcefully, and back it up: Employees must not ridicule questions asked by newcomers. In fact, they should encourage questions from their new coworkers. After all, everyone's safety depends on their knowing the answer.

Remind current employees that they must set a safety example for their new coworker. Your hard efforts to orient new hires to safety will be quickly undone if no one else takes it seriously.

WHAT you need to know

✔ Checklist

How your employees can help

Here are some more useful ideas from ToolBoxTopics.com—this time, on how employees can assist their new coworkers for the safety benefit of everyone:

◆ Offer yourself as a mentor, tell them your name, your job duties, and that they can ask any questions they have. Remind them that you were uncertain and had lots of questions when you first started, too. Tell them that if you see them doing something incorrectly, you'll stop them and explain the proper procedure. When you do so, do it tactfully and with respect.

◆ Include the new employee in the group on lunch and other breaks to make them part of the team as quickly as possible; you'll need to have a vested interest in each other to look out for each other's safety.

◆ Remember that a new employee is probably nervous and most likely doesn't remember all the instructions he or she received in safety training. Be sure the new employee understands the safety procedures that apply to his or her specific duties.

◆ New employees aren't familiar with new surroundings. Point out locations of first aid kits, fire extinguishers, emergency exits, and safety traps.

◆ If the work requires the use of protective clothing or equipment, be sure the new employee is wearing it, and doing so properly. Make sure you are too—a good example is critical.

◆ Even if your new coworker is a veteran in the occupation, your workplace will no doubt do things differently than at his or her last job. Don't assume knowledge that's not there because the new employee had been at it for awhile somewhere else.

◆ Most importantly, LEAD BY EXAMPLE!

> "Remember, getting new people started on the right path can help prevent an accident or injury to everyone on the crew. Don't think that helping to develop a productive coworker is a burden. Think of it as an investment in the future of your work group and your company."
>
> *(Source: ToolBoxTopics.com.)*

Other vulnerable employees

Which other employees are vulnerable, from a safety standpoint? In reality, all of your employees can be injured or made ill. But certain workers may be at greater than average risk:

Blue-collar workers

A national workplace survey sponsored by The Hartford Financial Services Group Inc, one of the country's leading providers of workers' compensation insurance, revealed that 58 percent of blue-collar households have a family member who was both injured on the job and required medical attention. Only 38 percent of white-collar workers reported the same hardships.

Young workers

Younger workers generally are more accident-prone, less attentive to rules and regulations, and more carefully regulated by the federal government.

Youth are less experienced at work and at life, lacking certain common knowledge acquired through living. This makes them more vulnerable. At the same time, teens are at an age where they feel they are invincible, so they're more lax about following safety rules and procedures.

A report released by the National Institute of Occupational Safety and Health in 2002 found that certain occupations like construction and garbage collection were too hazardous for teens. Injury rates for teenagers are almost twice that for adults. And *that* statistic applies to jobs that aren't already off-limits to teenagers due to their perceived danger.

Here's a crucial fact: Four-fifths of teen injuries occur when no supervisor is present. For this reason, some child labor advocates urge a restriction on unsupervised teen work altogether.

The Fair Labor Standards Act (FLSA), and many state laws as well, impose strict prohibitions on employees under age 18 taking on certain duties, like operating motor vehicles on public roads or using box crushers or food slicers. Many teenagers who have died on the job did so while doing such prohibited work. As a result, the U.S. Department of Labor has been stepping up enforcement in this area.

WHAT you need to know

> Do you have minors working in your organization? It's essential that you review the FLSA and the state law that applies to your organization to ensure that your minor-age employees are not engaged in unlawful dangerous work. Remind your supervisors of what type of work is off-limits to these employees, and insist that, whatever their job, teenage employees receive the proper training and supervision they need to do the work safely.

Immigrant workers and non-English speakers

Immigrants, even when working legally in the United States, often believe they are more likely to be terminated. They may be less willing to report workplace hazards or injuries because they don't want to lose their jobs.

According to data from the Bureau of Labor Statistics, the number of job-related deaths for Latino workers increased by 11.6 percent from 1999 to 2000, while deaths for other U.S. workers declined during this same period. Some of this trend is a result of where Latino workers are employed. According to Linda Chavez-Thompson, executive vice president of the AFL-CIO, "Latino workers are concentrated in high risk industries, yet they are often not provided with safety training or the most basic of protections." Chavez-Thompson also notes that some immigrant workers are unaware of the health and safety laws available to protect them because of the language barrier that exists.

WHAT you need to know

Do you have employees who don't speak fluent English? Non-English speakers are more likely to be injured or die because they often don't adequately understand the safety and operating instructions needed to perform their work safely.

Don't let this happen to your employees. Post your safety signs, exit notices, operations manuals, and other important information in more than one language if you have a large population of non-English-fluent workers.

Sick workers

Encourage employees to stay home from work when they are sick. When workers come to work with nasty colds and flus, they are less productive anyhow—and far more accident-prone. Then they spread these illnesses to coworkers, who in turn become less productive and more likely to have a workplace accident.

✓ Checklist

If sick employees simply have to come into work, use the following checklist, especially if they work in safety-sensitive positions:

☐ Ask that employees who are sick inform their supervisor.
☐ Consider assigning sick employees to less hazardous work for the day.
☐ Employees taking medication for a cold, flu, or other illness must alert their supervisor, and inform him or her what medicine they are taking. There are two reasons for this policy:
  1. Certain medicines impair judgment and dexterity to the extent that employees under their influence should not be operating heavy machinery or driving. Heed the warning labels on the bottles.
  2. In the event an accident or injury occurs, the response team may need to know what medicines the employee has ingested.

Employees with disabilities

> Tony has mild cerebral palsy—hemiplegia (muscle weakness on one side of the body) which restricts the manual dexterity in his right hand. You just offered him a job working in your research lab. He was a terrific candidate—seven years of lab experience, great references—it was an easy hiring decision to make. At the interview, you asked Tony whether he would require any special accommodations to perform the functions of the job if he were hired, and he answered no.
>
> After accepting the job, Tony discloses his medical information on the required paperwork, and brings it to your attention as well. (You hadn't even noticed during the interview! But thinking back, maybe his handshake wasn't as forceful as you'd expect...) Now you're worried about whether his condition can be a problem. He's going to be working with hazardous chemicals—what if he breaks a vessel, or spills some materials? He won't just endanger himself—his coworkers would be at risk too. What liability might the company face from a potential accident?

Certain employees with disabilities can pose greater safety risks, or be more vulnerable to injury from workplace accidents or hazards. Yet it's entirely likely that the disabled worker poses no higher risk or has no greater likelihood of injury. An employer cannot make assumptions without violating the Americans with Disabilities Act.

Don't assume that a person with cerebral palsy cannot work safely in a lab. Did you check Tony's references? Did he have a record of accidents during his seven years at his former lab employer? Tony told you that he didn't need special accommodations; it's certainly possible that he has adapted to his impairment and devised his own safe method of doing things.

On the other hand, perhaps he does pose a risk. And you don't have to hire an employee with a disability to work in a position where the disability might be a safety hazard. In fact, it would be a bad idea to do so, if Tony posed a real danger.

Tough questions, indeed. But you need to evaluate an applicant with a disability on an individual basis, according to the position at hand. Don't set a blanket policy that applicants with cerebral palsy cannot work in the lab. That's the very sort of discrimination the ADA aims to eliminate.

Safety and the ADA: What you can do

Hiring. An employer can refuse to hire a person with a disability if the employee would pose a *direct threat* to his or her own safety or to the safety of coworkers because of the disability.

Firing. An employer can defend itself against a charge of disability discrimination if the employee was terminated because he or she posed a *significant risk* or *high probability of substantial harm* to self or others. This is even truer if the employee is in a safety-sensitive position.

What does this mean to you? Here are questions to consider:

- Is the safety threat real, and verifiable, or perceived or assumed?
- How direct is the safety threat? Is it immediate, or remote?
- Is there a way that the disability can be accommodated so that the threat is reduced or eliminated?
- How great is the risk? High or just slightly heightened?
- How likely is the risk to cause harm?
- If harm does result, how serious would that harm likely be?

ADA quandary

Charles suffers from narcolepsy. His condition causes frequent and unexpected loss of consciousness. He applies for a carpenter position. An "essential function" of the carpenter job is to use power saws and other dangerous equipment (such as ladders) on the job. Should you hire him?

Solution: Ask yourself these questions as you make your decision:

- Is the safety threat real? Yes: the loss of consciousness is a verifiable symptom of his condition.
- Is the threat direct? Yes: because the loss of consciousness can't be predicted, the applicant can fall asleep while using a power saw at any time.

◆ Can the threat be eliminated or reduced? Not if Charles wants to be a carpenter. Perhaps if he were applying for an accounts receivable job—a calculator is unlikely to kill or maim if you fall asleep while using it.

In this example, Charles could lawfully be rejected for the carpenter position.

Charles could be terminated from the carpenter position as well, if the condition had emerged after his employment. His frequent and unanticipated losses of consciousness pose a significant risk of substantial harm.

HIV/AIDS in the workplace. *AIDS and HIV are recognized as disabilities under the ADA. Employers that are covered by the ADA cannot discriminate against applicants who have AIDS or are HIV-positive. Moreover, employers are expected to make reasonable accommodations for persons who are infected.*

While it is true that those infected with HIV can infect others, the condition is not spread through casual contact in the workplace. So there is no legitimate safety reason for asking applicants or new employees to undergo an AIDS test.

This principle applies even in the healthcare setting, where workers run a higher risk of infection due to needlesticks, the presence of bodily fluids, etc. The Centers for Disease Control does not recommend testing even for healthcare workers.

DON'T
miss
this

Shift workers

More than 20 million Americans work outside the traditional 9-to-5 work schedule. These workers are at greater risk than their counterparts on the day shift. Shift work and rotating shifts (working some days, some nights) place considerable physical and mental stress on employees. Shift workers can be more fatigued and less alert, and won't notice or respond to hazards as quickly, so they are more likely to have an accident. Also, those on the nightshift often lack seniority. That means they are less experienced, too. As we know, less experienced workers are more vulnerable.

So shift workers are more likely to commit unsafe acts or practice riskier behavior. But the unsafe conditions are higher for shift workers as well. Often the work itself is inherently more dangerous. Here's why:

◆ Out of sight, out of mind. The safety officer or human resources team might be readily available for the day shift, but seldom, if ever, around at night. Shift workers may not enjoy the benefits of safety meetings and occasional safety training.

◆ *You* might be a shift worker with seniority, but your coworkers aren't. And less experienced workers pose greater risks to their coworkers, too.

◆ Some companies schedule inherently hazardous work at night when fewer people are around. This reduces risk for all but the shift workers, of course.

◆ It's harder to see in the dark. Workers must rely completely on artificial light at night, but it can't illuminate every surface. Mishaps are therefore more likely.

◆ Shift workers are more likely to be victims of criminal behavior, which occurs more often at night.

(Source: adapted in part from ToolBoxTopics.com).

The human body just isn't wired for work during its physiological time of rest. Shift work disrupts the 24-hour circadian rhythm that regulates all body functions. Perhaps that's why research shows that health problems are higher among the graveyard shift. Shift workers are often less likely to eat, rest, and sleep properly. According to the American Federation of State, County, and Municipal Employees (AFSCME), shiftwork can cause a variety of health problems, including disturbed sleep, digestive problems, and heart disease as well as behavioral effects that impact mental and social well being too.

All of these are grave health and wellness concerns in their own right. But they also increase the chance of an accident or injury due to employees who are distracted, exhausted, in physical or emotional pain, or reckless, angry, or violent.

✓ *Checklist*

Easing the shiftwork problem

AFSCME recommends the following measures to improve shiftwork schedules and minimize the burden on workers:

☐ Provide enough rest breaks for jobs that require repetitive physical work. Brief rest breaks each hour seem to be the best for recovery from muscle fatigue.

☐ Improve lighting, ventilation, temperatures and noise control.

☐ Ensure proper safety training for your night shift, equal to your day workers.

☐ Offer safe travel to and from work, if possible.

☐ Keep long work shifts and overtime to a minimum.

☐ Consider different lengths for shifts. Heavier, more boring work should be done during shorter shifts and lighter, more interesting work should be moved to longer shifts.

☐ Avoid quick shift changes. 48 hours is the suggested minimum between shift changes.

☐ Keep the schedules regular and predictable. Workers should know their schedule well ahead of time, so they can plan their rest, childcare and contact with family and friends.

☐ Schedule as many weekends off as possible.

☐ Avoid scheduling several days on followed by four- to seven-day "mini-vacations."

☐ Keep consecutive night shifts to a minimum.

☐ Minimize the use of permanent (fixed or non-rotating) night shifts. Most workers never get used to the night shift because they go back to a daytime schedule on their days off.

(Source: AFSCME "Safe Jobs Now!")

WHAT you need to know

Do you award a shift differential? Consider other perks for valued shiftworkers. Perhaps an enhanced wellness benefit can alleviate the potentially damaging effects of the schedule:

◆ *Shift workers have to work harder to maintain health and fitness. For example, one study found that night-shift employees have higher blood cholesterol levels than day workers, even if they keep the same diet. A regular exercise routine is even more crucial to the graveyard staff, it seems. Perhaps you can subsidize a gym membership for your night crew.*

◆ *Or how about providing your shift workers with a gift certificate for some room-darkening shades?*

While we're on the subject of scheduling, here's an important point to keep in mind: Don't forget the safety and health implications of overtime work on your employees. As you'd expect, there's potential fatigue and carelessness and the other behavioral risks. But you also have to inquire whether your overtime workers might be dangerously over-exposed to certain workplace hazards. Perhaps exposure might be acceptable for eight-hour intervals, but unsafe for longer timeframes. Talk to your safety officer about the possible dangers before requiring, or even signing off on overtime.

Temps and agency workers

Chances are, your organization utilizes temporary or agency workers at least on occasion. If you hire temps from an agency, you're the "host employer," which means that you're the employer for compliance purposes, under federal health and safety law.

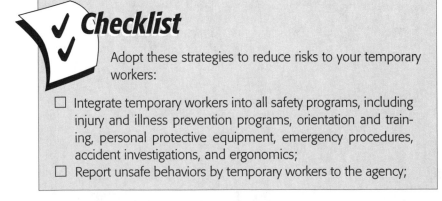

✓ Checklist

Adopt these strategies to reduce risks to your temporary workers:

☐ Integrate temporary workers into all safety programs, including injury and illness prevention programs, orientation and training, personal protective equipment, emergency procedures, accident investigations, and ergonomics;

☐ Report unsafe behaviors by temporary workers to the agency;

☐ Correct imminent danger situations immediately;

☐ Establish communication channels with the temporary agency;

☐ Become familiar with the agency's health and safety program;

☐ Review contracts with temporary agencies to ensure that they define safety/security responsibilities;

☐ Require proof of the agency's workers' compensation insurance coverage and spell out insurance obligations in the contract;

☐ Identify and segregate any medical claims for temporary workers; and

☐ Include safety issues in any company policy on temporary workers.

Don't forget about your part-time workers. They may be vulnerable for the same reasons as the temps: they aren't fully integrated into the employee culture. Do you always hold safety meetings in the morning? How can that accommodate your afternoon-only shift? Do they receive the same amount of training and supervision? Do they receive all of the safety memorandums that you send to full-timers? Do they know the HR staff so there's an individual they can go to with safety concerns? Do they have on-the-job mentors who can point out the safety hazards? Have you supplied the necessary protective equipment to accommodate the part-time employees?

Telecommuters

Did you know the average telecommuter gains six to ten pounds in the first six months of working at home? Think about the wellness implications of working at home and include a discussion of the issue in your organization's telecommuting policy.

Telecommuters tend to take less breaks because the natural social breaks that occur at the office don't happen at home. This can cause an increase in ergonomic injuries. Remind your telecommuters about the importance of regular rest periods and muscle stretches.

Be sure to keep your telecommuters in the loop when you provide safety and health information to your employees. This might mean providing literature about ergonomic furniture, or dialing them in to safety meetings if relevant to their work.

Also, think twice before allowing employees to perform activities at home that can involve inherently dangerous equipment or processes, such as manufacturing operations. These functions are best performed at the worksite, where you can control safety and health conditions.

Alcohol or drug abusers

An estimated 40% of industrial fatalities and 47% of industrial injuries are related to alcohol abuse and alcoholism.

Workplace accident rates are two to three times higher than normal for alcoholics.

A recreational drug user is 3.6 times more likely to injure himself or another person in a workplace accident.

Alcohol users also are more likely to be involved in accidents at work, and to endanger coworkers.

Those are some frightening numbers, gleaned from the National Institute on Drug Abuse and other sources. Drug and alcohol use by employees puts everyone in the workplace in imminent danger.

Consider this, too: A drug user is five times more likely to file a workers' compensation claim. Drug use in the workplace costs American business and industry between $75-$100 billion annually in lost time, accidents, and higher healthcare costs. (This figure doesn't even factor in the hidden costs associated with these incidents: diverted supervisory and managerial time, friction among workers, damage to equipment, poor decisions, damage to the company's public image, turnover... surely you can think of more.)

One more thought to ponder: the clear nexus between drug or alcohol use and violence. Is this a liability you can afford? You may want to consider drug testing, or instituting an employee assistance program. Organizations that don't test are in danger of becoming havens for drug users. Does that mean your workplace is less safe?

WHAT you need to know

"Do you want a drug user on your team?"

Here's what employees need to hear:

If a coworker is on drugs at work, he or she is endangering you—not just himself. It's your responsibility to talk to your supervisor whenever any performance or safety issue affects your job. A drinking worker could be just as dangerous as a defective saw. You wouldn't hesitate to bring the saw to your supervisor's attention, would you?

(Source: ToolboxTopics.com.)

Your employees generally know when a coworker is using drugs or alcohol. But usually, things will have to get really bad before they'll tell you or the supervisor about it. At first blush, it seems like a noble instinct, borne of an admirable desire to protect a colleague from discipline or termination. But it's a lot like giving him the keys to the car—and piling into the passenger seat next to him.

Medical costs and absenteeism are more than 50 percent higher for smokers than for nonsmokers. But the real surprise is that smokers' job-related accident rates are twice those of nonsmokers!

DON'T miss this

Employee health and safety off the job

Employees with personal problems

The well being of your employees is one of your top concerns as a human resources professional. But your interest in the health of your workforce is more than personal concern for colleagues. You know how integral your employees are to the success of your organization. You know that when workers are at optimal health, they are at optimal productivity. And you know all too well, especially after highly publicized incidents of growing workplace violence, that if employees aren't happy and healthy away from work, it can have dangerous consequences on the job.

Workers who are experiencing difficulties in their personal life, or poor physical or mental health, are at greater risk for accident or injury at work. Personal problems inevitably seep into the workplace. Your employees' health and safety on the job is interdependent with their general state of well being. It's unavoidable: work affects home life, home affects work life.

To create a safe workforce, your organization may want to integrate a wellness philosophy into its benefit offerings. Wellness extends workplace health and safety strategies to encompass overall employee well being.

We can't give wellness benefits the full attention it deserves here; it's beyond the scope of this book. Consult the "Work-Life Benefits" book in the CCH "HR How-To" series for a complete discussion of wellness and tips on setting up and maximizing the benefits of such a program.

WHAT you need to know

The number of accidental deaths in the home and community rose by 21 percent in the last ten years. The employer isn't responsible (or liable) for incidents that occur outside the workplace off the clock. But the National Safety Council suggests you give the issue your attention nonetheless. Why? It's in the company's direct economic interest.

It costs your organization money when employees go down, on or off the job. Medical expenses are typically the largest single cost component that hurts business. Setbacks such as rescheduling, lost or slowed productivity, overtime for other employees, reliance on temporary replacements, and reentry time for the injured worker all contribute significantly to the cost of an off-the-job injury, just like they do with injuries on the job.

The indirect costs from off-the-job accidents are a huge economic drain on American businesses—and potentially on your organization as well. Perhaps it's most cost-effective to include off-work safety precautions into your safety training and orientation as well.

A+ *Best Practices*

Focus on safety at home

Air Systems Components, a Tucson-based manufacturer, focuses on safety at home as well as at work. The company promotes awareness campaigns like National Safety Month and National Car Seat Safety Month in its safety program. At holiday time, employees receive brochures about fire prevention in the home. Anita Orozco, the organization's HR manager, notes of her employees that "If they are not getting hurt, that means they are coming to work."

Source: Arizona Daily Star, *12/17/02.*

Expatriates

In an increasingly global economy, more U.S. workers will be punching the clock in another country. Given recent international events and the 9/11 attacks on the United States and its workers, your employees traveling abroad must be made aware of the particular dangers they face as U.S. citizens. Today, extra precautions are necessary to avoid risks caused by crime or terrorist activity.

There's help in this vein, though. The U.S. State Department provides information to Americans who will be traveling or working outside the United States. It offers crucial advice on possible dangers in almost every country where your employees might conceivably travel. The State Department also alerts citizens as to when travel to a particular region or nation is not advisable.

There are numerous consulting firms that ready American employees for work and travel abroad. They can assist employees with language preparation, cultural orientation, and safety and health information as well.

To ensure the well being of employees abroad following the 9/11 attacks, the law firm of Curiale Dellverson Hirschfield Kraemer & Sloan, LLP recommends the following:

DON'T miss this

"Review your corporate travel security policies and procedures. Provide additional training to those who are at risk. Consult travel security updates routinely. Develop an emergency plan in case an employee is kidnapped. Enhance security measures if your company maintains its own aircraft for executive travel."

(Source: "Pondering the Unthinkable: Developing Corporate Protection and Workplace Violence Prevention Strategies After 9/11.")

Employees' safety rights and duties

What safety responsibilities do your employees have? You've tried to instill that they must assume responsibility for their own safety, the safety of their coworkers, and the importance of adopting a safety mindset.

✓ Checklist

Employee safety duties

The law outlines these specific safety duties for employees.

- ☐ Read the OSHA poster at the worksite.
- ☐ Comply with all applicable OSHA standards.
- ☐ Follow all employer safety and health rules and regulations.
- ☐ Follow safe work practices for your job, as directed by your employer.
- ☐ Wear or use prescribed protective equipment while working.
- ☐ Report hazardous conditions to the supervisor or a member of the safety committee.
- ☐ Report hazardous conditions to OSHA if your employer does not fix them.
- ☐ Report job-related injury or illness to the employer and promptly seek treatment.
- ☐ Visit a doctor selected by the employer, if requested, for workers' compensation claims.

A⁺ Best Practices

"The ten commandments of good safety habits"

Legal compliance aside, here's a useful breakdown of the responsibilities your workers must assume for their safety:

1. Set your own standards. Don't be influenced by others around you who are negative. If you fail to wear safety glasses because others don't, remember the blindness you may suffer will be yours alone to live with.

2. Operate equipment only if qualified. Your supervisor may not realize you have never done the job before. You have the responsibility to let your supervisor know, so the necessary training can be provided.

3. Respect machinery. If you put something in a machine's way, it will crush it, pinch it or cut it. Make sure all guards are in place. Never hurry beyond your ability to think and act safely.

4. Use your own initiative for safety protection. You are in the best position to see problems when they arise. Ask for the personal protective equipment or additional guidance you need.

5. Ask questions. If you are uncertain, ask. Do not accept answers that contain, "I think, I assume, I guess." Be sure.

6. Use care and caution when lifting. Most muscle and spinal injuries are from overstrain. Know your limits. Do not attempt to exceed them. The few minutes it takes to get help will prevent weeks of being off work and in pain.

7. Practice good housekeeping. Disorganized work areas are the breeding grounds for accidents. You may not be the only victim. Don't be a cause.

8. Wear proper and sensible work clothes. Wear sturdy and appropriate footwear that enclose the foot fully. Avoid loose clothing, dangling jewelry. Be sure that long hair is tied back and cannot become entangled in the machinery.

9. Practice good personal cleanliness. Avoid touching eyes, face, and mouth with gloves or hands that are dirty. Wash well and use barrier creams when necessary. Most industrial rashes are the result of poor hygiene practices.

10. Be a positive part of the safety team. Willingly accept and follow safety rules. Encourage others to do so. Your attitude can play a major role in the prevention of accidents and injuries.

(Source: ToolBoxTopics.com)

Your employees have certain rights and protections under federal health and safety law, as well as state safety and workers' compensation laws. There are other statutes that afford certain workplace health and safety rights too. The list is a long one and they are identified in detail in Chapter 9. Some of these rights are of particular relevance to HR professionals. You'll need to understand and be prepared to administer them. Let's look at these more closely.

Right to refuse unsafe work

Ronald, one of your traffic managers, came to your office in a rage. One of his drivers, Janelle, refuses to drive the delivery truck she's been assigned. She insists that a wheel is "out of whack" and it's not safe to drive. Ronald knows the garage inspected the vehicle two days ago and it was fine. He says "the truck's perfectly safe; she's just being belligerent and paranoid." He wants to have her fired for refusing to perform her job.

When workers believe that working conditions are unsafe or unhealthy, they have a duty to report the problem. But what if the employer takes no action—or disagrees that a hazard exists?

Of course, employers generally correct hazardous conditions that are brought to their attention. However, if a dispute remains as to whether there's truly a hazard, employees have the right to file a complaint with OSHA. The agency can investigate and resolve the matter.

In the meantime, they can refuse to perform the job. OSHA regulations provide for those occasions when employees are confronted with a choice between not performing assigned tasks or subjecting themselves to a risk of serious injury due to a hazardous workplace condition.

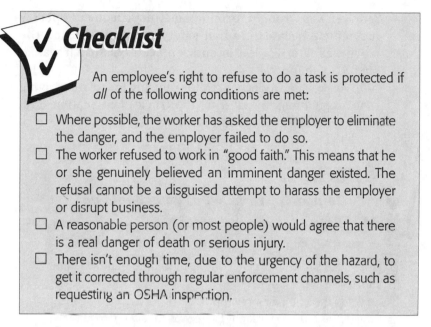

✓ *Checklist*

An employee's right to refuse to do a task is protected if *all* of the following conditions are met:

☐ Where possible, the worker has asked the employer to eliminate the danger, and the employer failed to do so.

☐ The worker refused to work in "good faith." This means that he or she genuinely believed an imminent danger existed. The refusal cannot be a disguised attempt to harass the employer or disrupt business.

☐ A reasonable person (or most people) would agree that there is a real danger of death or serious injury.

☐ There isn't enough time, due to the urgency of the hazard, to get it corrected through regular enforcement channels, such as requesting an OSHA inspection.

WHAT you need to know

If your employee has a ***good-faith belief*** that the work environment or a particular job is unsafe, and a "reasonable person" would think so too, he can refuse to work. It doesn't matter if the work environment is ultimately found to be perfectly safe; if the employee's belief that it was dangerous was reasonable, then his refusal to perform work was protected by law, and he can't be discharged on this account.

Here are some examples of "protected" work refusals, based on litigation:

◆ An employee refused to work on a 40-foot tower during a stormy night shift. The employee had a good faith belief that he would have exposed himself to a real danger of death or injury because it was windy and snowing and the tower catwalk and access ladder were slippery with ice and snow. While employees were required to work with flashlights held in their teeth, the foreman did not examine conditions on the tower before suspending the worker.

♦ A driver was wrongly terminated after refusing to operate his vehicle because he had safety concerns. In fact, the truck was later traded in and replaced because it was in such bad shape.

♦ A driver was improperly fired for refusing to violate "driving time" regulations by altering the truck identification on a required vehicle inspection report.

✔ Checklist
Refusal to work: what you should do

Take these steps when one of your employees refuses to work for safety reasons:

☐ Investigate the employee's complaint to determine whether there is a safety hazard.

☐ Reassign the complaining employee while you investigate.

☐ Correct the hazard quickly, if there was in fact a dangerous condition.

☐ Return the employee to his regular post, and be sure that his supervisor takes no adverse action against him.

☐ If there is no hazard, explain to the employee that you have found no threats to safety and assign him to his regular post.

☐ If you believe that the employee did not really have a good-faith belief that the site was dangerous, consider disciplinary action if you feel it is necessary to avoid costly work stoppages in the future.

Let's get back to Janelle, and her refusal to drive the vehicle she thought was dangerous. Here let's assume that the vehicle was actually safe to drive. Ronald has been vindicated. So how should you handle the situation as a performance issue? First, you need to ask some questions so you can better assess the situation.

Did Janelle offer to drive a different, "safer" vehicle? Or to drive the vehicle if it were repaired?

Did Janelle really believe that the truck she was assigned was unsafe?

If Janelle really believes the truck is unsafe, would a "reasonable person" in her position have the same belief?

If so, then Janelle's refusal to perform the work was permissible. You better tell Ronald to cool his jets.

Were Janelle's coworkers also somehow involved in this refusal to work? Or was she acting on behalf of her coworkers, for their safety as well as her own? If so, then Janelle was engaged in concerted, protected activity under the National Labor Relations Act (NLRA). The NLRA protects workers who are taking part in actions with or on behalf of their coworkers "for the purpose of mutual aid or protection." If Janelle's exercise of her safety rights was carried out jointly with coworkers, then it would be an ***unfair labor practice***—and disciplining her would be unlawful under the NLRA as well.

Protection from reprisals

Employees cannot be discharged or discriminated against for exercising any right created by the Occupational Safety and Health Act. That means you can't carry out reprisals for:

◆ filing complaints or starting proceedings under or related to the Act;

◆ requesting information under its right-to-know provisions;

◆ whistleblowing (reporting violations of health and safety standards); or

◆ acting on any of the other employee rights provided by the statute.

"Remember, the employee who brings safety problems to your attention is just trying to do his job and help you with yours. Such concerns should never be dismissed without a review."

(Source: ToolBoxTopics.com).

Encourage employees not to just report problems, though, but also to offer potential solutions to them. Often the worker who reported the hazard is in the best position to suggest ways of fixing it.

"Discrimination" can be any of the following adverse actions against an employee:

- Discharge
- Layoff
- Demotion
- Transfer (or refusing a desired transfer)
- Assignment to an undesirable shift
- Denial of promotion
- Reducing pay or hours
- Exclusion from normal overtime work
- Denial of benefits such as sick leave or vacation time
- Taking away company housing or similar essential perks
- Blacklisting with other employers
- Damaging credit at banks or credit unions.

Keep this important point in mind, though. You can't initiate reprisals against employees simply because they exercised their safety rights. However, you don't have to contend with a poor performer, or even an employee with a bad attitude, merely because she has filed an OSHA complaint or exercised her right to refuse to work.

If you have to terminate or discipline an employee for legitimate reasons such as inefficiency or misconduct, you should do so, even if the employee recently exercised a protected right. But before you do, ask yourself: has the employee simply raised your ire by filing a complaint? Or were you about to give your final written warning for excessive absenteeism, and the employee knew it and hid behind OSHA? Check your motivation. And make sure you've built an extensive record to back up your actions if the matter should be brought to court.

Employee safety rights: the union's role

A labor union is often the representative of your employees on health and safety issues. Therefore, "employee rights" can also mean the right to assistance from their union. Some rights extend to activities carried out by the union on the employees' behalf. For example, complaints made by an employee to the union are protected under OSHA. Under the NLRA, complaints made on an employee's behalf by a union can be protected as well.

You may have a union grievance rep or other union staff member who works at your workplace surveying or interviewing employees about dangers, hazards, and injuries that resulted. This is protected activity and it should be permitted where it doesn't unduly impact productivity.

The union also can conduct an investigation into a workplace injury or illness. Union representatives can review information regarding medical results and studies. (However, a union cannot review individual employee records unless the worker consents to their release.) The union representatives also have a right to review the OSHA 300 log. (See Chapter 9 for more information on this required form.)

Unions can play a positive role in building workplace health and safety. The large, affiliated labor organizations have significant resources of safety and health information, as well as training dollars for their members to learn safety procedures. On your worksite, the union's vigilance in protecting their members is far less of an annoyance than dealing with an injury's aftermath.

If a union represents some of your employees, then members of the labor organization should be key members of your safety team. They have a great deal to contribute. Plus, you can't make certain health and safety-related workplace changes without them, since they have a right to bargain collectively over many of these issues.

When it comes to safety, you definitely want the union on your side.

？The Quiz

1. An employer can refuse to hire a person with   ❑ True   ❑ False
   a disability if the employee would pose a
   direct threat to his or her own safety or to
   the safety of coworkers because of the disability.

2. Getting your line managers on board is a   ❑ True   ❑ False
   crucial step in building a safety mindset among
   your employees.

3. Workplace accident rates are two to three   ❑ True   ❑ False
   times higher than normal for employees
   who are alcoholics.

4. New employees are usually the least   ❑ True   ❑ False
   endangered since they are more careful
   on the job than the veterans.

5. Your employees should not be expected to   ❑ True   ❑ False
   play a role in assuring the safety of their
   coworkers. If every worker ensures his or her
   own safety, the workplace will be safe.

Answer key: 1. T; 2. T; 3. T; 4. F; 5. F

Safety programs and people

*Charisse, who works second shift for a printer, lost three fin-
gertips after the safety switch malfunctioned on the cutter she
was operating. It could have been much worse. Now she's out
for at least a month as her hand heals.*

    *The line supervisor asked Patrick to work overtime to cover
some of the second shift. Patrick works the cutter on the first shift.
When he heard about the injury, he said, "Well, I'm not surprised.
That safety mechanism was really starting to go. I learned that
about a month ago, when I almost got nicked myself."*

    *"Why didn't you tell someone about this?" Patrick's supervi-
sor demanded.*

    *"Are you kidding?" he responded. "You stick your neck out
around here, it gets chopped off. Besides, I'm not the safety
officer. It's his job to inspect the machinery, not mine."*

Introduction

The statistics are staggering:

> ◆ *5,915 workers died from traumatic workplace injuries in 2000.*
>
> ◆ *Occupational diseases kill 50,000 to 60,000 workers each year.*
>
> *(Source: U.S. Bureau of Labor Statistics. Note that the 2000 figures were used because they more accurately represent general workplace fatality rates than 2001 numbers. The 2001 fatality rate was sharply higher than the norm due to the deaths of workers in the 9/11 terrorist attacks.)*

A formal safety and health program is your starting point for meeting your duty to protect the safety and health of your employees—to prevent them from becoming statistics.

The benefits of a safety and health program

If a health and safety program can prevent one accident, it's probably worth the resources you've put into it. And not just in terms of lives or limbs saved.

What else do you have to gain? OSHA estimates that an organization can save up to 6 dollars for each dollar spent on implementing a safety and health program in its workplace.

The chart below shows why. Depending upon your organization's profit margin, it will take a lot of additional revenue to make up for a single injury. And of course, the higher the cost of the accident, the more profit you'll need to recover to make up the cost.

How many more widgets do you need to sell now?

Cost of accident	Additional sales 1% profit margin	Additional sales 5% profit margin	Additional sales 10% profit margin
$1,000	$100,000	$20,000	$10,000
$25,000	$2,500,000	$500,000	$250,000
$100,000	$10,000,000	$2,000,000	$1,000,000
$250,000	$25,000,000	$5,000,000	$2,500,000

(Source: ToolBoxTopics.com, "Accident Prevention—Painless & Profitable!")

Bring those numbers to the executive team if they're still not convinced of the importance of a safety program!

Could Charisse's injury have been prevented if her employer had a safety and health program in place? If the program had been carried out effectively and enforced vigilantly, the accident might well have been averted. Here's how the outcome might have been different:

- A machine safety inspection might have been carried out before the accident could occur.
- The safety officer would have conducted a walk-around at some point between Patrick's near miss and Charisse's injury; he might have spotted the danger.
- Patrick's supervisor would have understood the importance of motivating his staff to work with safety in mind. Patrick's attitude might have been more constructive.
- Patrick would have been *required* to inform his supervisor or the safety officer that the machinery was in disrepair and in need of attention.
- Patrick would not be fearful of "sticking his neck out"—rather, there would be an incentive for him to do so.
- Patrick would have been obligated to report his near miss that occurred weeks earlier.
- Patrick would understand that he has a responsibility to look out for his coworkers, and alert them to dangers that he finds.
- The safety device on the cutter would have been checked and its condition documented at the start of each shift.
- Charisse would have received instruction on identifying problems with equipment so she would have seen the danger.
- Charisse, on identifying that the cutter was in disrepair, would have the authority and responsibility to stop work because danger was imminent.
- The company wouldn't let Patrick or any other worker near the equipment until the safety switch was fixed.

Developing a safety and health program

OSHA recommends a four-point program for workplace safety and health:

1. Top management or the executive team leads the way by setting policy, assigning and supporting responsibility, setting an example, and involving employees.
2. The worksite is continually analyzed to identify all existing and potential hazards.
3. Methods are put in place and maintained to prevent or control existing or potential hazards.
4. Managers, supervisors, and employees are trained to understand and deal with worksite hazards.

Studies show that companies with the lowest accident rates tend to have health and safety programs with these characteristics:

◆ Top management commitment
◆ Functional responsibility for safety and health
◆ Frequent safety inspections
◆ Hazard and incident reporting systems
◆ Investigations conducted on all accidents
◆ Occupational disease prevention program
◆ Safety officials who report to top management
◆ Safety professionals with formal health and safety training
◆ Formal employee training
◆ Extensive safety communication to employees
◆ Employees' family involvement in safety consciousness
◆ Incentives for safe practices
◆ Safety and health committee
◆ Union involvement

WHAT you need to know

There are a number of elements of a successful program, but the bottom line is this: a successful safety program is not an appendage; it's an essential, integral part of your operations.

While quality safety programs have certain elements in common, there is no one-size-fits-all safety model. Hazards vary from company to company. Your program should therefore be different from the one your neighbor or competitor might use. Yours will address the unique hazards and physical demands of your workplace and workforce.

Should your health and safety program be in writing?

OSHA requires you to have a general safety program, but there's some debate over whether the agency requires that the program be put in writing. But ask yourself this: Is there a good reason *not* to put your program in writing?

There will be times when you'll need to show you have a safety plan in place for compliance or liability reasons. Isn't a written program invaluable when such an occasion arises? It's just like a contract—it doesn't have to be in writing to be enforceable, but it's sure a lot easier to prove you've got one when it is!

Besides, OSHA *does* require certain features of your safety program to be in writing. These include hazard communication, lockout/tagout, scaffolding safety and other programs. It makes little sense to put some provisions of your safety program in writing and leave others to word-of-mouth.

People take things more seriously when they are put in writing. And you want to show your employees that when it comes to safety, you mean business. Include your safety policy in your employee handbook. And while you're at it:

+ have your employees sign off that they've received and read the document;
+ have employees sign a pledge to work safely; and
+ include your progressive discipline policy in your written safety program.

Perhaps the most important part of your safety program is your safety policy. A written safety policy provides the foundation for every successful safety program and could help you avoid the expense, inconvenience, and other consequences of workplace accidents by making sure that employees know what is expected of them. Although you can orally inform employees of safety standards and procedures, for lasting impact there is no substitute for a written policy to which an employee may refer.

A safety policy should include:
- ◆ a policy statement identifying the goal of your safety program;
- ◆ an affirmative statement of the organization's responsibility for safety;
- ◆ safety personnel and support structures, and contact information for responsible individuals;
- ◆ an outline of safety rules and explanation of safety policies and procedures;
- ◆ hazard or rule violation reporting policies and procedures; and
- ◆ a statement of disciplinary policy for violations.

(A sample workplace safety policy is provided in the appendix to the book.)

DON'T miss this

A policy statement sets the tone for a company's safety program and spells out management's commitment to employee safety. Many companies include a safety policy statement as the introduction to their safety manuals. Some companies include it in their employee handbooks. OSHA suggests that employers post the policy next to the requried OSHA workplace poster where all employees can see it.

A safety policy statement should include the following:
- ◆ *a commitment to comply with all applicable laws;*
- ◆ *the overall objectives of the company's safety and health program, such as reducing or eliminating injuries and illnesses;*
- ◆ *designation of responsibilities among management, supervisors, and employees;*
- ◆ *a general statement about the consequences for employees who fail to comply with the company's safety program;*
- ◆ *a general outline of the company's safety and health program.*

Documenting your safety and health efforts

Not only should you put your safety program and policies in writing, it's a good idea to document *every* safety-related incident, communication, initiative, or event. All actions taken and their results should be recorded to reap maximum benefits and to demonstrate your compliance efforts.

You should document:

◆ Written work rules and policy statements;

◆ Communications and information distributed to employees;

◆ Training records (date, trainer, names of employees trained, topics discussed, materials used, and method of verifying learning goals achieved);

◆ Safety committee meetings and reports, including safety meetings at line level;

◆ Disciplinary records (date, name of employee, nature of infraction, action taken);

◆ Employee complaints and action taken;

◆ Hazard assessments (date, inspector, area, hazards found);

◆ Hazard controls (action taken on hazards found during the assessment);

◆ Schedule of periodic inspections and reports, with documentation of corrections;

◆ Accident investigation reports;

◆ Medical surveillance (industrial hygiene sampling, monitoring results, exposure records, medical removal records, and follow-up).

Safety and health reporting systems

Effective safety and health management depends upon an accurate reporting system. Your safety and health program should track and record injury and illness incidence rates, safety and health inspections, and accident reporting. The law requires it.

Maintain your safety information in a database system so that you can generate reports on a variety of categories and track accidents by employee name, supervisor, shift or work area, cause of accident, or other indicators.

WHAT you need to know

This exhaustive documentation might seem burdensome, but it will serve you well when you review and adjust your safety program. It will help you identify trouble spots, communication breakdowns, and how well everyone has been attending to their safety responsibilities. It aids formal recordkeeping and will be invaluable if an OSHA inspector comes calling or a workers' compensation dispute ends up in litigation.

Safety program review

Your safety program must be reviewed regularly. An annual review of safety policies and procedures is generally sufficient. But a review may be required sooner if:

◆ your organization has a substantial increase in accidents;
◆ new OSHA or other applicable safety regulations emerge; or
◆ your organization has substantially revised its equipment or operations.

There's an essential question to ask when assessing your safety plan: Does it continue to meet our safety goals?

Goal setting

A safety program identifies its specific objectives and a time frame for meeting them. Any program designed to avoid accidents, injuries and illness must set goals in order to succeed. Otherwise, how can you tell if your program is working?

Your safety program's goals should:

◆ be clearly defined;
◆ provide a clear understanding of expectations;
◆ be realistic; and
◆ allow for progress to be easily measured.

Your safety program will set goals based on keeping your workforce safe and productive and controlling costs for the organization's financial well being. Promoting safety, though obviously crucial, is not enough to protect the organization. Hazard prevention and control looks mainly to reduce the number of workplace injuries. But loss control seeks to reduce the *severity* of the injury as well, because lost workdays and large medical bills are what drive up the cost to the employer.

A safety program should set goals for reducing the number of accidents, near misses, and other elements indicative of workplace injury or illness. It must also set loss-control-based objectives such as:

◆ reducing the number of lost-time injuries per number of employees (frequency);
◆ reducing total lost workdays per number of employees (severity);
◆ reducing average lost workdays per lost-time injury; and
◆ reducing overall costs.

HR's safety role

We've talked about how your top-notch recruiting skills are a critical component of a safe and healthy workplace. But that's just the beginning of the role human resources plays in workplace safety.

Let's look at some of the other ways HR professionals contribute to safety policies and procedures in their organizations.

The face of safety

The HR department is, for many employees, the one-stop shop for all their employment needs. This includes safety, of course. That's a good thing, right? That's why you're there. You want your employees to know they can come to you with any problems they have, including concerns about their health and well being.

Conduct regular walk-arounds and encourage your HR colleagues to do the same. Let employees know they can come to you and approach you any time they see you in the hallway. Tell them to alert you of safety concerns at any time. A more visible presence will naturally make you more approachable. And the more they see you, the less likely you are to invoke *"uh ohs"* from the gloom-and-doomers when someone from HR visits their departments.

Don't just walk around to greet employees. Make an effort to take in the physicality of their workspace. How loud are those machines over in assembly? Are the Material Safety Data Sheets located where they should be? How cold is it when the dock entrance is open? If you want to convey your commitment to workplace safety and health, you need to show your desire to truly learn and understand the worksite.

✓✓ *Checklist*

Enhancing visibility

☐ Post your own policy on the importance of worker safety and health next to the OSHA workplace poster where all employees can see it.

☐ Hold meetings with all your employees to communicate that policy to them and to discuss your objectives for safety and health.

☐ Commit to an annual safety meeting to showcase activities and recognize achievement.

Employee safety meetings are a great way of connecting with your employees in groups and expressing the HR team's interest in communicating with the workforce about safety and health. Consider these suggestions when conducting employee safety meetings.

◆ Prepare and distribute an agenda in advance. Urge employees to contribute safety agenda items.

◆ Get feedback, review accidents or near misses, and inquire about whether any hazards have been spotted.

◆ Give a safety pep talk and acknowledge employees who have shown good safety habits.

◆ Though safety is a serious issue, you can lighten the tone a bit, too, by springing a surprise quiz on attendees. Ask a specific question from your organization's safety manual. Reward a prize for the correct response.

In addition to employee-wide meetings at the organizational or departmental level (depending upon the size of your company), encourage supervisors to hold smaller safety "rap sessions" at the line level. Weekly 5-10 minute informal chats are another way of conveying all-important messages. Both are useful components of your safety communication strategy.

WHAT you need to know

Safety communication is a two-way street. You need to relay concrete information about hazards and injury or illness prevention. You want to convey motivational messages too. But an equally important function of safety meetings is to hear from employees. It's probably the single most useful way of identifying workplace hazards.

Setting policy

Human resources professionals are in a key position to shape policies and procedures aimed at enhancing workplace safety and security.

First there are the safety rules, policies and procedures that will be dictated in part by OSHA requirements and the expertise of your safety professionals. Then there are the employment policies and procedures that aren't directly safety-related but clearly impact safety nonetheless. That's where your HR expertise is most valuable.

These policies include hiring procedures, job descriptions and qualifications, substance abuse provisions, absence policies, performance management, and numerous other employment rules. Consider also how your organization approaches social and recreational activities, corporate travel, telecommuting, and wellness benefits. How these functions are administered certainly can affect the safety and health of your workforce.

Dress code. *Here's an example of a policy area that falls squarely under the human resources domain, and it actually has quite a significant impact on health and safety. Consider how your standard dress code policy enhances or detracts from your safety goals. If you were drafting a dress code with safety in mind, these are some of the policy provisions you might add:*

◆ *All employees are required to where protective equipment where needed, in accordance with relevant safety policy and procedures.*

◆ *All employees performing outdoor work must wear appropriate outerwear, in accordance with relevant safety policy and procedures.*

◆ *Instead of high heels, lower, wider heels are encouraged to reduce the danger of falls.*

◆ *Do not wear loose clothing or jewelry around machinery. It may catch on moving equipment and cause a serious injury.*

◆ *Excessive perfume or cologne is discouraged in the workplace. Fragrances are chemicals, and some employees are highly sensitive or allergic to them. Employees with allergies can suffer headaches and other irritations from exposure to these odors.*

These are just a few. Open-toed shoes, shorts on the line ... these provisions might go into your safety policy. But with an eye toward integrating safety into every facet of your workplace, it's a good idea to note the safety-related dress provisions here. It seems natural to do so, once safety is truly an integral, not peripheral, part of your operations.

Consider some of the policies already on your books. Do you need to revise them to address their safety implications? Do a double-take of all your HR policies and procedures; integrate safety into each of them.

Of course, to many human resources professionals, setting policy is the easy part. "Complacency, apathy is the biggest battle," says Zrinka Allen, manager of employee relations at CCH Incorporated. "It's not a problem of putting systems in place; it's a problem of overcoming complacency among managers and employees."

How on earth will you do that? Read on.

Forging a safety culture

If the following statements are true, then you have a safety culture in your workplace:

◆ *All individuals within the organization believe they have a right to a safe and healthy workplace.*

◆ *Each person accepts personal responsibility for ensuring his or her safety and health.*

◆ *Everyone believes he or she has a duty to protect the safety and health of others.*

Show managers and employees that the organization cares about preventing accidents. Involve employees in designing safety training and programs. Make them accountable. Develop a "safety first" culture.

Wait a minute—didn't we discuss this already in another chapter?

We sure did. We talked about the importance of creating a safety mindset in your employees. But it's such a critical part of your unique role in workplace safety that it bears repeating. Making safety a vocal and visible priority in *every aspect* of the workplace will create an environment where "safety first" is more than a cliche. Don't just talk the talk.

Step one—conduct a "culture assessment." See how your organization fares using the criteria below.

✓✓ *Checklist*

Gauge your organization's current safety culture:

☐ Is there an overall commitment to safety?

☐ Where does safety rank in corporate objectives, strategies and policies?

☐ Is the message conveyed that top management is committed to safety?

☐ Do you provide adequate personnel and resources to staff safety and health programs?

☐ What is the reaction if a person sacrifices speed for safety? From coworkers? Line management? Executives?

☐ Is safety part of everyone's performance appraisals?

☐ Are safety contests used as motivators?

☐ If a manager saves on workers' compensation costs, does the money go back into the manager's department budget?

Do you see how almost each of these items involves human resources functions? Do you see how questions at the heart of corporate strategy can make or break a safety culture—and workplace safety itself? Do you see how much bigger your safety role becomes as the HR department enhances its position as a strategic partner in the organization?

Never underestimate your power to shape the organization's culture. As an HR professional, you do it every day: in the procedures you establish, the policies you enforce, the message you communicate to your workforce. Harness this power in service to safety.

An organization's injury and accident rate is really a reflection of the CEO's concern for employee safety and health. All of the other safety program features are only marginally effective without this top leadership commitment.

What about your executive team—how does it measure up?

✓ ✓ *Checklist*

Executive commitment to health and safety

Consider whether your executive team regularly does the following:

☐ Issues a written injury and illness prevention policy and visibly supports the policy.

☐ Wears appropriate safety equipment while touring the facility.

☐ Discusses health and safety issues with employees during periodic tours of the facility.

☐ Stays familiar with the details of the written health and safety program and develops action plans to implement the program.

☐ Presents safety recognition awards to employees.

☐ Participates, as a student, in some safety training programs (*e.g.*, first aid, fire extinguisher training).

☐ Occasionally attends, as an observer, employee safety meetings and training sessions.

☐ Reviews copies of supervisors' accident investigation reports.

☐ Interviews department managers and/or supervisors when one of their employees has a lost-time accident or serious near miss.

☐ Reviews agency safety performance and keeps informed of leading causes of accidents.

☐ Receives copy of safety committee minutes. Occasionally attends committee meetings.

☐ Reviews reports on safety achievements and inspections.

☐ Ensures that safety is an agenda item at staff and department meetings.

☐ Responds promptly to suggestions to improve workplace health and safety conditions.

(*Source: The* Guide to Developing Your Written Health and Safety Program, *State of Wisconsin, Department of Administration, Bureau of State Risk Management.*)

Has your CEO attended a safety meeting lately? How might you encourage him or her to do so?

Part of your power in shaping culture lies in your ability to influence the top brass. They rely on your expertise in workforce concerns, employment trends, compliance issues, and the effect each of these has on the bottom line.

Creating safety incentives

You use somewhat different strategies to influence the rank and file. One key tool is the use of incentives. Your managers have used this strategy to meet production goals and other desired outcomes. This motivator works for building good safety habits, too.

Incentives can take a variety of forms:

◆ Coffee and donuts

◆ Key chains or pens

◆ Company jacket or hat

◆ Savings bonds

◆ Pay bonuses

◆ Competitions

◆ Public recognition

Best Practices

One company holds two different monthly drawings for a $50 U.S. savings bond. One drawing is open to all employees who report at least one unsafe act or condition, submit a safety suggestion, or furnish some safety advice applicable to either the job or at home. To be eligible for the other drawing, an employee must have neither a lost-time injury during the month nor been disciplined for a safety violation during the period.

Organizations can get maximum effect from incentives by publicizing them extensively, making award presentations before the winner's peers, and including top management in award ceremonies. Some companies use annual awards and present them at dinners celebrating significant safety and health milestones.

Best Practices

Air Systems Components, a Tucson manufacturer, has a "caught in the act" program to recognize workers practicing good safety habits. A photograph of the employee is posted on the company bulletin board to acknowledge his or her safety contribution.

(Source: The Arizona Daily Star.*)*

Incentives—some caveats

DON'T miss this

It's important that your incentives for good safety practices are closely tied to your safety goals. If you offer substantial rewards like large cash bonuses you run the risk of creating a mindset that safety for its own sake isn't enough. A too-extravagant rewards program will become more important than the safety goals you want to attain!

Also be careful not to create incentive programs that have the effect of discouraging or underreporting incidents, injuries, or hazards. If this happens, you won't be building a safer workplace, you'll just be unwittingly fudging the numbers.

Safety people

Employees

Involving employees in making the workplace safer not only cuts down on accidents and the related workers' compensation and productivity costs, it also results in more committed and enthusiastic workers. Plus, tapping into workers' ideas about making the job safer can result in job modifications that make the workplace more productive too.

Your employees *must* play an active role in the following health and safety functions:

◆ inspecting for hazards and recommending corrections or controls;

- analyzing jobs to locate potential hazards and develop safe work practices;
- developing, reviewing, and revising safety rules;
- training new employees and coworkers in safe work procedures;
- preparing and presenting programs for safety meetings;
- serving in accident investigation teams;
- participating in OSHA walk-around inspections and interviews; and
- taking functional responsibility for their own health and safety.

Best Practices

OSHA urges employers to encourage and authorize employees to stop activities that present potentially serious safety and health hazards. Employees of Johnson Control Northern New Mexico who work at Los Alamos laboratory understand their vital role in safety. They know the safety procedures and hazards, and they have this "stop work" authority if a hazard arises.

Safety committees

Employees can play a concrete, ongoing safety role through participation in health and safety committees. When properly organized and administered, safety and health committees are invaluable tools for employees to contribute to a safe and healthy work environment.

Who should participate? Consider rotating employees so they all can play an active part in safety and health programming. You can rotate employee assignments into various safety teams, or seek volunteers to participate. A union may appoint members to the labor-management safety committee, or coworkers might elect them. A committee might require a certain number of employees from each of your departments or occupational categories. Of course, certain employees simply will have to participate in particular safety committees by virtue of their job functions, expert knowledge, or safety-sensitive role.

Safety committee members typically serve one or two years. Sometimes, members serve staggered terms to prevent a complete turnover when member terms expire.

How do you prepare committee members? Usually new members are oriented in their duties and receive more extensive health and safety training and instruction in hazard identification and regulatory issues. Regular briefings from management reps on the committee keep employee members in the know about current safety and health matters that arise. Some organizations provide committee members with subscriptions to safety and health newsletters or other informational tools.

In addition to acquiring safety knowledge, committee members might need skill building in conflict management, problem solving, leadership skills, business communications, or related abilities in preparation for their committee work.

What functions can committees serve? There are a variety of ways to set up your committee structure according to your employee population and your various safety needs:

◆ Your program might have one safety and health committee for the entire organization. Or you can have one safety committee for each worksite or in every large business unit.

◆ One committee might address all of your organization's safety goals. Or you might devise individual committees to attack particular issues, like coworker involvement in safety, improved compliance, or a reduction in risky behavior.

◆ You might set up a separate committee to study each specific hazard or safety issue at hand, like chemical and air conditions, industrial hygiene, noise abatement and hazard communications.

WHAT you need to know

It's a good idea for your safety program to provide for separate committees for the "big" safety issues. A specific ergonomics team, for example, can devote its time solely to gaining expertise in this increasingly complicated area. Team members might not have that luxury if they were required to spread their efforts across your many safety needs. A disaster readiness team or workplace violence response team should be discrete groups as well.

How can committees enhance communication? Safety committees are effective communication channels between employees and management, assuming employees know their committee reps and their efforts are well publicized. To ensure this, list the names of safety committee members in employee newsletters. Encourage employees to discuss their safety and health concerns with committee members. Some unions have their safety committee representative write columns in the local union newsletter and make presentations at union meetings. This might be a nice idea for your employee intranet!

How do committees work? Committees may meet monthly or quarterly, depending upon your organization's safety needs. Meetings are typically run on agendas, and minutes are distributed and action items developed. Your safety plan should identify how committee proceedings will function.

Safety committees are most prevalent in unionized workplaces. Often the committee structure, membership selection, and committee responsibilities are determined by a collective bargaining agreement.

Seneca Hospital Safety and Health Committee Meeting Minutes

January 15, 2003

Attendance: Sue Gardner, Paperworkers Union; Jacob Ginns, IBEW; Murial Roswell, Paperworkers Union; Roy Senn, Safety Officer, Jennings Sisky, American Nurses Association; and Josephine Waters, Human Resources Director.

Action Items (old business):
#22—Mopping the floor during shift changes on Saturdays causes a slipping hazard. Item referred to Joe Landrigan in Plant Maintenance.
Action: Mr. Landrigan sent memo to the committee stating the mopping will be done on the second shift when the staffing levels are lowest and when most patients are sleeping.

*Sometimes state laws require employers to form safety commit-
tees. For example, Oregon's workers' compensation law mandates
that employers with more than 10 workers must establish a safety
committee. An employer with 10 or fewer employees must establish a safety committee if the employer has a lost workday rate in
the top 10 percent in the industry or if its workers' compensation
premiums are in the top 25 percent of all classes of employers.*

Unions

Unions are keenly interested in employee safety and health, and
they spend considerable resources protecting their members. For
example, unions in the healthcare industry use audio-visual materials, pamphlets, and safety and health training courses to teach
employees about hazards in healthcare facilities. They lobby Con-
gress to introduce legislation aimed at tougher safety and health
laws. Unions pressure OSHA to reduce exposure limits on hazardous substances and materials. They are especially watchful of any
reduction in the enforcement of safety and health laws, regulations,
and standards.

Given these vigorous activities, it may appear that unions and
employers are at odds over safety and health issues. It might seem
like labor-management cooperation is not feasible. But this is simply untrue.

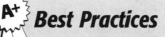

Best Practices

Union-management cooperation

Levi Strauss and Company has enjoyed a long productive partnership with the Union of Needletrades,
Industrial and Textile Employees (UNITE!), the union rep-
resenting much of its workforce. Speaking about its Labor-
Management Partnership at an October 2001 session of the
"Unions and Management Working Together" conference
in Chicago, the company's director of industrial relations
and the international union vice-president jointly presented
the organization's "LEAP" ergonomics action program. The

team included representatives from the company's health and safety, engineering, and HR staff, as well as union representatives. The program's goals were to create more safety awareness in order to avert potential injuries, and to train employees on ergonomic risk factors and on how to work safely and comfortably.

Efforts have paid off. Levi Strauss reported a reduction in the frequency and severity of ergonomic injuries, quicker return to work and, just as important to this company, increased employee involvement in the organization through its union.

If you have a union, you most likely have a traditional joint labor-management safety and health committee in accordance with the union contract. The union almost certainly has an independent safety and health committee too. The union local's safety committee is usually composed of members working for various employers. It addresses the safety needs of members at numerous different worksites. It's *not* a substitute for union participation in your organization's safety committees.

WHAT
you need
to know

A union perspective

"Don't let the [health and safety] committee become part of the problem!," warns the American Federation of State, County and Municipal Employees at its "Safe Jobs Now" website. It tells members that management can misuse the committee structure as a way of feigning concern about safety without actually addressing hazards in the workplace. It urges its union members to judge the success of a safety committee by asking themselves:

- Are hazards seen as real and serious?
- Has the committee made good and workable recommendations?
- Has the employer put the committee's recommendations into practice?
- Does it take longer than it should to get action?
- Is management more interested in slogans and putting up posters?
- Does management prefer to run "safety" contests than make real changes?

It's a good reality check to hear what employees and their labor union reps are thinking.

So you don't have a union in your workplace. Do you want one? If your workers aren't currently represented by a labor union, one of the quickest ways for a union to come in is for an employer to neglect workplace safety. Safety concerns are one of the top issues used by unions during organizing drives. In fact, in many elections, safety surpasses the bread and butter issues like wages and benefits.

Supervisors

Of course, supervisors have critical safety roles in the organization. As we noted earlier, they are crucial to forging a safety mindset. Let's take a look at the full scope of their functions in your health and safety program:

Train and motivate

◆ Know the organization's safety policies and programs inside and out.

◆ Follow personally all company safety rules and safe work practices.

◆ Provide complete health and safety instruction and training for employees.

◆ Conduct a thorough safety orientation for new and transferred employees.

◆ Instill a high level of safety awareness through leadership and positive reinforcement.

◆ Encourage employee participation in safety committees and suggestion programs.

◆ Reinforce the organization's safety message by "walking the walk."

Team-build and communicate

◆ Conduct group safety meetings at least quarterly.

◆ Hold informal safety rap sessions a few times each month.

◆ Conduct frequent one-on-one safety talks with employees.

◆ Attend safety meetings and training sessions when requested.

Manage performance
◆ Consistently enforce all safety rules.
◆ Take disciplinary action for repeated safety rule violators.
◆ Recognize positive safety efforts.
◆ Assess safety performance in performance reviews.

Manage hazards and unsafe conditions
◆ Don't order unsafe work speed-ups or make unreasonable production demands.
◆ Provide adequate personal protective equipment and training on its proper use.
◆ Ensure that appropriate protective devices are installed and intact on all machines.
◆ Ensure that good housekeeping practices are maintained at all times.
◆ Conduct periodic planned safety inspections in your work area.
◆ Issue work orders and written requests to address hazardous conditions.
◆ Follow up to ensure timely correction of the problem.

Manage the aftermath
◆ Immediately investigate all accidents and near-miss incidents in your area.
◆ Report accidents and near misses promptly to the appropriate safety personnel.
◆ Ensure that injured and ill employees are referred for proper medical treatment.
◆ Get your area up and running at optimal levels as soon as *safely* possible.

(Source: adapted in part from The Guide to Developing Your Written Health and Safety Program, *State of Wisconsin, Department of Administration, Bureau of State Risk Management.)*

The safety officer

Ideally, your organization has a safety specialist on staff—your go-to person for conducting hazard analysis, recommending safety measures, and overseeing compliance. If you don't have a safety officer, consult with outside professionals for guidance on your programs, policies, and safety law.

Sources of safety and health expertise include consulting services sponsored by OSHA, insurance companies (for whom safety consulting is integral to loss prevention), and private consultants. There are various safety professionals who can assist you:

◆ **Safety professionals** identify and evaluate hazardous conditions or practices, and develop procedures or systems to control or reduce them.

◆ **Industrial engineers** design, install, or improve integrated systems of people, material, information, equipment, and energy.

◆ **Ergonomists** fit workplace conditions and job demands to the capabilities of individual workers to maximize comfort, safety, and job performance.

◆ **Industrial hygienists** identify and control workplace chemical, biological, or physical factors that cause sickness, impaired health, or significant discomfort.

◆ **Occupational health professionals** assess and treat workplace illnesses and injuries. They perform physical exams, job placement assessments, periodic examinations, and may provide screening related to specific chemicals or exposures as well.

Safety training

Roderick is always willing to lend a hand, so when Minkyu joined the warehouse staff, Roderick stepped up and offered to train him. They did the same job, and Roderick had been relatively accident and error-free, so Miguel, the warehouse supervisor, was confident delegating the training to Roderick.

Things were going smoothly; Minkyu trailed Roderick as he worked, Roderick gave quick how-to's with each new task, and then Minkyu would step in and help. Miguel was especially pleased when he passed the pair and heard Roderick telling Minkyu about the importance of proper loading to avoid dangerous shifting of cargo when the truck is in motion.

So Miguel couldn't believe his eyes when he saw Roderick show Minkyu how to unload a 50-gallon drum. The way he rolled the drum to position it on the lift was downright reckless. Was that how Roderick always unloaded drums? How has he evaded injury thus far? Miguel would have to intervene. He didn't want his new worker to pick up this unsafe practice.

Training is essential for employees to know how to protect themselves at work. But to be successful, training must be conducted by qualified persons. While Roderick's intentions were good, he didn't have the safety knowledge to instruct Minkyu. In fact, Roderick needed more training himself!

Your general safety orientation is broad enough to encompass the varied roles and hazards that all your employees share. But the intensive, hands-on training should be job- and site-specific. Had Roderick been properly trained himself and been given some basic train-the-trainer education, he might have been an ideal trainer for Minkyu. Because he had the same job, Roderick would best know the hazards and hazard control strategies unique to Minkyu's position.

OSHA says: *Safety training is most effective when it is incorporated into other training about performance requirements and job practices.*

DON'T
miss
this

✓ ✓ ✓ *Checklist*

Whom do you train, and when?

Training generally should be conducted according to the following needs:

☐ Train supervisors to familiarize them with the hazards to which workers under their supervision may be exposed.

☐ Train all employees when the safety and health program is established.

☐ Train all newly hired employees.

☐ Train all workers as they transfer to new job assignments.

☐ Train all affected workers whenever new substances, procedures or equipment are introduced in the workplace.

☐ Train all affected workers if you uncover a new or previously unrecognized hazard.

☐ Train your safety committee members (short but intensive instruction in safety and health principles).

☐ Train members of your labor-management safety committee (usually pursuant to a union contract).

☐ Train members of your crisis or emergency management team.

Training content

To be effective, training should be done in person, with interaction between the trainer and the workers to ensure that the training is understood. Videotapes, computer-based training or written materials are not enough by themselves, but they can be an excellent component of a safety training program. If the workforce includes non-English speaking workers, the training program should include a method for instructing workers who do not speak or read English.

Sending some of your employees to attend train-the-trainer sessions conducted by a safety professional allows you to provide professional quality in-house training.

Best Practices

OSHA voluntary training guidelines

OSHA has voluntary training guidelines that offer these training tips:

◆ Determine whether you can solve a worksite problem by training.

◆ Determine what training is needed using a job safety analysis or other measure.

◆ Use specific, action-oriented training objectives.

◆ Design learning activities that simulate the actual work environment to facilitate learning reinforcement and application.

◆ Motivate employees to learn by pointing out the benefits of training to them personally.

◆ Evaluate the training to gauge its continued effectiveness, and revise your program as needed.

◆ If training cannot be given to all employees due to budget or other constraints, establish a priority for such training, which includes these considerations:
  ◆ Train employees who have the greatest need to be trained; and
  ◆ Train employees in the most hazardous occupations.

Like every other component of your health and safety program, your training program needs periodic review to make sure its content, scope, and frequency are sufficient for your safety needs. Modify the training curriculum as needed based on newly emerged hazards and newly promulgated OSHA regulations. You may need to deviate from your standard training schedule, too, if circumstances require.

Worksite hazard analysis and audits

A *job hazard analysis* breaks down each job function into its most basic steps. Then the hazards associated with each step are identified. Hazard controls are established for each identified hazard.

Then a chart is prepared, which lists the basic job steps and the associated controls. The chart is used to determine the events and the conditions that led to the accident, such as the failure to follow a step or the failure to control for a hazard.

Hazard identification and analysis is one of the major functions of a safety program. A good safety program will include an initial "baseline" analysis of the hazards (and potential hazards) already existing in your workplace. The program should also provide for a system of ongoing hazard evaluation, to identify and analyze hazards that emerge later.

✓ *Checklist*

Conducting an initial hazard analysis

An effective safety program provides the following steps in conducting a rigorous baseline analysis:

☐ Determine which OSHA standards, state regulations, or other agency provisions your workplace *must* comply with.

☐ Research the types of hazards prevalent in your particular industry, and the industry standard for controlling them. Consult national consensus standards, industry publications, trade associations, and equipment manufacturers.

☐ Analyze your organization's accident, injury and illness records over time to identify patterns that emerge or problem
areas. (This analysis is especially important for preventing or
controlling occupational illness hazards.)

☐ Conduct a comprehensive, systematic worksite survey to
identify existing or potential hazards. Obtain outside expertise
if you need help determining appropriate methods for
the assessment.

☐ Conduct a detailed job hazard analysis for each position.

☐ Document all identified job hazards and worksite hazards.

Doing the research is an important precursor to your worksite
hazard analysis. It's important, for example, to first identify what
OSHA expects of your organization given its particular production and
industry characteristics. Even if no specific OSHA worksite standard
applies, though (such as hazard communication, scaffolding safety,
construction training requirements), its "general duty" clause does.
You *must* comply with the agency's general mandate that employers
provide their workers a safe and healthful work environment.

Computing the incidence rate. Your worksite hazard analysis
should include a review of your organization's incidence rates.
The incidence rate is the percentage of full-time employees (or the
number of workers out of every 100) who suffer a recordable injury
or illness during a calendar year. To compute your incidence rate,
you need to know:

◆ the number of employee injuries within a set period of time
◆ the number of employee hours worked during that period
◆ that "200,000" is used as a standard base for comparing rates.
(This figure represents the equivalent of 100 employees
working 40 hours a week for 50 weeks. It assumes 2 weeks
off work per employee.)

Here's the formula:

No. of injuries and illnesses x 200,000 = A;

Divide A by the number of employee hours worked;

That's your incidence rate.

Example. *Friendly Furniture Co. had five (5) recordable injuries and illnesses during 2002. The total hours worked by all its employees during this period were 125,000.*

   5 injuries x 200,000 = 1,000,000
   1,000,000 divided by 125,000 work hours = 8.0
Friendly Furniture had 8.0 injuries and illnesses per 100 full-time employees during 2002. That's the company's incidence rate.

Continuing hazard evaluations

Your safety program must entail an ongoing system for monitoring hazards and hazard controls. Ongoing hazard evaluations allow you to identify hazards that were previously missed and those that just emerged. They also help you gauge the effectiveness of the hazard controls you've implemented since your initial baseline check.

Your baseline record will provide a checklist for later routine inspections. Once your initial worksite analysis has been conducted, you'll have a clearer picture of what steps your periodic hazard evaluations will entail.

In crafting specific procedures for your routine hazard evaluations, keep the following principles in mind:

◆ Use workplace safety rules as an inspection checklist. Find out if safety rules are being followed. If not, analyze why.

◆ Encourage employees to report safety hazards, observations, or concerns without fear of reprisal, and make sure that employees get a timely and appropriate response.

◆ Continue to analyze injury and illness trends and incorporate new data to identify problem patterns; adjust your safety program accordingly.

◆ Include routine monitoring of noise, toxic substances, and other industrial hygiene hazards as part of your regular safety and health inspections.

◆ Undertake "change analysis" to detect potential hazards in advance when modifications, new facilities, processes, or equipment are being introduced.

◆ Conduct periodic *update surveys* like your initial hazard analysis. These provide an opportunity to step back from routine checks of known hazards, and look for other hazards that may have been missed.

OSHA recommends monthly self-inspections for most workplaces, and weekly inspections for construction worksites.

Safety audits and inspections

A *safety audit* is a comprehensive evaluation of an organization's entire safety and health program. A *safety inspection* is a periodic evaluation of various departments or operating units to determine if any unsafe conditions exist and whether safety and health procedures are followed. Both are powerful tools for ensuring optimal safety conditions and legal compliance.

Hazard prevention and control

Your safety program should encompass and identify the hazard prevention and control strategies outlined in the following chapter. You'll see that some of the hazard prevention strategies at your disposal include engineering controls (like redesigning poorly structured workstations), administrative controls (adopting "ramp-up" policies for new employees), and personal protective equipment.

Integrate these additional guidelines into the hazard prevention and control provisions of your safety plan:

- ◆ Involve employees in devising hazard control methods.
- ◆ Use engineering controls first, and to the maximum extent feasible.
- ◆ Provide personal protective equipment and adopt written rules for selecting, using, and maintaining the equipment.
- ◆ Establish safe work practices for equipment ("use only with guards in place"), workplace conditions ("ventilation system must be operating effectively"), and work practices ("do not operate vehicle in reverse with obstructed rear vision").
- ◆ Follow manufacturers' recommendations and industry and consensus standards for equipment maintenance. OSHA advises the use of a comprehensive safety and preventive maintenance program to maximize equipment reliability.
- ◆ Check and document the condition of safety devices on equipment and machinery before each shift.
- ◆ Use well-defined job descriptions that include specific training requirements, especially for occupational disease

prevention in jobs requiring exposure to toxic and hazardous substances.

◆ Correct hazards in the shortest possible time, given the complexity of the technology required, the degree of the risk, and the availability of materials and staff to make the correction.

◆ If immediate correction is not possible, provide interim protection.

The practice of correcting identified hazards is usually referred to, in safety talk, as *hazard abatement.*

Don't forget to prevent and control human errors, too. Analyze them as you would machinery or system breakdowns. Is there a frequent departure from a particular safety rule? If so, has management failed to communicate the danger the rule seeks to minimize? Perhaps the rule is unnecessary. Perhaps it should be modified because it's too difficult to follow under the circumstances. Or maybe additional training is needed to enable workers to follow the rule.

Medical program. An effective hazard prevention and control strategy should include a medical component. Your program should provide for medical surveillance, monitoring, removal, and reporting, as required by applicable OSHA standards.

Injury or illness: the aftermath

Despite the most well-executed health and safety program and the most conscientious, highly trained workforce, a workplace accident or hazard exposure will more than likely occur at some point during your organization's operations.

An outstanding safety program minimizes injuries, physical damage, and economic consequences for the employee and the organization. An organization with a true safety mindset immediately tends to the workers involved as well as their coworkers and gets back on track as quickly as safety will allow. Then it evaluates what happened and learns from the incident to reduce the risk of similar events in the future.

Accident response

Omar was injured after a platform he was standing on was hit by a forklift Tom was driving in reverse. Omar was knocked off the platform and took a fairly steep fall. It wasn't clear how badly he was hurt, but pandemonium broke out quickly. Tom seemed genuinely concerned and sorry, but he was more intent on figuring out how to cover up his mistake. Garth, Omar's good friend, was angry and started to go after Tom. Tom got so distracted he didn't secure the forklift. Mike and Lupe argued over whether they should try to move Omar, who was still too stunned to join the debate—all he could think about was the horrible pain in his right leg and abdomen.

Ahmad, always the instigator, was already ranting about how dangerous "this place" was, and that Omar should sue. In the meantime Deb, the shift supervisor, was out on break, and no one was making the slightest effort to try to locate her, let alone call for an ambulance...

Once an accident happens, quick response is critical. The quality of your team's response can determine the well being of the affected employee and the extent of the damage done. The initial response requires caring for the injured, preventing secondary accidents, and preserving evidence. It must be carried out as follows:

◆ Take control of the accident scene. Accidents affect people differently, and may make them curious, irrational, confused, or even unable to act. A leader or supervisor needs to take charge immediately.

◆ Administer first aid if necessary and call for emergency services. Assign someone to keep the injured employee calm. A member of the human resources team, or a trusted coworker of the injured employee, are best able to keep the employee at ease.

◆ Control potential secondary accidents. An accident scene can be a trap for those seeking to help. Spot potential dangers and warn others.

◆ Identify sources of evidence that may be moved or removed during the emergency response and rescue efforts.

◆ Prevent evidence at the scene from being altered or removed. Use employees to block off the evidence and preserve it for investigation purposes.

◆ Notify appropriate managers. Some may need just a courtesy notification; others may have to be called to the scene.

Ensure that first aid and emergency care is readily available in case of injury or illness. Resources must be on-site (or at a nearby hospital emergency room) on every shift. If your organization is a highly hazardous worksite, employees trained in CPR and certified in first aid skills should be available on every shift.

Omar's accident is a good illustration of how quickly things can get out of hand. But a good safety program that trains supervisors and employees on accident response and reinforces the training with reminders or role-plays in safety meetings, can help prevent some of the problems that followed the incident.

On the other hand there are times when, in the heat of the moment, training, policy, and reason go out the window. That's why the presence of a supervisor, safety officer, or human resources team member should be sought out immediately. A leader needs to be on the spot to control the situation until cooler heads prevail.

Accident Investigation

Thorough investigations can prevent future accidents and minimize the damage of the incident that just happened. Getting to the root cause helps eliminate the hazard and therefore, further incidents. A well-documented investigation can control the extent of the organization's liability in the event of legal action as well.

Conduct your accident investigation immediately, once the worksite has been stabilized and it's safe to investigate. Why is prompt investigation so critical?

◆ to record what happened and why when the incident is freshest in the minds of witnesses;

◆ to determine quickly if a similar hazard exists elsewhere at the worksite that must be abated;

◆ to shorten downtime caused by investigation needs; and

◆ to assess whether safety rules were violated so that timely disciplinary action can be taken.

Some studies show that property damage and downtime resulting from accidents cost organizations 5 to 50 times more than workers' compensation costs of the accident.

Accident investigations should be conducted by trained individuals. Ideally, they are the responsibility of the safety director. However, this should not be mandated if your safety officer's limited resources would prevent *all* relevant incidents from being investigated, including minor accidents and near misses. Supervisors should be involved and trained in your safety program's investigative procedures, in either case.

The investigator should ask:

1. What occurred? (Describe in detail what took place: for example, an injury to an employee, an incident that caused a work stoppage and production delay.)
2. Why did it occur? (Uncover all the facts: who was involved, whether the individual was qualified and properly trained to perform the function he was doing, whether proper safety procedures were used.)
3. What should be done? (What is the problem that requires attention? This is not to establish blame, but to determine what constructive actions can prevent further incidents.)
4. What has already been done? (Note any actions that have been taken to reduce or eliminate the hazard. Interim or temporary precautions should also be noted. Identify any corrective action that is pending, and why it hasn't been implemented yet.)

Four basic types of evidence will be uncovered and pieced together to tell the whole story:

Position evidence. This evidence explains the physical environment of the site when the incident occurred. Where was each worker at the time? Where were the materials and equipment?

People evidence. To gather information from accident witnesses, interview them. Interview employees separately so they don't influence each other's recollection. Never challenge the employee's story.

Wherever possible, conduct interviews in the employee's native language. However, if a translator assists you, make sure the employee's message isn't conveyed to you in looser or slightly varied terms. There is no room for interpretation here. You can't be satisfied with just getting the "gist" of it; you need a precise account just as the employee conveys it. If necesssary, ask the employee to write out a detailed description in his or her language. Then you can seek a more methodical translation of the employee's report at a later time.

Parts evidence. This evidence includes the tools, equipment, and materials used in the course of the incident. Review standards for usability, condition, guards, safety features, and hazard warning labels. Look for failures in equipment and structures, and ensure that suspect parts are saved and examined.

Paper evidence. A primary goal in investigating accidents is to prevent recurrence. To achieve this goal, the investigator has to find the underlying or systemic causes in addition to the immediate cause of the accident. To this end, the investigator reviews:

◆ Training records (if an employee failed to use the right procedure or equipment);

◆ Maintenance logs and records (if equipment was worn, previously damaged, or in disrepair);

◆ Shift schedules (if employees were servicing and operating equipment at the same time, or there was evidence of congestion, interference, fatigue, or stress); and

◆ Job procedures and practices (to identify current job standards for the position in question).

Accident follow-up

The investigation has been completed. Now your organization needs to do the work of reporting and analyzing the findings, assessing the potential loss, and adopting remedial measures.

The evidence is now to be analyzed so that causes can be identified. While the immediate cause generates a great deal of attention, it's the underlying causes that must be remedied in order to prevent future incidents. Ask these critical questions: How serious might the accident have been? How likely is it to occur again? When you know the underlying cause of the incident, and the answers to these follow-up questions, you'll be able to adopt corrective actions.

The safety incident report. There is no standardized incident form that is required by law, but you can create one that includes the following information:

- ◆ Type of incident
- ◆ Date and time of the incident
- ◆ Location of the incident
- ◆ Name and other relevant personal information of the injured employee
- ◆ Position, employment status, rate of pay of injured employee
- ◆ Name of supervisor and other operating personnel on duty at the time of the incident
- ◆ Name of paramedic and medical facility that treated the employee, if any
- ◆ Names, addresses, phone numbers of witnesses to the incident
- ◆ Detailed description of the incident: the sequence of events, extent of damage, type of accident, source of energy or hazardous material)
- ◆ Date and time of report preparation
- ◆ Name of preparer of the incident report

Include all witness testimony and forms too; you want a thorough and complete record of what happened. The report might well be used in a legal proceeding if an injury becomes a workers' compensation issue that must be litigated. It should be written accordingly.

The accident investigation report is one of your organization's critical safety documents. It should be reviewed by management, the safety officer (if the officer didn't conduct the investigation), and the safety committee. Don't treat the document as a mere exercise in recordkeeping. Your organization can't learn from an accident if its follow-up report is filed away with no further action taken. That would be *bad* safety policy—one that would undermine the health and safety program you worked so hard to create.

The Quiz

1. If the HR training team does its job right,   ❏ True   ❏ False
   new employees will show up to their department
   armed with all the safety instruction they'll need.

2. You should avoid getting the union involved   ❏ True   ❏ False
   in your safety program at all costs.

3. It's best to keep your safety policies entirely   ❏ True   ❏ False
   distinct and separate from your other policies
   and procedures.

4. The most extravagant safety incentive reward   ❏ True   ❏ False
   isn't necessarily the best one.

5. Where accident investigations are concerned,   ❏ True   ❏ False
   the best strategy is "the sooner, the better."

Answer key: 1. F; 2. F; 3. F; 4. T; 5. T

A safe workplace

So your boss has asked you to take on the workplace safety role in your HR department. You're excited by the challenge and increased responsibility—that is, until you start to do the research. Bloodborne pathogens? Material safety data sheets? What's a "hazmat," anyway? Now you fear you're in over your head. You chose a career in human resources because you're a people person. How did you ever manage to get yourself into this?

Introduction

Ensuring a safe and healthy workplace is no small task. It requires an exhaustive review of your organization's work environment to assess the health hazards and safety risks that threaten your workers. And that's just the first step. Actually preventing and controlling the hazards is even more complicated, of course. These functions require the expertise of a safety professional, and you probably aren't expected to go it alone. If your organization doesn't have an in-house safety officer, you'll need to collaborate with your maintenance and building staff, in addition to outside experts, in order to find and minimize workplace risks.

The nature of your business will determine the type and extent of the workplace hazards your employees face. Manufacturers, warehouses, healthcare providers, construction companies—these employers have unique or heightened dangers that may require an on-site safety officer to manage.

We won't focus on these industries for our purposes, though. We'll direct our attention to the more general workplace and the common dangers present there. You don't want to become an occupational safety engineer, after all; you just need a general understanding of the hazards and issues so that you can coordinate HR's role in your organization's overall safety efforts.

To this end, a simple overview is in order. We'll take a quick look at some of the occupational health and safety hazards of the industrial workplace, but our main focus will be on the more common dangers present in the typical office setting.

WHAT you need to know

*Different workplaces pose different dangers. Healthcare employees are at a greater risk from bloodborne pathogens or radiation exposure. Construction workers and road crews are more susceptible to workplace accidents. Office workers, insulated though they may seem from occupational hazards, also face ergonomic stressors that can debilitate. Yet despite the variety of workplace dangers that exist, there are basically two ways your employees can be jeopardized at work. They can be made ill because of an **unhealthy work environment,** or they can be injured (or even killed) due to **unsafe work conditions.***

The "general duty" clause

The federal government and most states expect employers to keep workers safe in the workplace. While it's impossible to eliminate all the hazards that employees face, going to work should be as safe as reasonably possible. Under the Occupational Safety and Health Act, employers are required to "provide a workplace free from known hazards that are causing, or are likely to cause, death or serious physical harm to employees." This obligation is referred to as the "general duty clause."

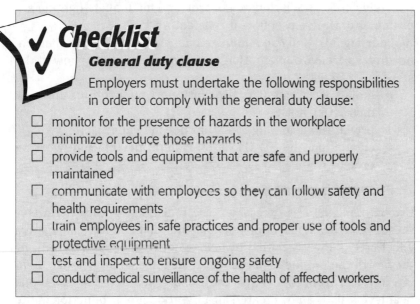

✓ Checklist

General duty clause

Employers must undertake the following responsibilities in order to comply with the general duty clause:

- ☐ monitor for the presence of hazards in the workplace
- ☐ minimize or reduce those hazards
- ☐ provide tools and equipment that are safe and properly maintained
- ☐ communicate with employees so they can follow safety and health requirements
- ☐ train employees in safe practices and proper use of tools and protective equipment
- ☐ test and inspect to ensure ongoing safety
- ☐ conduct medical surveillance of the health of affected workers.

In addition to establishing general provisions to keep employees safe and healthy, OSHA sets particular standards to regulate aspects of the worksite that need careful attention. Here are some examples of particular areas that have been regulated:

- ◆ orderliness and maintenance of worksites
- ◆ handling of hazardous materials
- ◆ electrical standards
- ◆ mandated use of protective gear or equipment for certain employees
- ◆ temperature and ventilation
- ◆ clear ingress/egress, stairways
- ◆ fire evacuation, emergency exits, alarm systems, sprinklers
- ◆ noise levels.

These standards apply to all organizations and their workplaces. They are aimed at reducing health hazards and illnesses, as well as safety dangers and workplace injuries.

Health hazards and illnesses

An unhealthy work environment can cause occupational illnesses, or it can simply create general discomfort. Whether the unhealthy worksite causes a full-blown illness or simple lethargy, however, it has a marked impact on employee well being and productivity. Excessive noise, poor climate control, and inadequate lighting are examples of work-environment risk factors.

Your organization can minimize many of the elements of an unhealthy work environment. Here, for example, are just a few of the steps you can take:

◆ isolate equipment or operations that produce loud or distracting noise
◆ provide sufficient lighting that doesn't cause glare
◆ ensure that the HVAC system is in proper, efficient working order.

Physical hazards

Extreme temperatures, excessive noise, radiation, electrical hazards—these are all examples of physical agents that can have a negative effect on employee health. Physical agents can occur naturally, or they might be produced in the workplace itself. For instance, heat is a physical agent that is the result of the weather. But dangerous heat levels also can be created as a byproduct of production in the workplace. You need to be cognizant of both the natural and "man-made" dangers that employees may be exposed to at work.

Noise. Too much noise can be hazardous to your health, especially when workers are exposed to it on a continuing basis. ToolBoxTopics.com, a website dedicated to workplace safety, defines noise as "unwanted sound that can effect job performance, safety, and your health." The physical effects of excess noise can include hearing loss (temporary or permanent), and perhaps surprisingly, pain and nausea.

Too much noise does more than damage your ears and jeopardize your hearing, though. Excessive noise also increases physiological hazards like blood pressure and stress. So it's important for a number of reasons to monitor the noise levels in your workplace.

Employers can take engineering steps to reduce the hazard. These measures might include:

◆ enclosing or muffling loud machinery, or installing acoustical material that absorbs sound, like acoustic ceiling tile;

◆ rotating workers in and out of noisy areas to reduce extended exposure; and

◆ keeping machinery well maintained to reduce the noise emitted.

Personal protective equipment is critical to protect employees from the hazardous effects of too much noise. Earplugs and earmuffs serve as barriers to the ear, reducing inner ear noise levels.

DON'T miss this

Should your employees be required to wear such protection? According to ToolBoxTopics.com, here are some signs that they should:

◆ *They have to speak in a very loud voice or shout at their immediate coworkers in order to be heard and understood.*

◆ *They have roaring or ringing noises in their ears at the end of the workday.*

◆ *Speech or music sounds muffled to employees after they leave work, but sounds fairly clear in the morning before they arrive at work.*

It's also important to keep in mind another incidental danger of excess noise: loud noise at work interferes with effective communication—talking to and hearing your coworkers on the job. These communication difficulties can cause workplace accidents, or make it difficult to convey safety and evacuation instructions in the event of an accident or emergency. That means there are even more reasons to keep excessive noise in check.

Extreme cold. More than 700 people die each year from hypothermia in the United States. Given the grave dangers cold weather can pose, it's critical to learn the signs and symptoms of cold-induced illnesses and what to do to help an ailing worker. According to OSHA, employers can take steps to help protect their cold-weather workers from potentially deadly working conditions.

Know about the two most serious hazards employees face from the cold—frostbite and hypothermia:

Signs of frostbite.
◆ Pale, waxy-white skin color
◆ Skin becomes hard and numb
◆ Usually affects fingers, hands, toes, feet, ears, and nose

How to help. Move the employee to a warm, dry area. Do not leave the employee alone. Remove wet or tight clothing. Do not rub the affected area. Instead, slowly warm the affected area in a warm water bath, but do not pour the water directly on the area. Seek medical attention ASAP.

Signs of hypothermia.
◆ Fatigue or drowsiness
◆ Uncontrolled shivering
◆ Cool bluish skin
◆ Slurred speech
◆ Clumsy movements
◆ Irritable, irrational, or confused behavior

How to help. Call for emergency help. Move the employee to a warm, dry area. Don't leave the employee alone. Remove wet clothing and replace with warm, dry clothing or wrap the employee in a blanket. Give the employee warm, sweet drinks if he or she is alert. Have the employee move the arms and legs to create muscle heat, or place warm bottles in the armpits, groin, neck, and head areas. Do not rub the employee's body or place him or her in a warm-water bath.

Extreme heat. Heat exposure carries a number of health hazards to the outdoor worker, including dehydration, sunburn, fatigue, cramps, fainting, heatstroke, cancer, and in the worst case, death. In fact, in 2000, 21 workers died and 2,554 others experienced heat-related occupational injuries and illnesses serious enough to miss work days.

OSHA imposes obligations on employers whose workers face heat hazards. The agency requires employers to provide protective equipment to employees who are over-exposed to the sun's radiation.

✓ Checklist

✓

Combating heat risks

OSHA has compiled a checklist to help combat the heat risks faced by outdoor workers:

☐ Encourage workers to drink plenty of water: about one cup every 15-20 minutes.

☐ Help workers adjust to the heat by assigning a lighter work-load and longer rest periods for the first five to seven days of intense heat.

☐ Encourage workers to wear lightweight, loose-fitting, light-colored clothing.

☐ Use general ventilation and spot cooling at points of high heat production.

☐ Alternate work and rest periods, and take longer rest breaks in a cooler area. Shorter, but frequent, work-rest cycles are best.

☐ Monitor temperatures, humidity and workers' responses to heat at least hourly.

☐ Learn to spot the signs of heat stroke, which can be fatal. The symptoms are severe headache, mental confusion/loss of consciousness, flushed face and hot, dry skin. If someone has stopped sweating, seek medical attention immediately. Other heat-induced illnesses include heat exhaustion, heat cramps, skin rashes, swelling and loss of mental and physical work capacity.

☐ Train first-aid workers along with all employees to recognize and treat the signs of heat stress. Be sure all workers know who has been trained to provide first aid. Also train supervisors to detect early signs of heat-related illness and permit workers to interrupt their work if they become extremely uncomfortable.

Consider a worker's physical condition when determining fitness to work in extreme temperatures. Obesity, lack of conditioning, pregnancy, or inadequate rest can increase susceptibility to heat stress. Chronic medical conditions like heart disease or diabetes make workers vulnerable too. Certain medications or regimens like low-sodium diets heighten the risks from heat exposure. In short: seek medical advice before sending medically vulnerable employees out into the heat or cold.

Indoor air quality

Irene is out sick again today. She came back yesterday after three days off due to what her doctor said was a sinus infection. But Irene felt lousy again as soon as she returned to work. Now she thinks it's an allergy to something here in the office. Come to think of it, you noticed a different fragrance in the restrooms recently. After checking with building management, you've discovered that the custodial staff began using a new cleaning agent in the past few weeks. Maybe Irene is right. Could she be having a reaction to the cleaning chemicals?

Irene may very well be suffering from the adverse effects of a new cleaning solution. Even if other employees didn't have the same response to the switch, it doesn't mean Irene's reaction is overstated. Individuals react differently when exposed to certain chemicals and to the numerous other factors that alter indoor air quality in the workplace. Air contaminants like chemical agents and tobacco smoke are an even greater problem when the worksite has a poor central ventilation system.

In its publication "Safe Jobs Now," the American Federation of State, County and Municipal Employees (AFSCME) offers the following signs of poor indoor air quality to look for:

◆ Odor from dumpsters, garbage, food preparation, chemicals or stale air

◆ Moisture damage or water stains on walls, windows, ceilings and floors

◆ Visible fungal growth

◆ Dust, soot and other dirt coming out of vents

- Tobacco smoke
- Dirty and clogged ventilation filters
- Improperly stored chemicals
- Unsanitary conditions or equipment
- Areas that feel too hot or too cold, or that have little air movement.

(Source: AFSCME, "Safe Jobs Now")

Some employees have allergic reactions to strong perfumes in the workplace. Sufferers must contend with headaches, congestion, eye irritation, and other symptoms. Employees with asthma or bronchitis may be especially sensitive. Discourage your employees from wearing strong fragrances to work.

Smoking. Many states and local municipalities have legislation banning indoor smoking in public places. If your locality doesn't require that you ban smoking in your workplace, strongly consider banning it anyway.

Even a separate smoking lounge will not suffice to prevent damage to indoor air quality, especially if your building has a single common ventilation system. The health risks of smoking and the danger to coworkers of passive smoke are clear. Make sure you do what you can to protect your employees and your organization.

Biological hazards

Occupational illnesses can be caused by exposure to asbestos, solvents, mold, dust and dust mites ... it seems like there's an endless list of hazards. That's why careful attention to building and HVAC system maintenance is such a critical component of a safety program.

Microbiologic exposure. The Environmental Protection Agency (EPA) reports two different types of adverse exposure to biological hazards at work:

- "building-related illnesses," caused by hazards such as asbestos and radon (usually in the foundation of a building);
- "sick building syndrome," which describes the health effects brought on from building materials like insulation and carpeting. Sick building syndrome can cause headaches,

dizziness, nausea and fatigue, eye, nose and throat irritation, and sinus and respiratory problems.

Mold. According to the Society for Human Resource Management (SHRM), nearly 9,000 lawsuits have been filed in the U.S. as a result of mold in the workplace. A November 2002 SHRM article notes that indoor mold growth and toxic mold have been dubbed by some as "the new asbestos."

According to the EPA, mold has the potential to cause harmful health effects if unchecked. Moisture from leaky roofs or pipes is often the breeding ground for mold in today's workplaces.

DON'T miss this

Some employees may be more vulnerable than others to biological hazards in the workplace. This includes employees with compromised immune systems caused by AIDS or other conditions, dialysis patients, organ transplant recipients, cancer patients, or smokers. You may need to take added precautions to ensure the safety of these workers.

Infectious diseases. These are illnesses that workers can catch from other people (or animals). They can be spread through blood contact (bloodborne pathogens), air, or other means. Infectious diseases pose a particular danger to healthcare workers. Environmental controls and engineering measures such as improving ventilation or enhancing housekeeping practices can help reduce the spread of disease. Personal protective equipment may also be used by workers in high-risk jobs.

Chemical hazards

Toxic chemicals can be an especially dangerous occupational hazard. The health problems associated with chemical hazards at work can result from contact with agents that are used in manufacturing operations, or from incidental exposure to chemicals that happen to be present in the environment, like lead paint. There are also everyday chemicals all around you at work, like correction fluid, copier toner, or cleaning supplies, that must be factored into an assessment of chemical hazards.

Just because employees don't smell a hazardous chemical or feel an immediate impact doesn't mean that they are not suffering its effects. Some health hazards have an acute impact, like losing consciousness after inhaling certain fumes. Others, however, are chronic and only show up after a prolonged period—such as cancer from asbestos exposure. Don't assume that a lack of apparent symptoms on your employees' part means that they are safe from illness.

WHAT you need to know

OSHA intensely regulates the presence of chemicals in the workplace. If you have hazardous materials on-site, your organization will need effective chemical hazard management. To best minimize danger and ensure full compliance with the law, an occupational safety officer or other professional with needed expertise should take on this crucial role.

✓ Checklist

Hazard communication standard

OSHA requires employers to follow its hazard communication standard if they have hazardous materials in their worksites. The hazard communication standard has these requirements:

- ☐ a written hazard communication program
- ☐ a list of hazardous chemicals known to be present in the workplace
- ☐ a completed Material Safety Data Sheet (MSDS) for every chemical on the list
- ☐ labels for all hazardous chemicals, updated as necessary, including the chemical identity of the contents, hazard warnings, and the name and address of the manufacturer or supplier
- ☐ an explanation of the methods used to train employees and to inform them of the hazards associated with chemicals.

The Material Safety Data Sheet. The Material Safety Data Sheet (MSDS) is a bulletin that provides specific information about the chemicals that employees use. It describes the chemical's physical and chemical properties, physical and health hazards, and routes of exposure, as well as precautions for safe handling and use, emergency first-aid procedures, and control measures. The MSDS helps employers and their workforce respond effectively to daily exposure and to emergency situations.

The MSDS is prepared by the manufacturer or importer of the chemical. However, it is ultimately your organization's responsibility to make sure that an MSDS is on hand for each chemical in your workplace.

Your organization must maintain a binder with an MSDS for every substance on the list of hazardous chemicals. Make the binder available to employees at their workstation during their shift.

DON'T
miss
this

OSHA requires employers to inform their workforce about the hazardous chemicals they work with, and to explain how to avoid injury in dealing with the chemicals.

Under OSHA's hazardous communication standard, employees must be told about:

◆ OSHA's hazardous chemical communication requirements;
◆ where hazardous chemicals are located in their work area; and
◆ the location and availability of your written hazard communication program.

WHAT
you need
to know

> **"HAZMAT," "HAZCOM"—What's the difference?**
>
> Here are phrases that get tossed around readily by safety professionals. Know the difference: HAZCOM refers to the hazard communication standard that requires employees to be trained about the hazardous chemicals they use at work. HAZMAT refers to the hazardous materials themselves, usually when discussing their use, disposal, cleanup or emergency response.

Ergonomic hazards

Ergonomic hazards are those dangers that can cause musculoskeletal disorders and repetitive stress disorders like carpal tunnel syndrome (the most well known of ergonomic disorders, though certainly not the most common). Ergonomics isn't only about the rickety office chair, though; it's a study of the way humans work and the way their bodies interact with their work and work environment. Ergonomics also focuses on the dangers of poor lighting, heavy lifting, and other factors.

We'll discuss ergonomics in greater detail in the next chapter.

What is an occupational illness?

Health hazards like those described above can cause occupational illness. An occupational illness is any abnormal condition or disorder caused by exposure to environmental factors at work. An occupational illness can be acute, in which the symptoms are severe and emerge immediately for a short term. An illness can also be chronic, where the symptoms only emerge over time, after ongoing exposure. While not necessarily severe, the symptoms of a chronic illness are nagging and ongoing.

OSHA has identified the following categories of occupational illness:

◆ occupational skin diseases or disorders
◆ dust diseases of the lungs
◆ respiratory conditions due to toxic agents
◆ poisoning—the systemic effects of toxic materials
◆ disorders due to physical agents other than toxic materials (such as exposure to extreme heat or cold), or elements such as non-ionizing radiation or a welding flash
◆ disorders associated with repeated trauma, repetitive stress or motion (ergonomic disorders)
◆ other illnesses, such as infectious hepatitis, that were contracted at work.

It's natural to think of ergonomic-related conditions as "injuries," but they're actually classified as "illnesses." The reason: ergonomic disorders aren't caused by a single incident or accident. Rather, they are usually the result of ongoing interaction with a hazard and emerge only after prolonged exposure to the danger.

Occupational illnesses can have a wide range of severity. Some workers might suffer the nagging pain of a mild ergonomic disorder. Others may need to transfer to a different worksite due to an allergic condition. Still others will end up on disability as a result of their symptoms. And some workers will be left fighting for their lives.

Safety hazards and injuries

Ashok broke his ankle after he slipped on a puddle near a freezer in the grocery section of the warehouse store where Maria heads up human resources. After the accident, she was reviewing the incident with the shift manager. Dmitri, one of Ashok's coworkers, came over to tell her that he took a similar fall just last week, but fortunately escaped injury. "That freezer is in bad shape. It's been leaking for awhile," he tells her. Maria is not happy. Why didn't she hear about this sooner?

What causes accidents at work?

Accidents can be caused by unsafe conditions. Unsafe conditions are the safety hazards that an effective safety program aims to eliminate, reduce, or at least control.

Some hazards are avoidable. On the other hand, some work conditions or jobs are inherently and unavoidably hazardous. Can you identify the avoidable hazards? Those are the dangers you can eliminate with a concerted effort. What about the ones you can't get rid of—what do you do then? Here's the short answer: you train your employees in how to manage the hazard and remind them to exercise care, caution, and common sense.

WHAT you need to know

Accidents don't "just happen"

Don't buy into the faulty notion that "accidents will happen." This mindset robs your organization of the opportunity to see that accidents are the result of specific events or conditions, and to apply that insight to prevent future accidents. Almost every accident is caused by some personal or mechanical failure. Just because a hazard is unavoidable, it doesn't mean an accident will unavoidably result.

Accidents can be caused by unsafe acts. This is where negligence and recklessness come into play. One study of business insurance claims showed that 97 percent of losses incurred due to accidents were related in some manner to human error.

These kinds of human failings are made within a climate that in some way allows for them, or didn't do enough to discourage them. It's the job of your trainers, supervisors, and safety team to build a safety-conscious environment and make sure your employees are trained to avoid accidents. Your organization's culture, as shaped by the HR department, front-line managers, and the executive leadership, can help make or break employees' safety attitude as we discussed earlier in Chapter 3.

Virtually all accidents are preventable! One study reported that perhaps one or two percent of accidents should be considered nonpreventable (that is, caused by acts of nature and unpredictable).

There are three types of accident causes:
- ◆ **Basic** cause (the climate that allowed for the accident, such as poor safety management practices or failure to train)
- ◆ **Direct** cause (the actual source of the accident: a wet floor causing a slip-and-fall, a metal ladder touching a high-voltage electrical line)
- ◆ **Indirect** cause (unsafe acts, like operating equipment too fast; or unsafe conditions, like poor housekeeping)

...and six sources of failure that might lead to one of these causes:
- ◆ **Human** failure (employees who are under stress, ill, incapable of following instruction)
- ◆ **Technical** failure (insufficient instructions for operating machinery)
- ◆ **Organizational or managerial** failure (failure to train or set safety procedures)
- ◆ **Material** failure (the breakdown of equipment, materials or components)
- ◆ **Design** failure (a deficiency in the design or structure)
- ◆ **Natural** failure (an act of nature that led to the accident cause).

Knowing these causes and potential sources of failure allows you to audit your workplace accordingly and to identify and prevent many of the conditions that lead to accidental injury.

The National Safety Council says that 75 percent of all accidents are preceded by at least one near miss. Let those near misses be a warning.

Accidents can be caused by unsafe employment practices. Take job speed-ups, for example. Working at a rapid-fire pace might be OK every once in a while when there's a rush job. Occasional overtime or requests to reduce production time are to be expected. But steady, regular increases in the productivity required per hour will also boost work-related injuries or illnesses. A faster work pace inevitably means short cuts, which increase risks and lead to more injuries.

So what was the cause of Ashok's accident? We could point to a number of culprits. First, the unsafe condition: A material failure that led to the leaky freezer. Now we have the unsafe condition—the accident just waiting to happen. But what about the unsafe acts? After all, extra caution could still have prevented the injury.

Let's start with Dmitri: Should he have alerted his supervisor to the danger last week when it first became known to him? In fact, he probably knew of the hazard before that first slip. Did he tell Ashok about it? Or did Ashok already know of it himself? Maybe he didn't exercise proper caution and was working recklessly when the accident happened. Perhaps he was carrying more than he should have been, and couldn't see the hazard. There may have been some human failure that contributed to this incident.

And what about unsafe practices? What organizational and managerial failures might be to blame? Is the shift supervisor the kind of manager that Ashok and Dmitri could have gone to and reported the hazard? Maybe they would have just incurred his wrath for doing so. Or perhaps they already told him about it. Was the manager pushing his employees too hard to get their work done so that they worked quickly instead of safely?

Now think about what would have happened if the manager had been informed, and had come to your office or the safety manager to discuss the hazard. What would the response have been? Would your building office have tended to the danger immediately? Would the shift manager have been encouraged instead to keep quiet about it? Would store management have complained about the costs of repair or replacement?

Keeping your employees safe will require you to take a cold, hard look at the realities of your workplace culture as well as the physical hazards at hand.

Some hazards are unknown or unexpected. On the other hand, some are right in front of your eyes. Don't let an injury occur from something that is obviously hazardous—there are enough hidden hazards in the workplace!

Occupational injuries and hazards

An occupational injury results from unsafe conditions at work. An occupational injury may be a cut, fracture, sprain, amputation, or other injury that occurs from a work accident or a single incident of exposure at work. Incidents such as animal bites or the results of a one-time exposure to chemicals are also considered injuries.

Occupational hazards cause the accidents or conditions that result in injury:

- *Slips or falls* cause sprains, broken bones, etc.
- *Faulty electrical systems* cause electrocution.
- *Fires or explosions* cause burns and other injuries.
- *Machine and equipment accidents* cause lost limbs or worse.
- All of these accidents or conditions can also result in complete disability or death.

✓✓ **Checklist**

Common safety hazards at work.

Consider whether some of these dangers are lurking in your workplace:

☐ Blocked aisles
☐ Blocked fire doors
☐ Blocked fire extinguishers, hose sprinkler heads
☐ Dangerously piled supplies or equipment
☐ Directional or warning signs not in place
☐ Evidence of smoking in nonsmoking areas
☐ Leaks of steam, water, oil, etc.
☐ Loose handrails or guard rails
☐ Loose or broken windows
☐ Loose scaffolding
☐ Missing (or inoperative) entrance and exit signs and lighting
☐ Oily rags
☐ Open doors on electrical panels
☐ Open or broken windows
☐ Poorly lit stairs
☐ Roof leaks
☐ Safety devices not operating properly
☐ Slippery floors and walkways
☐ Tripping hazards, such as hose links, piping, etc.
☐ Unlocked doors and gates

Let's take a quick look at some other common safety hazards:

Poor housekeeping practices. All of your worksites must be kept neat and orderly; employees should understand that housekeeping is everybody's responsibility. It's not just about appearances; it impacts safety. When the worksite is in disorder, workers can't find the tools they need to do the job safely. They can fail to see hazards because they're hidden by a mess. A worksite in disarray is a breeding ground for slips, falls, and other accidents.

Negligent equipment use. Equipment might be in good working order but used in a negligent fashion. Or equipment might be faulty, or in disrepair—in which case using the equipment at all was the negligent act that caused the avoidable hazard. On the other hand, some equipment is inherently dangerous, or used in inherently hazardous settings. (This may be the case with ladders or scaffolds, for example.) Again, the presence of an unavoidable hazard doesn't mean an accident is inevitable, though; it simply means that extra care and vigilance must be applied to ensure safety while using it.

Equipment is being negligently used if being employed when it is running hot or overheating, or if machine, power transmission, or drive guards are missing, damaged, loose, or improperly placed. Electrical equipment left operating is another example of negligent equipment use.

What is "lockout/tagout"?

Equipment that is being serviced or maintained could be turned on inadvertently. Or the machinery could unexpectedly release stored energy, causing an accident. These dangers can cause injury or death to those working on the machine. In order to prevent the danger of unintended turn on of machines as they are being serviced or maintained, employers are required by OSHA to develop programs for:

WHAT you need to know

♦ deenergizing equipment;
♦ isolating equipment from its energy sources; and
♦ verifying deenergization before the servicing or maintenance begins.

If equipment can be locked, then "lockout" is required, unless an employer can show that "tagout" (putting a "do not use" or "not in service" tag on the machine) will fully protect employees. This requirement is referred to as "lockout" and "tagout" by safety pros.

Be sure that employees who use equipment know their role in ensuring proper maintenance. Part of this role is in reporting unsafe equipment before any accidents or injuries occur. As noted in ToolBoxTopics.com, "...the person who sees a situation that should be fixed and fails to report it may well end up being the victim of his or her own neglect."

What should employees look for to ensure the equipment they are using is safe and in proper working order? Here's what ToolBoxTopics.com suggests they keep an eye out for:

◆ Belts that are slipping
◆ Broken plugs and receptacles
◆ Broken switch on a tool
◆ Burned switch
◆ Continually sparking motor
◆ Crossovers in poor repair
◆ Damaged extension cord
◆ Lack of a jump-out or idler roller where two conveyors meet
◆ Loose conductors
◆ Loose conduit
◆ Loose or cracked shaft housing
◆ Loose or missing machine guard
◆ Missing fact plate
◆ Missing nuts or bolts
◆ Moving parts with too much "give" or "play"
◆ Sharp corners on conveyors
◆ Unguarded parts on power-driven conveyors
◆ Unlubricated machine.

Electricity. Electricity can kill. Danger can strike in the form of lightning, contact with power lines, or a current from equipment that uses electricity. The American Federation of State, County, and Municipal Employees (AFSCME) provides extensive information on its website about the hazards of electricity.

✔ *Checklist*

AFSCME provides its members with a checklist of work practices that can prevent shocks and electrocution:

☐ Have only qualified workers install and maintain electrical systems.
☐ Use proper electrical outlets, and do not overload extension cords.
☐ Keep electrical cords away from water.
☐ Ground electrical equipment.

□ Use ground fault circuit interrupters (GFCI).
□ Keep a safe distance from overhead power lines.
□ Locate underground utility wires before digging.
□ Find shelter during rainstorms when there is lightning and thunder.

Confined spaces. Manholes, sewers, or tunnels pose unique physical hazards, including excessive heat, insufficient oxygen (or too much oxygen), toxic or flammable gases, and the danger of becoming trapped. Employees who will be working in a confined space, and their supervisors, must be trained about the hazards and the measures that can be taken to reduce them. OSHA has a regulation for confined space work with very specific safety requirements.

Identifying hazards and preventing loss

You pass the smokers in the employee entrance on your way inside. They're huddled close to the building to stay out of the rain. Damon opens the door for Judy—a new hire who just started a few days ago, who forgot her entry card. You're sure Damon has never seen Judy in his life!

Susan drops a lit cigarette on the ground and heads back in. I suppose the rain will extinguish that butt, you think to yourself as you enter the building.

There's Patrick, the security guard. He barely looks up from his paper when he hears the door open. A puddle is forming where wet employees stop to shake off the rain. You ask Patrick to page maintenance to come and mop up the spot.

As you head to your office, you barely escape the employee barreling towards you with a cup of hot coffee (uncovered!). You head up the side stairs for a meeting on the second floor, and encounter a huge stack of photocopy paper boxes in the stairwell. You stop at a house phone to call the copyroom and insist they move this fire hazard ASAP. Now you're a few minutes late for your meeting. You try to sneak unnoticed into a seat near the door and nearly trip over a phone wire hanging off the conference table.

Just another day at the office, you mutter to yourself...

Now that you're on heightened alert, you feel like there's danger lurking at every corner. Well, you just may be right! Now it's time to seek out the hazards you haven't already found, and consult with the safety experts for help as you carry out your organization's efforts to protect its workers.

Many employers have taken on the challenge of creating and maintaining a safer and healthier workplaces because it makes good economic sense, and also because it's so critical to the well being of employees.

A+ *Best Practices*

Derst Baking Company worked with Liberty Mutual Insurance to reduce its safety costs and accident rates. To accomplish this, it implemented a program to reduce workplace injuries. In the end, the company lowered its loss rate by 54 percent, its injury frequency rate by 33 percent, and disability days lost rate by 66 percent. According to Liberty Mutual, the employer realized a financial impact for its workplace safety efforts that was the same as if it had generated $3.6 million in revenue (assuming an industry profit margin of 5 percent).

Identifying hazards

To establish a safe working environment, institute occasional safety inspections so that you can spot conditions that are unsafe. Walk through the facility regularly with your safety officer or a member of the safety team. Inspect for problems together. This partnership is crucial. You know your employees, their jobs, and their workplace needs. The safety pros know about the hazards and how to eliminate or reduce them. In collaboration, you make a great workplace safety team.

The American Industrial Hygiene Association (AIHA) offers free online brochures on workplace safety. It's also a good way of locating an Occupational and Environmental Health and Safety (OEHS) professional, if your organization doesn't already have one on staff. Check them out at www.aiha.org.

✓ Checklist

Workplace hazards

Examine the worksite and workers in general as to comfort and safety. Here's a laundry list of things to look for when searching for hazards in your workplace:

- ☐ Adequacy of tools
- ☐ Chemical emissions that give rise to dust, gases, or vapors
- ☐ Chemical storage and containers
- ☐ Condition and maintenance of facility
- ☐ Confined spaces
- ☐ Emergence of eye or respiratory irritations or other symptoms during the walk-through
- ☐ Emergency equipment and first aid kits
- ☐ Equipment in disrepair
- ☐ Housekeeping
- ☐ Immediate dangers to life or health
- ☐ Lighting and harmful electromagnetic frequencies
- ☐ Materials handling
- ☐ Mold or other elements that can breed microbiologic hazards
- ☐ Noise and vibration exposure
- ☐ Poorly designed workstations
- ☐ Sanitation
- ☐ Signs and labels
- ☐ Temperature, humidity level
- ☐ Unsafe or ergonomically unhealthy furniture
- ☐ Ventilation

Also observe your employees at work to detect obvious and foreseeable hazards. Is there a great deal of avoidable heavy lifting? Unnecessary repetitive motions? Routine job requirements that force risky positions and behaviors? Reckless horseplay?

It's important to evaluate the potential for psychological stress as well. Is your workplace overcrowded? Are the employees' physical surroundings sufficient given their job assignments?

WHAT you need to know

Do HR policies allow workers a sufficient outlet to complain or make suggestions? Is there reasonable job stability at your organization? Is employee morale relatively high?

Don't underestimate the effects of stress and depression on workplace safety. And not just on employees' mental health, either, but on their ability to carry out their work safely and to avoid negligent behavior.

Quandary

Did my job make me sick?

An employee is ill. He thinks it was caused by an unhealthy condition at work. Coworkers are also symptomatic. Here's how to narrow down the causes:

Solution.

- ◆ Pinpoint the scope of the problem. Ask your employee: When did the symptoms start? Do they occur at particular times of the day? On certain days or in certain areas? While doing particular tasks or using certain equipment?
- ◆ Investigate the problem. Don't dismiss your employee complaints, even if they seem rather vague. Often, employees will just feel generally lousy, and won't be able to point to a specific illness. Or at best, they'll identify cold or flu-like symptoms. That doesn't mean they're just complainers, or exaggerating their symptoms. That's just the nature of how "sick buildings" impact occupants.
- ◆ Look for patterns in where complaining employees are located at the worksite. Find out from your building manager if any changes were recently made to the HVAC system, cleaning agents, or other potential environmental variables. All of these can have an adverse effect on air quality.
- ◆ After identifying the specific nature of the complaints and when and where they emerge—or if you're having trouble doing so—consult the professionals.

Your safety officer would ideally perform the role of identifying hazards. If your organization doesn't have such a professional on staff, then contact an industrial hygienist or engineering specialist. He or she will examine the ventilation system, measure the air for contaminants, and review other materials in the worksite, such as the chemicals used in production, etc.

When identifying hazards in your workplace, don't concern yourself only with the major health and safety hazards. Employees will usually take great pains to exercise precautions around known hazards. But sometimes it's the minor safety infraction that can cause the injury. Employees let down their guard, they don't perceive the environment as dangerous, and an injury results. Remind employees that with regard to safety, sometimes it's the little things that can harm them.

Furthermore, those minor injuries can become major ones if not properly cared for. Don't ignore these dangers.

Preventing loss

A 24-year-old drilling company employee died after he became entangled in the truck-mounted auger he was operating. He suffered multiple amputations and was decapitated.

A similar accident had taken the life of another employee of the same company a few years earlier. In that accident, the worker became entangled in a cable attached to a similar drilling rig and was pulled into the machinery. The employee suffered multiple fractures of both arms and legs, and his right leg and the arteries in his abdomen were nearly severed. He was conscious as rescuers tried to free him; he asked, "Am I going to die?" One hour after arrival at the local hospital, the employee was pronounced dead.

Thousands of Americans are killed each year because of on-the-job accidents. (Many more U.S. workers contract occupational illnesses or incur work-related disabilities.) What a frightening toll.

And there are very high economic costs attached to workplace injuries and illnesses as well. Employers must calculate lost production time, the salary they must pay to sick and disabled employees, and the wages of replacement workers who take over for them. Add on to these costs the damaged equipment, insurance claims, administrative and recordkeeping costs. And finally, there's the incalculable cost of pain and grief that injured workers, their families and coworkers must bear.

The incident illustrated above shows what can happen when an organization lacks an institutional memory and the resolve to learn from its safety mistakes. Employers should be required to review the details of such tragedies in excruciating detail, however horrific those details may be. The employer and workforce must be able to identify precisely what went wrong, and why. This communication is a crucial means of preventing similar incidents in the future. The employer above didn't take this step. Had it done so, perhaps a life could have been saved.

When designing and operating a safety program, it's essential to have an accurate picture of the accidents occurring in your plant or office. Investigating and recording accidents, computing injury rates, and determining the monetary costs of accidents will give you the information you need to focus your safety efforts on where they are most needed.

DON'T miss this

When implementing a safety program, the steps you take will depend in part on the specific goals you hope to achieve. Do you hope to reduce:

◆ *the number of accidents?*
◆ *the number or severity of injuries that result from accidents?*
◆ *employee lost workdays and disability days?*

These are all different targets. Set your measurable goals after you've evaluated how each of these variables impact your organization's overall direct and indirect costs. These goals should then inform the focus of your safety initiatives.

As you strive to set your organization's safety goals, be careful to accurately identify the cause of your workplace injuries, illnesses, and financial losses. Look at the numbers—and check your assumptions. Don't assume you know where the danger lies. Carefully evaluate hazards.

Liberty Mutual, an insurer of employers that conducts research in workplace safety, ranks the leading causes of injury and illness and develops a Safety Index based on the findings. It identified a gap between perception and reality among employers as to the leading causes of disabling workplace incidents.

When measured in terms of the direct costs of the incidents, most employers, for example, assume that repetitive motion is the leading cause of injury. In reality, though, overexertion is the leading cause. (This includes injuries from excessive lifting, pushing or otherwise moving an object.) Repetitive motion injuries actually ranked only sixth. Employers also thought highway accidents were the third-highest source of injury or fatality, but this cause only ranked seventh. On the other hand, employers paid little attention to the dangers of injuries due to falls on the same level, yet these incidents were the second leading cause of workplace injury.

Again, these numbers were based on direct costs to employers—the expense to the employer in payments to injured workers and the medical costs of treating the injuries—not on the *number* of injuries. As you set your safety priorities, consider whether you want to reduce overall incidents, or incidents that are most expensive to your organization, or both. Your answer to this question will help you prioritize your workplace safety efforts.

A closer look: the office workplace

Six million people get hurt at work each year. More than 400,000 of those people work in offices.

Most people think of manufacturing, construction, and other industrial work when occupational safety comes to mind. But we can't overlook the fact that those who work in the modern office setting—a segment of the workforce that has grown steadily in the last few decades—can also suffer injuries at work. It's true that the white-collar workplace poses less of a risk than the construction site. But there are still potential hazards there that cannot be ignored.

White-collar work at all levels has become increasingly automated. That's why safety and health concerns in this area have focused on illness and injuries caused by limited movement or lack of movement. In the old days, even those who did office work regularly rose from their desks. They went down the hall to speak with a colleague rather than sending off an email. They stood up to retrieve a file from the cabinet rather than from the hard drive at their fingertips.

But now, the overwhelming majority of the workday is spent in front of the computer. It's not the way the human body was meant to operate. And at some point, the body will revolt. Long hours at your computer means little muscle movement, insufficient circulation to your muscles, and eventually, muscle fatigue.

So most of the jobs at your worksite require employees to sit in one place for long periods of time. What to do to stay healthy? Encourage your employees to move! Stretch! Take a break! Have them shrug their shoulders, shake their fingers, roll their heads around their necks. Sometimes it's better to put down the phone and go talk face to face with your coworker down the hall.

DON'T miss this

In addition to hazards posed by the sedentary nature of office work, tendinitis, carpal tunnel syndrome, and other illnesses related to computer use are increasing costs to employers and pain to employees. Office injuries occur most often right at your desk.

However, accidents can happen away from your desk as well.

✓ Checklist

Here are some suggestions for avoiding office hazards:

☐ Avoid walking and reading at the same time. If it is important enough to read, then stop and read it.

☐ Never leave file cabinets open and unattended. How long does it really take to open a file cabinet?

☐ Never run in the office. Nothing is so important that you risk running into a coworker.

☐ Leave your shoes on. If your shoes are too uncomfortable to wear all day, then wear different shoes. Running around the office barefoot is a sure way to stub a toe or pick up a staple.

☐ When you must carry files, don't carry more than you are capable of. If you're grunting or your muscles get tired, you're carrying too much. Use a cart or make more trips.

☐ Avoid placing extension cords on the floor. These are tripping hazards and can also become fire hazards.

☐ Never put your fingers in an automatic stapler or stamper. Always unplug any equipment before you try to unjam or fix it.

☐ Always keep your aisleways clear. Never stack boxes or supplies in the aisles or in front of egress paths. Never arrange offices with desks in front of exits.

☐ Don't carry boxes or other items in a manner that blocks your vision as you walk.

☐ Use a stool or stepladder when placing items or removing them from high shelves.

☐ Don't try and fix copiers or other office equipment unless you know how it's done. Notify your maintenance staff.

☐ Don't use chairs for anything other than sitting. Don't use them as ladders or stools.

(Source: adapted in part from ToolBoxTopics.com.)

Did you know that falls are the primary cause of injuries within the office setting? What hazards cause slips and falls?

DON'T miss this

◆ *Spills on floor*
◆ *Torn carpets or exposed carpet seams*
◆ *Electrical cords running across the floor*
◆ *Open desk or file drawers*
◆ *Boxes or supplies stored in aisles*

Slips or trips result in falls that can injure. Eliminate any hazards that can lead to these accidents.

Mind your stairways

"If your office has stairs or steps, watch out!," ToolBoxTopics.com advises. "Falls on stairs cause more than 33,000 disabling work injuries each year. About two-thirds of the workers falling on stairs were not using handrails when they fell. Many were carrying objects, or slipped on something left on the steps. Accidents on stairs are usually serious—80 percent of these falls result in lost workdays."

Prevention is key: Building maintenance staff should conduct periodic checks of stair handrails to make sure they haven't become loose. They should also ensure that enclosed stairways have proper lighting. Your organization's safety policy should prohibit the use of your site's stairways for storage of any kind. Stairs should be free of any objects that a user would not expect to encounter when using them.

A closer look: the off-site workplace

In the modern work environment it's not unusual for employers to have much of their workforce scattered in home worksites across the city or sales territories across the country. Your field sales reps, for example, most likely spend most of their time in their cars or home offices. As telecommuting grows in feasibility and popularity, more of your workforce will be spending the day off-site. What safety considerations arise? What obligation does your organization have to protect these workers?

Don't falsely assume that workplace safety is "out of your hands" simply because your workers are out of your building!

Drivers

Whether truck drivers or sales reps, your employees can injure or kill themselves or members of the general public by unsafe driving. Courts have held some employers liable for the negligent driving of their employees, too. Of course, transportation safety is highly regulated and beyond the scope of this book, but the following common sense rules apply universally:

- ◆ Ensure that your company vehicles are checked regularly and are not used unless in proper working order.
- ◆ Drivers must pull over when making a cell phone call, eating lunch, applying makeup, or performing a task that requires attention to anything but the road. Make it company policy; enforce it with vigilance.
- ◆ Provide all of your employees who drive with copies of the rules of the road in your state. Remind them to observe speed limits and other regulations at all times.
- ◆ Restrict employees from driving excessive distances without taking a break. Too much time behind the wheel can cause ergonomic stress in addition to potential accident-causing fatigue.
- ◆ Remind employees that driving safely also means being mindful of pedestrians and other drivers.

Telecommuters

As computer use increases both in the office and at home, and tele-communications equipment becomes more affordable, accessible, and user-friendly, the home has emerged as a workplace for the new century. In fact, millions of people now work at home. (And that doesn't count the growing number of workers who still toil every day at the office, but bring work home at night or on weekends.) Telecommuting presents great advantages to businesses and their employees. But it also raises questions about the employer's role in ensuring the health and safety of its telecommuting employees.

While OSHA oversees safety in the American workplace, it doesn't regulate home offices, and the federal workplace safety law does not apply to private homes. On the other hand, you still must keep records of work-related injuries and illnesses, wherever they happen. That's a compliance reason why you should care about the condition of your employees' home worksites.

To maximize the safety of all of your employees, you should provide telecommuters with basic information to enable them to set up a safe and healthful workstation. You might also implement home visits to examine proposed home office sites, especially if you have a structured telecommuting program and a large number of employees working at home.

✔ Checklist
Telecommuting safety

Here's a checklist to review the safety elements of a telecommuting site:

☐ The workspace is neat and clean.
☐ The workspace is reasonably quiet.
☐ The workspace is adequately ventilated with good-quality air.
☐ The workspace is equipped with ergonomically friendly furniture and equipment.
☐ The workspace is not overly crowded with furniture.
☐ File cabinets, shelves, and other storage units are secure and stable.

- [ ] Floor surfaces are clean, dry, level, and nonslippery. Carpets are well secured to the floor and free of frayed or worn seams, with slip-resistant pads underneath.
- [ ] Phone lines, electrical cords, and extension wires are secured under a desk or alongside a baseboard.
- [ ] Circuit breakers and/or fuses in the electrical panel are labeled for intended use.
- [ ] Circuit breakers clearly indicate if they are in open or closed positions.
- [ ] Electrical outlets are three-pronged (grounded).
- [ ] Extension and power cords are being safely used and are not overloaded.
- [ ] Electrical equipment is free of recognized hazards that would cause physical harm (frayed wires, bare conductors, loose wires, flexible wires running through walls, exposed wires fixed to the ceiling).
- [ ] Heated surfaces such as coffee makers, hot plates, and portable heaters are away from the workspace, where they could trigger a fire.
- [ ] The workspace has a working smoke detector within hearing distance.
- [ ] The workspace has a fire extinguisher within easy access.
- [ ] Aisles, doorways, and corners are free of obstructions.
- [ ] Stairs with four or more steps are equipped with a handrail.
- [ ] The workspace has safe exit paths (at least 36 inches wide).
- [ ] The telecommuter has an established evacuation plan. (This might require installing a ladder as an escape route if the office is on the second floor.)
- [ ] The workspace has first aid supplies available.
- [ ] The name, location, and phone number of the nearest healthcare facility is readily accessible.

In older homes, existing electrical circuits may be unable to handle the additional electrical load from fax machines, computers, scanners and other office equipment, in addition to air conditioning units used in the home office. Require your telecommuter to have a licensed, bonded electrician inspect the existing electrical system and upgrade it if necessary to assure the current protection and load will meet electricity demands.

Keep the following compliance issues and best practices in mind when coordinating safety efforts for your telecommuters:

◆ As long as an employee is engaged in work-related tasks at home, you'll be required to report any accidents that happen there. And your organization can incur workers' compensation liability for those accidents, too.

◆ If you provide office equipment or other items for employees who work at home, then you're liable for injuries resulting from their use. (Unsafe materials or tools that are brought into a private home at the employer's request can cause liability for the employer too. An example would be a pieceworker who was injured while making clothes or other consumer goods out of materials provided by the employer.)

◆ Require that your employee agree to arrange for an energy audit of the home by the local utility company and fire safety inspection by the local fire department within 30 days of signing a telecommuting agreement, if requested.

◆ Have a member of your safety team visit and inspect the home workspace, to confirm inspection was completed, and to sign off on the safety of the workspace. Note the date of the inspection and sign-off, and keep the document in your records.

◆ Allow your telecommuters access to consultation with your safety officer for advice on any particular safety concerns that they have about their home worksites.

⁇The Quiz

1. Most accidents are preventable. ☐ True ☐ False

2. Information about chemicals and their hazards should be restricted to the safety officer or building management only. ☐ True ☐ False

3. Employers need to track and report their employees' work-related injuries, even if they don't happen on the employer's premises. ☐ True ☐ False

4. Identifying the cause of a workplace accident is a critical means of preventing future accidents. ☐ True ☐ False

5. Excessive noise at work is an annoyance, but not a health hazard. ☐ True ☐ False

Answer Key: 1. T; 2. F; 3. T; 4. T; 5. F

Ergonomics

> *Your benefits colleague comes to you clearly dismayed. "I just don't get it," Patrick says. "We don't have any assembly plants. We're not construction contractors. Most of our workforce sits behind a desk. So why the heck are our workers' compensation costs so high?"*

Introduction

Musculoskeletal disorders cost the U.S. economy more than $50 billion annually. According to an AFL-CIO fact sheet on ergonomics, every year employers pay between $15 billion and $18 billion in workers' compensation costs alone. Maybe that's why the national labor organization calls ergonomic hazards "the biggest safety and health problem in the workplace today."

The National Academy of Sciences and Institute of Medicine reports that 1 million U.S. workers experience serious work-related ergonomic injuries each year.

Ergonomic hazards and injuries have been around a long time. And today's workers are no safer from ergonomic hazards since moving off the assembly line and into the office cubicle. Computer workstations, and the sedentary work habits they foster, pose unique ergonomic hazards of their own.

What, then, can you say to Patrick, your benefits colleague? The fact that much of your workforce sits behind a desk no doubt contributes to the potential for ergonomic risk—and costly injuries—rather than minimizes that risk.

"People are different in size, shape, strength, and in other ways. Too often, workers have jobs that ignore these differences," notes a government workers union. In its Guide to Health and Safety in the Workplace, the American Federation of State, County, and Municipal Employees points out that workers get injured when they try to adapt their bodies to the way their job, workspace, tools or work processes are designed. When the workspace is adapted to the individual workers, in contrast, employees are less likely injured and more content and productive, too.

Ergonomics defined

Ergonomics is the study of human work and the science of fitting jobs to people. How do people interact with the equipment they use each day? With their workflow and processes? With their office or plant environment? It's a science that looks at the employee as he or she interacts with tools and equipment, methods and tasks, and overall work environment.

Ergonomics strategies seek to reduce the pain and cost of injuries caused by work conditions that don't accommodate the individual

worker. To do this, ergonomics tries to make the job fit the employee, rather than making the employee fit the job.

It's this quality that distinguishes ergonomic measures from other HR issues and solutions like recruitment or performance management. You don't normally write job descriptions to suit particular employees, or set performance criteria based on an employee's unique strengths. However, attention to the individual needs and characteristics of your employees *is* the best way of approaching ergonomic comfort and safety.

An ergonomics program is a systematic method of preventing, evaluating, and managing work-related disorders. Its aim: to reduce injuries by getting rid of conditions that put a harmful strain on workers' muscles, nerve, and joints. An ergonomics program can play a key role in keeping your employees happy and healthy—and in alleviating workers' compensation costs and diminished productivity.

Who is at risk?

What jobs pose ergonomic hazards? There are very few occupations that don't present some type of ergonomic risk. However, certain professions are more dangerous, ergonomically speaking, than others.

Here are some workers who should be on heightened ergonomic alert:

- ◆ *Computer users*
- ◆ *Assembly line workers*
- ◆ *Cashiers and supermarket checkers*
- ◆ *Hospital employees*
- ◆ *Truck drivers*
- ◆ *Construction workers*
- ◆ *Meatpackers*
- ◆ *Poultry workers*
- ◆ *Sewing machine operators*

The Occupational Safety and Health Administration (OSHA) and National Institute for Occupational Safety and Health (NIOSH) issue ergonomic recommendations for industries that are shown to pose greater than average hazards. For example, OSHA developed a 30-page booklet on Ergonomics Program Management Guidelines for Meatpacking Plants. As a general employment sector, service industries were found to be of greater than normal risk. So NIOSH conducted health hazard evaluations identifying ergonomic hazards and recommending solutions for certain retail and service industries.

Women workers are affected more by ergonomic injuries. According to the AFL-CIO Department of Occupational Safety and Health, although women account for only 46 percent of the workforce, they suffered 64 percent of repetitive motion injuries and 71 percent of carpal tunnel syndrome cases in 1998.

Ergonomic problems

You notice it every morning as you walk in the front door. Soraya, your organization's receptionist, deftly negotiates a flurry of activity: signing for packages, signing in and directing visitors, greeting arriving employees. Plus you've got her inputting the results of an employee survey. All the while, the phones ring incessantly.

While juggling her many tasks, Soraya cradles the phone between her neck and shoulder and contorts her upper extremities so her hands are free to write, point, or wave. By 2:00 p.m., she is inevitably rubbing her neck, which has been overstretched by her distorted posture.

Today she pokes her head in to HR and pleads, "I'd like to leave a little early today. I have a horrible headache and my neck is killing me." As a result, there goes your administrative assistant—she's grudgingly heading off to the reception desk to provide front-desk coverage.

Ergonomic injuries—those associated with repeated trauma, repetitive stress or motion—are usually called "musculoskeletal disorders," or MSDs. Musculoskeletal disorders are illnesses and injuries that affect one or more parts of the musculoskeletal system, which is composed of bones, muscles, tendons, ligaments, cartilage, nerves and blood vessels.

MSDs include sprains, strains, inflammation, degeneration, pinched nerves or blood vessels, bone splintering, and stress fractures. Symptoms include discomfort, pain, fatigue, swelling, stiffness, burning, cramping, or numbness and tingling. Other signs of a musculoskeletal disorder are a decreased range of motion or grip strength, deformity, or loss of function.

There are a number of terms used to describe the ergonomic injuries characterized as musculoskeletal disorders:

DON'T miss this

- ◆ *cumulative trauma disorders (CTDs);*
- ◆ *repetitive stress injury (RSIs);*
- ◆ *repetitive motion injury (RMIs);*
- ◆ *overuse injuries.*

Ergonomic hazards cause a number of different work-related disorders and illnesses. In fact, OSHA reports that more than 100 different injuries can occur as a result of repetitive motions that produce wear and tear on the body. These disorders (considered by OSHA to be an "illness" rather than an "injury") make up 67 percent of workplace illnesses reported, according to the Bureau of Labor Statistics (BLS).

However, these numbers don't reflect the full extent of the problem. The figures don't include injuries suffered by public sector workers or postal employees, and don't reflect underreporting of injuries by employers. (OSHA estimates that for every MSD reported, there is another work-related MSD that is *not*.) Also, these figures only include cases that involve one or more days away from work, the only incidents for which the BLS collects detailed reports. (Source: AFL-CIO, "*Death on the Job: the Toll of Neglect*.")

There are often simple and inexpensive ways to fend off ergonomic disorders. Even costlier preventive measures are worth the resources though, since treating ergonomic injuries can be expensive. To illustrate, for injuries to the upper extremities, the average cost is $3,000 without surgery and $30,000 with surgery. One major insurer estimates the individual cost per claim to be $8,000, or double the average for other injuries or illnesses.

DON'T miss this

Back disorders. *Back disorders are especially troublesome MSDs. They cause a significant loss of productivity and large workers' compensation costs. With the exception of the common cold or flu, back disorders are the reason most often cited for job absenteeism. Pulled or strained muscles, ligaments, tendons, and disks are the most common back problems.*

The majority of back disorders result from chronic or long-term injury to the back rather than a single incident. Back problems often result from the cumulative effects of excessive twisting, bending, and reaching; carrying, lifting, or moving loads that are too heavy or too big; staying in one position for too long; and poor posture. Prolonged sitting stresses the lower back and is a common complaint of office workers and truck drivers.

Causes of ergonomic problems

Ergonomic disorders have physical causes. Yet it would be short-sighted to end the analysis there. The big picture is important too—you have to consider the systemic issues that underlie the physical stressors. What are the systemic causes that make employees put such strain on their bodies? Until you look at these larger variables, you won't have a clear picture of the problem.

For example, ergonomic hazards are often the result of techno-logical advances in the workplace. More specialized tasks, higher assembly line speeds, and increased repetition coupled with a lack of ergonomically designed technologies create the danger zone. These are all systemic factors. Consequently, the physical risk factors emerge. Because of the work "system" in place, workers' hands, wrists, arms, shoulders, backs, and legs may be subjected to thousands of repetitive twisting, forceful, or flexing motions during a typical workday.

✓ ***Checklist***
✓
What causes the risk factor?

Consider which of these factors might be the culprit that threatens injury:

☐ the method used or required to do the task?
☐ the effort or strength required to do the task?
☐ the location or position of parts, equipment, or tools required to do the task?
☐ the speed or frequency of the work?
☐ the duration or repetition of the tasks?
☐ the design of the parts, equipment, or tools?

Determining why risk factors exist is the essential first step to reduce ergonomic hazards and protect your employees. You can't craft the solutions until the underlying causes are found.

Systemic risk factors

Systemic factors can be broken down into "engineering" and "admin-istrative" variables. Outmoded equipment design and inadequate seating are examples of engineering-related factors that can cause ergonomic hazards. Administrative practices that exacerbate ergonomic dangers include:

◆ Lack of recovery time between shifts or individual hazardous duties

◆ Stressful work organization

◆ Speedups in productivity demands

◆ Insufficient pauses or rest breaks

◆ Excessive overtime

◆ Unfamiliar or unaccustomed work

◆ Inadequate training

DON'T miss this

Overtime—it's not just a pay problem! According to OSHA, working overtime can overstress your employees' bodies, especially when the overtime hours are added on to a standard workday. Body muscle and tissue need rest and recuperation. Adding hours to the job adds to the cumulative effects of stress on the body, and also takes away its healing time.

OSHA advises that employers eliminate overtime wherever possible to reduce ergonomic problems. If it can't be eliminated, consider asking employees to work their off-days instead of tacking hours to their shift. That way their bodies will still have between-shift recovery time.

Physical risk factors

"Risk factors" are the characteristics of a job that increase the chance of an employee developing an ergonomic disorder. The main risk factors that cause MSDs are:

◆ Repetitive motion

◆ Long periods of the same repetitive activity

◆ Rapid hand and wrist movement

◆ Contact stress (from direct contact with equipment or tools) such as chafing, pinching or bruising

◆ Awkward posture

◆ Static postures that must be sustained for extended periods

◆ Overhead or extended reaching

◆ Heavy lifting

- Forceful exertion or movement (the amount of physical effort required to perform a task)
- Hand-arm vibration

The more an employee is exposed to these risk factors, the more likely he or she will develop an ergonomic condition. A combination of these hazards can increase the chances of ergonomic illness as well.

Best Practices

Do you have ergonomic problems?

In 1991, Siemens VDO Automotive in Auburn Hills, Michigan, started an ergonomics program after 43 percent of its 250 office employees complained of pain in their shoulders, back, elbows and fingers. The organization conducted evaluations of each workstation, and brought in ergonomically designed chairs as well as back cushions, lumbar supports, keyboard/mouse rests and document holders. The organization also encouraged its office staff to take regular, short exercise breaks.

The company implemented a training component in its program as well: offering new hires office ergonomics training, and regular instruction for all employees in correct posture, exercises, workstation adjustment and back safety. In September 2002, the company reported that it has not had *any* lost work time due to ergonomic injury *in the past two years*. It also noted that, over the decade since its program was implemented, it estimates a savings of 20,000 hours per year in time lost to pain, doctor visits, and time off from work.

So now you know some of the key physical risk factors for ergonomic hazards and the underlying systemic variables that can cause them. Are these dangers present in your workplace? Here's how to find out.

- **Analyze your positions.** Look at the job functions throughout your organization. Think of all the daily work tasks your employees perform. How many of these functions carry the risks listed above?
- **Consult with employees.** Conduct regular symptoms surveys to identify employees who may already be experiencing

discomfort. Use employee questionnaires to assess the extent of the problem, but also get out and talk to employees individually to see firsthand how they are being impacted.

◆ **Check your records.** Find out which workers have been injured and look for trends in job functions or sites. Look for repetitive strain injuries in your OSHA log. Review your workers' compensation first notice of injury reports, accident and near-miss reports.

◆ **Research your industry.** There may be common ergonomic problems across your industry or within certain job classifications. Obtain information about problems faced by other companies whose employees are engaged in similar tasks. Problems elsewhere can serve as useful predictors of injuries in your own workplace. You can also consult with OSHA; the agency has such information available for research purposes.

DON'T miss this

Here are some sure-fire clues that you might have an ergonomics problem in your workplace. Be on the lookout for:

◆ *Employees self-modifying their workspace (makeshift footrests, VDT "awnings," etc.)*

◆ *Awkward work positions*

◆ *Low productivity*

◆ *High absenteeism*

◆ *High turnover*

◆ *The four "G"s: groans, grimaces, grumbling, and grabbing (of sore backs, arms, necks, wrists, and other agonized body parts)!*

The job hazard analysis

A job hazard analysis is a structured way of spotting jobs and workstations that pose ergonomic dangers. The analysis is a four-step process:

1. **Select the job(s) to be analyzed.** This will require you to prioritize ergonomic needs and dangers within your organization. Follow up on employee complaints of ergonomic problems. Review accident and injury records, identify patterns that suggest problem areas, and prioritize these problem areas

for attention. Rank departments, job classifications, and job activities in descending order according to the need for intervention. You'll determine the extent of this need based on the injury incidence rate (the number of injuries in the past year weighted by the number of employees in the department, classification, or activity) and by the severity of the particular injuries employees have suffered.

2. **Investigate top-priority jobs and departments.** Consult with employees in "problem jobs." Break down the jobs into individual activities and observe how employees perform each activity. For example, to find the cause of carpal tunnel syndrome for library clerks, a job analysis should look at computer work, book handling and other repetitive tasks performed with the hands.

3. **Identify the hazards of each activity,** including the physical risk factors and systemic factors at the root of these hazards.

4. **Develop corrective action plans and improvements to reduce or eliminate the hazards.** Set target dates for improvement.

Preparing ADA-compliant job descriptions is a good way to help you analyze jobs from an ergonomics perspective.

DON'T miss this

Under the Americans with Disabilities Act, you're required to determine the "essential functions' of each position because you must return an injured worker to his or her position if the employee is able to perform the essential duties with or without a reasonable accommodation. That means you must stop and think about what employees actually are required to do in their jobs.

In defining the essential functions of a job for ADA purposes, an employer needs to write job descriptions that are ability-specific rather than task-specific. For example, to perform essential functions, a meatpacker must be able to "reach above his or her shoulders, pull on a heavy carcass, and bend backwards." At this point you should be thinking, "Wait a minute. Isn't there a way we can design this job so that it won't be so hard on people? Does that meatpacker *have* to reach up and bend backward while pulling on a 120-pound carcass of meat? Is this really necessary?" Soon you'll be thinking about how you might be able to redesign your positions to comply with ergonomic principles.

Ergonomic solutions: The employee's role

Paul, an order input clerk, came to human resources to request short-term disability leave. It turns out he's developed carpal tunnel syndrome in his left hand, and surgery will be required to repair the injury. He's got the medical report to back him up. "I'm sorry," he said, with all sincerity. But it's been plaguing me for over a year now, and my doctor said I can't put it off any longer."

Could Paul have possibly avoided surgery? Probably so. Immediate attention to the early warning signs of an ergonomic disorder can alleviate the need for more serious (and expensive) treatment in the long run. Paul should have informed his employer far earlier so it could have taken preventive measures. Employees have a responsibility to report promptly in order to stay healthy.

Employees should also be involved in ergonomics initiatives well before symptoms of injury begin to emerge, though. They have a larger policy role to play in order to prevent injury. Your job is to ensure they play it.

Identifying hazards. Send each department a one-page safety checklist, and ask employees to define any problems they have discovered at their worksites. Urge them to identify potential hazards in their own workspace as well as in common areas or with shared tools and equipment.

Setting policy. Employee representatives should be key members of your organization's ergonomics team. Workers who face ergonomic hazards every day must help to shape policies to alleviate them. Even if they don't know how to solve ergonomic problems, they can surely identify them!

DON'T miss this

Tell your employees how important their input is. You don't want to hear from them only when they become injured. Encourage them to talk to you before an injury happens and advise on the best ways to do their job, the equipment they need to do it safely, and the trouble spots they see every day.

Following policy. Communicate the organization's expectations about the role employees must play. Convey the message right in your policy handbook:

> *"All employees must use safe work practices. Employees are responsible for learning and applying the safe working practices they are taught during their general safety orientation and their task-specific training. Employees who refuse to comply with ergonomic guidelines or who recklessly disregard the guidelines can be subject to discipline."*

Working safely. Offer guidance to employees on how they can reduce exposure to cumulative trauma disorders and other MSDs.

✓ *Checklist*

Working safely

Share these tips with your workers and encourage your front-line supervisors to support their staff in these safety efforts:

- ☐ Plan ahead. If you will be doing a job that requires awkward motions or positioning, think about ways of making it easier.
- ☐ Do warm-up exercises before you take on a task that is physically demanding.
- ☐ Rotate workstations or functions with a coworker to minimize repetition resulting from a single task.
- ☐ Shift and change your position so that you alter the muscles being used and the way they're being used.
- ☐ Avoid repeating awkward movements or holding yourself in awkward positions.
- ☐ Stretch your muscles regularly to improve blood circulation and relieve tension.
- ☐ Take frequent breaks from repetitive motion tasks.
- ☐ Use proper lifting techniques—back strain is one of the most common cumulative stress disorders.
- ☐ Use two hands instead of one for a task to reduce excess demand on a single muscle group.
- ☐ If you use hand tools, keep your wrists in a "neutral" position, instead of bending them up, down or sideways during a task.

☐ Use tools that are right for the job and right for you—that is, proportioned to your body.

☐ Use power tools instead of manual tools when possible.

☐ Be sure that the tools you use are kept in proper working order.

☐ Use proper protective equipment if needed, such as anti-vibration gloves, anti-fatigue insoles, etc.

☐ Take a rest break when you're getting tired. Just a few minutes can make a big difference.

☐ Stay in the game: Don't get distracted, and always think about the best posture and the safest technique for doing the job.

☐ Listen to your body! It will begin sending you messages long before a severe cumulative trauma disorder can set in. Don't think you have to "tough it out" just because a co-worker doesn't seem bothered by a physically demanding task— people have different strengths, weaknesses and pain points.

☐ Report symptoms of chronic discomfort as soon as you experience them. The sooner you can be accommodated with a different tool or work position, the more likely you are to quickly alleviate your discomfort and avoid a more chronic injury.

(Source: ToolBoxTopics.com)

Reporting promptly. It bears repeating: employees must immediately report MSD signs, symptoms, or injuries. It's the only way early intervention can happen. Your ergonomics policy will inform employees whether to report to their immediate supervisor, safety officer, or ergonomics team member.

In developing an ergonomics program, view your employees as part of the solution, not part of the problem. Maintain a positive, proactive attitude toward your workforce, and reinforce this philosophy with a written policy setting forth the crucial contribution they can make to their own health and safety.

Distribute a flier with these "ergo-cises" and encourage employees to do them regularly throughout the workday:

- *Make the hands into tight fists and then slowly stretch the fingers out and apart.*
- *Flex the wrists up, down, and around.*
- *Gently stretch the upper body with arms over the head while either standing or sitting.*
- *Roll the shoulders forward and then backward in a circular motion.*
- *Focus on a distant object for 20 seconds to relax the eye muscles. (Don't focus on a bright object, though.)*
- *Breathe deeply several times; close your eyes while inhaling, open them when exhaling.*

Ergonomic solutions: The employer's role

Your employees can only do so much to alleviate the physical risk factors of their jobs. When it comes to the systemic variables that can cause ergonomic hazards, you'll need to step in. In collaboration with your safety and facilities pros, employees and union, upper management, and even the purchasing department, you'll want to shepherd the creation and implementation of a full-scale ergonomics program.

Ergonomic solutions can be very simple. MSDs are often easy to prevent. Sometimes all it takes is adding a book under a monitor or padding a tool handle. There are also relatively inexpensive system interventions that can be carried out. For example, many heavy lifting and materials handling injuries can be avoided by putting work supplies and equipment within comfortable reach, or repackaging items to reduce the weight and size that workers must lift.

And let's face it: Even more expensive preventive measures are less costly than curing ergonomic illnesses once they emerge.

The key strategies

Employers have a number of options at their disposal to correct or control ergonomic hazards:

◆ **Engineering controls** like workstation, tool, and equipment design or redesign. These efforts aim to "engineer out" the hazard.

◆ **Administrative controls** such as worker rotation, reduced production demands, and increased rest breaks. These strategies control the amount and duration of exposure to the hazard.

◆ **Personal protective equipment** like footrests and gloves. These items are a barrier to the hazard.

◆ **Work practices redesign** including altering job processes and training employees in using safe work habits. This is the step to take when no other measures are feasible.

Engineering controls

Engineering controls are the preferred means of resolving ergonomic hazards because these permanent changes can eliminate the hazard's root cause. The other strategies are really ways of "getting around" the hazard, not eliminating it.

Engineering control measures include altering the workstation design and workspace layout, adjusting the walking or standing surfaces, or replacing unsafe seating.

For example, the controls and displays employees use when operating equipment or tools might require an adjustment to make sure they are visible and easy to operate. They should be located where they can be viewed or used while employees maintain neutral body postures, without having to stretch, twist, or bend. Controls and displays should be readily accessible by both right- and left-handed operators.

Another engineering control is a change to the surfaces workers must stand or walk on for long periods. Rather than having employees walk on a concrete floor, an employer can put rubber anti-fatigue mats in standing and walking areas to give employees greater comfort and better traction.

Administrative controls

After assessing the physical makeup of your workstations and making the necessary engineering adjustments, consider the way your workflow policies and administrative behaviors impact the ergonomics of the work environment. We talked earlier about some of the systemic factors contributing to ergonomic problems. Let's look at some of these with an eye to crafting solutions:

- **Job rotation.** Provide for job rotation or a variation of duties to reduce duration of work that poses high ergonomic risks.
- **Avoid speedups.** Set reasonable production goals. Ensure that your front-line supervisors' work demands aren't unrealistic or unhealthy.
- **Rest breaks.** Allow for a sufficient number of recovery pauses or rest breaks in employee workflows. In an office setting, computer workers should be allowed to leave their workstations for at least 10 minutes for each hour of intensive keying and at least 15 minutes after every two hours of intermittent keying.
- **Overtime.** Reduce mandatory or excessive overtime.
- **Training.** Provide adequate education in ergonomic hazards and training on safe work methods.
- **Ramp-in.** Institute "ramp-in" periods for new employees. They aren't accustomed to the work rates established for your more experienced workers. Allow them a gradual introduction to work.

WHAT you need to know

OSHA notes that employees experience fewer MSDs when a 15- to 30-second break is taken every 10 to 20 minutes, or a five-minute break is taken every hour. "During these breaks, employees should be encouraged to stand, stretch, and move around a bit," the agency advises, as this "allows the muscles enough time to recover."

Personal protective equipment

Minimize ergonomic hazards with equipment that reduces their impact. Personal protective equipment (PPE) can make the job easier and safer.

Personal protective equipment, such as gloves, footwear and kneepads, helps to protect your employees. Provide them with equipment appropriate to the task being performed, and make sure the gear is properly sized for each individual worker.

Devices such as wrist splints and back belts are not considered personal protective equipment. Employees should not use these items unless a qualified healthcare practitioner has prescribed them.

Work practices redesign

If hazards can't be eliminated through the use of engineering or other controls, your employees will need to adopt work practice controls so that they can safely work around the hazards they face each day. This may mean adopting different workflow procedures or following new work safety rules.

Work methods design. Work methods should be designed so work can be completed safely and comfortably. Work processes should allow employees to maintain neutral postures, avoid stooping and reaching, and minimize time spent working with arms overhead.

Here are some examples of work method redesign strategies:

◆ Automate tasks.
◆ Redesign the job so repetitive actions are properly paced and conducted with minimal stress to the worker.
◆ Change the job to include tasks that use different muscle groups. Mix non-computer tasks into the work.
◆ Buy supplies in smaller containers to reduce the weight of materials that must be lifted.

Insist that employees take their breaks! OSHA notes that without proper rest periods, body tissue cannot rest and recover. "Workers who consistently work through their breaks are at greater risk of musculoskeletal disorders (MSDs), accidents, and performance or poor quality work due to operating at higher muscular fatigue levels." Make sure your supervisors aren't skimping on employee breaks or setting inappropriate production expectations.

Remember Soraya, our beleaguered receptionist? What measures can you take to solve her ergonomic distress? First, you'll want to review her work responsibilities. Reevaluate what tasks Soraya can be expected reasonably and safely to carry out at one time. (And not just for Soraya's own safety, by the way. As a receptionist, she has an important security function, and she should not be distracted from that critical role.) Offer ergonomics training so that Soraya can be educated about the causes of her discomfort. And for goodness sake—buy a headset for her phone!

Workstation design. Do you know what your ideal employee looks like? Who was your workplace designed to accommodate?

> *Bill started working in your tech department several weeks ago. By all accounts, he was acclimating well to his group and his work. But last week you got a call from Sam, the tech supervisor. Bill keeps complaining to him about his workstation. "He says the desk is too low, his keyboard is at his knees, his neck is sore from looking down at his monitor.*
>
> *"Frankly, I think this guy's a real prima donna," Sam continues. "His setup is just fine. Azra (Bill's predecessor) never complained about it."*

What if Azra stood 5'1" to Bill's 5'11"? Can the workstation you provide realistically be a one-size-fits-all package? *Is this really the best way of getting productivity from your workforce?*

Keep in mind that not every workspace configuration will work for everyone. We're all different shapes and sizes, different heights, leg lengths, and arm spans. An ergonomic office is one whose individual workspaces are readily adjustable for the particular employee using the space.

Redesigning the workstation to fit the worker and the job is one of the most effective solutions to ergonomic problems.

✓ *Checklist*

Workstation Design

In designing workstations, keep in mind that they must:

☐ conform to the employee actually using it, not the "average" worker

☐ permit the worker to adopt several different but equally safe postures and still perform the job

☐ accommodate the employee's full range of motion

☐ minimize the need for awkward bending, stretching, or twisting

☐ reduce or eliminate repeated manual lifting

☐ comfortably accommodate both computer and non-computer work

☐ ensure a comfortable level and angle of work surfaces and shelves.

Proper seating should:

☐ be adjustable while sitting (height, depth and angle)

☐ be approximately 18 inches wide

☐ be padded

☐ have armrests that support the wrists and forearms during prolonged keying

☐ have armrests that don't interfere with chair adjustment and fit easily under the work surface

☐ have armrests that are adjustable (up/down, in/out, swivel)

☐ have an adjustable backrest (depth, angle, and height) that provides lumbar support

☐ have a stable, five-point star base with casters that are suited to the flooring

☐ isolate the employee from vibration

☐ be positioned so the user can maintain a neutral, balanced posture while at the keyboard or desk.

Work surfaces (desk or tabletop) should:

☐ have a thin work surface to allow legroom and posture adjustments

☐ be height adjustable

> ☐ be large enough to accommodate the keyboard, mouse, monitor, and documents
> ☐ have rounded furniture edges
> ☐ be organized for users to view the monitor and a document without turning their heads back and forth.

A variety of document holders and clip devices are commercially available so workers can view documents directly beside their computer monitor.

DON'T miss this

Computer station design. These days, workstations are utilized mainly for working on a computer. This means added opportunities for discomfort or injury to surface. To prevent them, follow these additional guidelines:

Keyboards

♦ should be placed directly in front of the user
♦ shouldn't slip when in use
♦ should have rounded edges
♦ should be detachable and adjustable to allow straight/parallel hand-forearm
♦ should adjust to vary slope and height from the floor
♦ should slope no more than 15 degrees
♦ should have enough workspace so the user can switch hands to perform mouse tasks
♦ should be at the same height as the mouse and other devices (such as a pointer or calculator).

Did you know that keystrokes on a computer keyboard cause less strain on your elbow and shoulder than using a mouse? Get to know some of the keyboard strokes for software commands and give your arm a rest.

DON'T miss this

Monitors
- should be set slightly less than an arm's length away from the user (18-30 inches)
- should be equipped with flexible document holders at the same distance from the user
- should be adjustable, capable of swiveling vertically and tilting or elevating vertically
- should be positioned so that the top of the display screen is slightly below eye level
- should be situated so the user's head is upright in a neutral posture.

Display screens
- should include brightness and contrast controls for adjustments
- should be clean and free from flickering or waviness
- should have a clear display of characters and images
- should display characters brighter than the screen background
- should face away from windows
- should be positioned to avoid glare
- shouldn't be positioned directly under overhead lights
- shouldn't have bright light sources in the periphery of the screen
- should be equipped with anti-glare filters, if necessary.

Avoiding vision problems and eye strain

Employees who spend their days staring at computer screens can experience discomfort and vision problems, too. In fact, eyestrain or "computer vision syndrome" is the number one complaint of computer users.

Too much time at the computer can lead to the following ailments:
- headaches
- blurred vision
- dry and irritated eyes
- slow refocusing
- light sensitivity
- double vision.

✓ Checklist

Minimizing vision problems

Your employees don't need to suffer. Here are some ways to minimize the risk of injury or discomfort:

☐ Provide desk equipment so that reference materials can be placed close to the computer monitor and at the same distance from the eyes.

☐ Reduce room lighting in the area to about half the brightness of the customary office lighting.

☐ Shade windows to reduce glare on computer monitors.

☐ Provide desk lamps for work away from the computer.

☐ Allow breaks or time for tasks that don't require close concentration and staring at the computer screen. Encourage computer users to follow the "20/20/20 rule": every 20 minutes, take a 20 second break and look 20 feet away.

☐ Blink! We blink less when staring at our computers, and that can be a real source of discomfort. Consider keeping commercial "artificial tears" on hand for those dry-eyed days.

☐ Educate employees on how prolonged staring at a computer monitor may affect their eyesight.

☐ Encourage computer users to have a thorough eye examination annually and ensure they have the correct vision prescription.

A closer look: ergonomic tools. The repeated or long-term use of improper tools is a common cause of ergonomic disorders. Choosing the right tool for the job can solve many ergonomic problems. Most hand tools are designed for only occasional use, not repetitive use over long periods. When acquiring tools for regular use in an industrial setting, work with your purchasing department to ensure that the tools have the following ergonomic features:

◆ Tools should be designed for use with either hand.

◆ Tools should be available in various sizes to fit the needs of different-sized employees.

◆ Tools should allow employees to maintain neutral body positions while working.

◆ Tools should be made of material that is nonconductive.

◆ Tools should be lightweight.

- ◆ Tools should have a textured, nonslippery surface.
- ◆ Tools should have rounded (not sharp) edges and corners, a positive stop or flanged end, and no fluting.
- ◆ Tools should minimize vibration transferred to the hand.
- ◆ Tool handles should be designed to allow a relaxed grip so the wrists can remain straight.
- ◆ Tool handles should be shaped so they contact the largest possible inner surface of the hand and fingers, and are fitted to the anatomy of the hand.

Here are some more safe tool-use tips:
- ◆ Tools should be sharpened and maintained within manufacturers' specifications.
- ◆ Use power tools to reduce the amount of human force and repetition required.
- ◆ The weight of the power tool should be counterbalanced, whenever possible, to reduce vibration.
- ◆ Fit absorbent rubber sleeves over the power tool handle to reduce vibration.
- ◆ When vibrating tools are used, install rubber-backed, low-pile carpet sections on the work surface to diminish vibration.
- ◆ Urge employees to use gloves in order to minimize the effects of vibration and force.

DON'T miss this

Make the purchasing department your friend—you'll need them to help carry out your ergonomic vision for the organization. Make sure that your purchasing and procurement colleagues are involved in the early stages of any workspace redesign. Include them in your ergonomics training initiatives; you'll need to share expertise both ways. They need to be trained to understand basic ergonomic concepts of tool, equipment, and furniture design so they can make informed purchasing decisions. Communicate both to the procurement group and the front-line managers with purchasing authority that your organization must purchase only ergonomically suitable tools, equipment, and office furniture.

A closer look: heavy lifting. Lifting injuries make up 25 percent of workers' compensation cases. But employers can make a number of systemic adjustments to minimize the risk of lifting injuries to their employees. After all, the best way to avoid a back injury is to avoid lifting altogether—to engineer it right out of the job, if possible. How might this be done?

◆ Talk to your safety officer or building manager about evaluating the workflow and workstations in the warehouse. Consider whether there are ways of further reducing the need to carry:
   ◆ Can you relocate the storage, production, receiving, or shipping areas?
   ◆ Can the containers or materials be made smaller so that the objects being moved all day have less weight?
◆ Do you have the proper equipment available for your employees' use, and in good working order, such as mechanical lifts, conveyer belts, cranes, and dollies?
◆ Consult the National Institute of Occupational Safety and Health (NIOSH) Work Practices Guide for Manual Lifting to help identify and mitigate risk factors associated with lifting operations.

Remind your employees of this simple axiom: work smarter—not harder. Especially where heavy lifting is involved.

DON'T
miss
this

Building a business case for ergonomics

You've finished your proposal to implement an ergonomics program. You're sure there will be some costs involved—especially in getting the warehouse up to speed, ergonomically speaking. But you know it's a worthy expenditure of resources. When you present your proposal to the VP for human resources, however, it's met with resounding disinterest. "The executive team is still reeling from these abysmal fourth-quarter figures," she moans. "Just tell me this: will OSHA fine us if an inspector shows up on-site? Are we breaking the law? If not, I don't want to hear about it."

It looks like you've got your work cut out for you. But you know how important an ergonomics program is to the health of your employees and your organization's bottom line. So it's your job to advocate on behalf of the policy and the employees it will protect.

To convince your organization's upper management to initiate an ergonomics program, you'll need to build a business case for ergonomics. According to Franz Schneider, a certified professional ergonomist, the key to building support is to show that an ergonomics program adds value to the business. Ergonomics programs can produce short-term gains in productivity and long-term reductions in injury rates and costs.

Reduced cycle time. Show management the short-term gain the organization can achieve by investing in ergonomic solutions. Use the concept of "lean manufacturing." If you can reduce the time necessary to perform a job, you save money. The "cycle time," or the length of time necessary to produce a product, can be affected by point-of-motion constraints such as excessive reach, awkward postures, and excessive task frequency.

Your organization can reduce cycle time by ergonomic interventions. You can get employees to work faster with increased efficiency and also drive the risk of injury down. One company saw a 24% reduction in production time while its injury incident rate fell after launching its ergonomics program.

DON'T
miss
this

Ergonomics is "a blinding flash of common sense," says ergonomist Franz Schneider. As he notes, there's a simple rationale for ergonomics programs: Healthy people perform better than sick people do.

Ergonomic solutions will produce short-term improvements in productivity and long-term reductions in injury rates and costs. Convince your organization's decision-makers by appealing to the bottom line. You can move your ergonomics agenda from one that management tolerates, at best, to an initiative that management owns and drives.

Implementing an ergonomics program

Best Practices

Quad Graphics, a Wisconsin commercial printing and lithography company, set out to reduce occupational injuries and the workers' compensation costs that accompany them. It enacted an ergonomics program that began with training on how musculoskeletal injuries occur. Employees were instructed on recognizing early signs and symptoms, workplace biomechanics, and the importance of early reporting.

The organization also created employee management teams in areas that they found to be high-risk. The employee teams were charged with the function of identifying ergonomic stressors and possible controls. The teams consulted with management, other employees, engineers, safety and healthcare professionals in carrying out their role.

Four years after rolling out the ergonomics program, lost workdays were reduced by 60 percent, and workers' compensation costs decreased by 10 percent. By the end of eight years, the organization enjoyed the following benefits:

◆ lost time days decreased by 25 percent (per 100 employees)

◆ restricted days decreased by 115 percent (per 100 employees)

◆ reported work-related injuries decreased by 25 percent

◆ back injuries due to material handling decreased by 39 percent; the cost of these injuries decreased by 25 percent.

Even though federal law does not currently require employers to have a concrete ergonomics program in place, it's clearly a best practice to do so. Employers who have implemented such programs have decreased employee injury rates and healthcare costs, increased productivity and product quality, and enhanced worker morale.

The federal government's General Accounting Office (GAO) released a study of ergonomics programs that had already been undertaken by private employers. Which ones were successful? Those with the greatest benefits to show had devised programs with the following core elements:

◆ management commitment
◆ employee involvement
◆ identification of problem jobs
◆ development of solutions for problem jobs
◆ training and education for employees, and
◆ appropriate medical management.

What *didn't* these successful programs have? A hefty price tag. The GAO found that the best programs didn't necessarily involve costly or complicated processes or controls. Often employers achieved results through a variety of simple, flexible approaches.

We've talked about a number of the core elements of an ergonomics program earlier in this chapter, including the importance of management commitment and a strategy for bringing them on board, the critical role employees must play, and methods for identifying ergonomic hazards and reducing them. Let's look at the other components of an ergonomics program: the training and medical management functions. We'll also discuss ergonomics program review—an important step for fine-tuning your efforts as you go.

Ergonomics training

Training and educating employees on work-related ergonomic disorders is critical to the success of your ergonomics program. Your workforce must be instructed about the hazards and armed with the knowledge of how to protect themselves. Effective training is the best way for employees to reap the health benefits of your ergonomics program.

Training and education should give supervisors, employees, and key members of your safety staff an understanding of MSD injuries, causes, prevention and treatment, signs and symptoms, and the importance of early reporting.

New employees. New hires should receive ergonomics training as part of their safety orientation. Line supervisors should provide employees with task-specific ergonomics training, in consultation with your organization's ergonomics team.

Instruct the new employee on proper lighting, seat height, angle and position relative to their computer screen, and the proper way to type and use the telephone. You should also educate new workers about the importance of taking periodic breaks to rest their strained muscles and tendons, and to vary their workflow in order to use different muscles and postures.

Ergonomics training included in employees' general safety orientation will cover:

◆ Types of musculoskeletal disorders often associated with the job;

◆ How to prevent these disorders from occurring;

◆ Risk factors that may contribute to MSDs, and how to recognize them;

◆ Recognizing signs and symptoms of ergonomic injuries;

◆ Procedures to request an ergonomic evaluation of their job, equipment, or worksite;

◆ Reporting protocol and the importance of prompt reporting of injuries and hazards; and

◆ Injury management and methods for seeking medical attention.

Current employees. An ergonomics refresher course should be a regular component of your training program. As a rule, employees should be given brief refreshers every two years or so. However, certain workplace changes or a rising tide of injuries will require a more assertive training schedule. Be sure to schedule special training when:

◆ an employee has been off the job for more than 30 days or transfers into a new position;

◆ new processes, equipment, or procedures are introduced into the workplace; and

◆ accident rates go up, injuries become more severe, or performance drops.

Key safety players. Ergonomics team members must be educated about their role in establishing and/or managing your organization's ergonomics program. They need perhaps an even broader understanding of the means for identifying and analyzing MSD hazards and measures available to eliminate or reduce them. Team members must be advised of criteria and measures for evaluating the effectiveness of the ergonomics program and specific ergonomic controls. Your engineers and building or safety personnel must also receive more extensive instruction in ergonomic risk factors and prevention strategies. These professionals should be able to expertly recognize hazards and identify workstation modifications that can reduce them.

Medical MSD management

"An ounce of prevention," as the saying goes. But regrettably, there will be times when your organization will have to pay for that proverbial pound of cure, and an injured employee will need to seek medical attention for a musculoskeletal disorder. That's where an efficient medical management system comes in. It's an important part of your ergonomics program. In fact, according to OSHA, employers without a medical management program in place have less general awareness of musculoskeletal disorders, so employee symptoms are more likely to be left untreated until they become disabling injuries.

Here are the key strategies for achieving medical management goals:

◆ a system to report early signs and symptoms;
◆ access to trained healthcare providers experienced in the detection and treatment of MSDs;
◆ standardized procedures for healthcare providers;
◆ medical surveillance that includes baseline and any subsequent evaluations;
◆ evaluation, treatment and follow-up for individuals after treatment and/or return to duty; and
◆ a list of light-duty jobs to reduce exposure to risk factors.

Workers who have an MSD, are returning to work after an injury, or are experiencing symptoms may need accommodations to reduce exposure to ergonomic risk factors. Light-duty positions or job transfers, either temporary or permanent, can help injured workers who want to rejoin the team.

Ergonomics program review

Your ergonomics team should undertake periodic evaluation of its ergonomics program to ensure that it is meeting its stated goals. Evaluate the ergonomics program annually, in consultation with employees, to gauge its effectiveness.

How useful are the solutions you've implemented? Monitor injury records to look for reductions in the numbers. Observe evidence of decreased lost or restricted work time, sick leave, medical, and other costs. Conduct periodic symptoms surveys to ensure health complaints are beginning to taper off. If you can't see the benefits of your efforts by reviewing these numbers, then it's time to step back and identify the deficiencies and take prompt action to correct them.

You've done a great job of convincing your organization's leadership of the importance of an ergonomics program. You've shepherded the creation of such a program, bringing in all the key stakeholders. You've attained buy-in among employees, supervisors, your ergonomics team, and top brass. But now is not the time to rest on your laurels. Another risk factor, no doubt, is looming.

A word on enforcement

Technically there is no federal law requiring your organization to have an ergonomics program in place. But you're not completely off the compliance hook. Remember that the federal occupational safety act has a "general duty" clause. As an employer, you're still obligated to furnish a workplace "free from recognized hazards that are causing or likely to cause death or serious physical harm" to your employees. If your workplace poses recognized ergonomic risks, you might be in violation of this obligation. In fact, under the general duty clause, OSHA has initiated more than 400 enforcement cases involving ergonomics-related injuries.

Also keep in mind that several states have adopted mandatory ergonomics regulations, or are currently taking action to do so. Be sure to refer to the employment and safety laws and regulations in your state to make sure your organization is in compliance with any applicable state ergonomics standards.

A+ *Best Practices*

Intel Corporation seeks out the most stringent ergonomics regulations it can find—throughout the world—and then raises the bar on its own ergonomics program based on these standards. The approach has paid off: the world's largest chip manufacturer saw its lost time rates plummet an average of 33 percent from 1995-1999, while its employee population tripled during that same time. Further, according to an AFL-CIO fact sheet on ergonomics, Intel reported a 72 percent reduction in the rate of MSDs from 1994 to 1998, with 20,000 days away from work avoided, to the benefit of more than $10 million in direct and indirect savings.

Intel initiated its ergonomics program way back in 1992, when it found that a large number of injuries at its manufacturing and office sites, such as sprains, strains, and cumulative trauma injuries, could be attributed to ergonomic risk factors. First they benchmarked other hi-tech companies to see what they were doing in this area. The program that resulted is applied to Intel employees across the globe.

Doing the right thing

Even though in some countries with Intel employees, ergonomics is unrecognized, and even though no regulations exist even in the U.S., the company's commitment to its ergonomics program hasn't wavered. "It's completely voluntary," remarked Intel corporate ergonomist Robbie Walls, in a 1999 interview. "But we feel it's the right thing to do."

Compliance issues aside, however, adopting an ergonomics program is a win-win strategy for your employees and your organization. As many employers have already discovered, it's the right thing to do, and pays bottom-line benefits in increased productivity and reduced injury rates and costs.

⁇ *The Quiz*

1. The move from the factory to more sedentary deskwork hasn't reduced the number of ergonomic injuries.   ❏ True   ❏ False

2. The best ergonomics strategy is to hire employees who fit the physical specifications for the equipment and workstation already in place.   ❏ True   ❏ False

3. Setting up an ergonomics program is an expensive regulatory undertaking and just another unnecessary but legally mandated cost burden for business.   ❏ True   ❏ False

4. Injuries resulting from heavy lifting make up 25 percent of workers' compensation cases.   ❏ True   ❏ False

5. A job hazard analysis can help identify the specific source of an ergonomic hazard.   ❏ True   ❏ False

Answer key: 1. T; 2. F; 3. F; 4. T; 5. T

Chapter
7

Preparing for
the unthinkable

September 11, 2001. 11:00 am. Ann is the HR director for a large accounting firm located in Chicago's Sears Tower. Everyone is reeling from the terror still unfolding at the World Trade Center. It seems like the entire company is clamored around the breakroom TV, watching in stunned silence. But Ann's thoughts have already turned to the danger they still may be facing. This building could be a target too, she quickly realizes. As she picks up the phone to call the head of security, he walks into her office. "We got a call from building management. We're going to evacuate," Kwame tells her. "Let's figure out how we're going to handle this situation."

Twelve years in human resources, but nothing has prepared her for this. Ann is frightened (naturally) but calm as she and the security chief quickly forge a plan. "My team will get everyone out of here," Kwame says. "You just figure out what happens from there..."

Introduction

What could possibly have prepared Ann for the role she was to assume on that horrible day? Ann was a skilled, seasoned HR veteran, but she had never experienced anything like this. So many things to think about, and such precious little time to think.

It's hard enough sometimes to manage the issues and events that you have some control over! But trying to steer your employees and the organization through an unexpected crisis over which you feel powerless yourself—like an incident of workplace violence, an emergency, a natural disaster, or a major terrorist attack—is an even greater challenge.

In this chapter, we'll talk about HR's critical role in preparing for, responding to, and coping with a crisis that impacts your organization. Many functions are to be carried out when an organization responds to an emergency or disaster. Some of these may fall under the purview of your security department, building office, or executive team. But others will require the HR department's steady hand.

So many questions will emerge: what does an evacuation mean in terms of paid time off? What if an incident results in an employee's death—do you expand your standard bereavement policies for employees? How fast can you get a grief counselor on-site? How do you educate managers to help move employees through the inevitable cycle of mourning, grief, and resentment, and get your organization up and running again? The best time to think about these questions is *before* an incident arises. When it comes to crisis management, planning is everything.

Once the dust began to settle and her organization returned to business as usual, Ann immediately gathered a team to begin drafting an emergency readiness plan. She hoped that she would never have to use it, but she knew that if there *was* a next time, her organization would be prepared. Yours should be, too.

Best Practices?

Perhaps you'd think that after 9/11, most organizations have implemented some form of crisis management system to prepare for the possibility of an attack or other disaster. But in fact, an August 2002 survey conducted by the American Management Association suggests otherwise:

◆ 54 percent of organizations surveyed had designated a crisis management team; but

◆ only 49 percent of organizations surveyed had a crisis management system in place;

◆ only 39 percent had conducted crisis drills or simulations; and

◆ only 35 percent offered employees formal training on security procedures.

Yet all of these measures are crucial for helping your organization and employees withstand attacks, disasters, or other emergencies.

Readiness

A workplace emergency is an unforeseen situation that threatens your employees or the public; disrupts or shuts down your operations; or causes physical or environmental damage. Emergencies can be natural (floods, hurricanes, tornadoes) or manmade:

◆ Fire or explosion

◆ Toxic gas releases, chemical spills, radiological accidents

◆ Terrorist acts

◆ Workplace violence.

An HR professional has no control over terrorist attacks or earthquakes. And while you can do your best to minimize the likelihood of fires or workplace violence, you still can't immunize your organization completely. But you *can* prepare how the organization will respond to the crisis. How do you ready your organization and employees?

◆ Implement a crisis management plan and identify a crisis management team.

◆ Train employees throughout the organization in emergency preparedness.

♦ Devise a contingency plan to keep the organization up and running.

♦ Craft human resources policies for the crisis and its aftermath.

Here are the steps you'll take:

Assess the risk(s).

First, assess the risk to your organization. Consider what would need to be done in the worst possible scenario. What if a fire broke out in your boiler room? Or a hurricane hit your building head-on? Or an angry former employee entered the building with a loaded gun?

In each of these scenarios (and as many others you can think of), gauge which areas of your worksite would be most vulnerable. In each instance, what would be the best strategy for protecting employees? Which functions would be the hardest to resume operations? Devise your crisis management plan based on these answers.

The risk assessment is a good time for your organization to consider whether the insurance coverage that it currently carries is enough to meet the company's needs.

Draft a plan.

The process of creating a crisis management plan is a useful tool in itself. It forces you to consider your organization's vulnerabilities. It allows you to make critical decisions in a noncritical setting. And with a crisis management plan, if a crisis does hit, many of the hard decisions will have been made already. You can devote your full attention to the emergency at hand as it unfolds.

Your plan will need to address the unique needs of your worksite, your employees, and the particular vulnerabilities you've identified during the risk assessment. Keep these suggestions in mind, however, as you customize your plan:

♦ Consult with individuals who have specific training in emergency response. Have your local fire department review the plan you've composed.

♦ Recruit employees to help draft the plan. "The best emergency action plans include employees in the planning process," OSHA suggests. Encourage employees to offer suggestions about potential hazards, worst-case scenarios, and proper emergency responses.

◆ Prepare evacuation provisions; they are one of the most crucial plan elements. An effective emergency evacuation plan has specific provisions for alarm locations and evacuation routes, and other procedures for leaving the scene safely. Devise a system for accounting for each employee once evacuation is complete. What other post-evacuation issues must you prepare for?

◆ Consider: How many ways are there to get safely in and out of your workplace? Do your employees know about them all? If a fire started near your front door, could everyone get out safely by some other route? Are there known hazards that require special steps to be taken in the event of, for example, a power outage?

◆ Outline clear procedures for whether and how to contact emergency response personnel. First determine whether employees will directly respond to workplace fire, chemical, or weather emergencies, or under what conditions outside emergency response professionals should be called. Describe how the organization will coordinate with local authorities.

◆ Specify the circumstances that will require the facility to be closed. Who will make that decision? How will the decision be communicated? Will employees be compensated during the closure of the worksite? (Your organization might have already devised such a policy for weather-related closures. It's the same principle, albeit on a broader scale.)

◆ Designate employees to continue or to shut down critical operations during the course of an evacuation. Include orders that set forth the conditions under which these employees will know when to abandon operations and evacuate themselves.

◆ Devise a contingency plan for an alternate worksite during the emergency, especially if your facility suffers more long-term damage. Where will your staff work? How will you quickly amass telephones, computers, and other necessary resources?

◆ Include provisions for property protection to ensure the long-term well being of the organization. This includes protecting the facilities, equipment, and vital records that are mission-critical and essential to restoring full operations. Be available as a resource to assist your organization's building and facilities team, technology, and purchasing departments.

- Identify the important contacts within your organization—who must be reached first? What are their responsibilities? Require your line managers to have a ready list, maintained as current at all times, of their employees' phone numbers. Managers should have the list ready to bring with them in case of evacuation, and keep a copy at home or elsewhere so employees can be quickly contacted in the days following the emergency.
- Post copies of the crisis management plan in numerous locations in the worksite. Keep copies of the plan at an offsite location as well. For example, individuals with key responsibilities can keep copies of the emergency plan at their homes.
- Continue to review and revise your emergency plan to accommodate new dangers or vulnerabilities that you identify. Review and update the plan at least once each year.

Communicate the plan.

Communicate the plan so that, in the event of a real emergency, employees know their roles, functions and exactly how to respond. Provide employees with copies of the plan and discuss it in detail in your safety orientation training.

As with all policies, employee buy-in will be critical to the plan's success. Remind employees that following the plan and its procedures will save lives.

What does OSHA require? OSHA requires an Emergency Action Plan for employers who are required to comply with particular standards. The following standards require emergency action plans:

- Means of egress (employee emergency plans and fire prevention plans);
- Medical services and first aid;
- Fire prevention plans: fire protection (fire brigades, fire suppression equipment; fire detection systems; employee alarm systems);
- Hazardous waste operations and response;
- Toxic and hazardous substances.

Before implementing an emergency action plan, employers must train a sufficient number of persons to assist in evacuation. Employers must review the plan with all employees.

Avoid these mistakes:

The National Safety Council identified the ten most common errors found in implementing emergency response plans:

1. No upper management support
2. Lack of employee buy-in
3. Poor or no planning
4. Lack of training and practice
5. No designated leader
6. Failure to keep the plan up to date
7. No method of communication to alert employees
8. OSHA regulations are not a part of the plan
9. No procedures for shutting down critical equipment
10. Employees are not told what actions to take in an emergency.

Consider your special needs employees.

Your crisis management plan must include provisions for the safety of employees who have disabilities. Recruit your employees with special needs to assist you in drafting these provisions; they should be an integral part of the emergency planning process. What means of exit or safe refuge areas will be available to employees in wheelchairs? How will employees who are hearing-impaired receive evacuation orders and communicate with emergency workers? Some of your employees with disabilities may be completely independent in emergency situations, while others may be totally dependent on assistance. Prior consultation and practice with each employee will determine what assistance may be needed under specific circumstances.

Use the buddy system. Assign a coworker in advance who will assist a disabled employee if it ever becomes necessary to evacuate the building. These pre-selected persons are frequently referred to as buddies or monitors. Alternates, or back-up helpers, should also be named to assume the responsibility during the absence of the normally designated buddy. Assign a corps of employees who are trained and ready to assist disabled coworkers. Ensure that your disabled employees and their designated "buddies" coordinate in advance what steps they will take in the event of an emergency.

Employees who use wheelchairs. Under many emergency conditions, elevator use is not possible. Ensure that buddies are trained in proper lifting and carrying techniques for employees who are unable to use stairs. Under what conditions can the employee be carried down with the wheelchair? When must the chair be abandoned?

Employees with a hearing impairment. Employees and their assigned buddies should devise a system of pre-determined hand gestures to convey an emergency message such as an evacuation order. In addition, audio warning signal systems can be supplemented with visual or other sensory information.

Employees with a visual disability. Employees who are visually impaired may require a buddy to lead them to safety. Even if an employee has a guide dog, the dog may become disoriented in smoke or other emergency situations. In some instances, acoustical and tactile cues along the route of egress may be valuable. For example, tape or other tactile material such as a border placed along the corridor walls can serve as a series of directional feelers for sighted as well as visually impaired employees.

DON'T miss this

*Under some emergency conditions, such as a smoke-filled, multi-storied building without interior lighting, **all** employees will become visually impaired. Your emergency management system must prepare for this possibility.*

Questioning employees about disabilities. It's true that an employer cannot ask job applicants about disabilities during an interview. However, under the Americans with Disabilities Act, once a job offer has been made, an employer may ask whether an employee with known disabilities needs special assistance in emergency situations. Attorneys Sheila Engelmeier and Susanne J. Fischer, and Security Consultant Paul A. Jaeb, spoke on this topic in a session on "Post 9-11: Disaster Preparedness and Heightened Security—What All Employers Should Know," at a May 2002 conference in St. Paul. They advised that, for individuals with unknown disabilities, employers can ask employees of their special needs in the event of an evacuation, "in as much detail as is necessary to ensure safety, about what type of assistance is needed by the employee." But employers shouldn't inquire about the employee's underlying medical condition.

It's a legitimate information request, and an important one to ensure the safety and well being of your employees. But keep the following points in mind:

Keep information confidential. The disability information the employee provides is to be kept confidential, and distributed only to individuals with a legitimate need to know for purposes of disaster planning. Those with a need to know may include medical professionals, emergency coordinators, colleagues who will act as buddies, and building security officers who need to ensure evacuation is complete.

Provide a specific, detailed list of everyone who is entitled to information about employees with special needs in evacuating and reaching safety. Explain why those individuals listed have a need to know.

Assure the employee that the confidentiality of the information will be maintained.

> Your emergency plan must also include a plan for communicating evacuation orders and other emergency messages to employees who do not speak English.

WHAT you need to know

Assemble a crisis management team.

Another essential measure of an organization's crisis management initiative is creating an emergency response team. This team should be assembled well in advance of a crisis situation. It must be ready to react on a moment's notice; select team members accordingly. The emergency response team will assume primary responsibility for:

◆ Arranging the evacuation of employees;

◆ Rendering first aid; and

◆ Salvaging and restoring company operations.

According to Engelmeier, Fischer, and Jaeb, "the system for managing resources, analyzing information and making decisions in an emergency is called direction and control." This is the emergency response team's essential role. The direction and control system your organization will implement can depend on a number of factors, including the size and resources available.

The emergency response team will play a critical safety role in the event of an emergency. But it will serve other interests as well: the team must protect the larger interests of the organization and its employees. That means the team may need to interact with the media and the external community, it may deal with liability issues, and there will be operational concerns post-crisis. Given these roles, in addition to its safety responsibilities, the team must include representation from the following functional areas of your organization:

◆ Human resources
◆ Security, building management
◆ Safety department
◆ Legal, risk management
◆ Public relations
◆ Executive team
◆ Leaders from mission-critical operational units

Once the crisis management team has been identified, convene to review the crisis management plan and guide implementation strategies. Train the team in emergency preparedness, ideally with assistance from local emergency officials. Establish a clear chain of command, and identify which members will have authority to order an evacuation of the worksite. Once the team and plan are in place, it won't be necessary to meet regularly—only to be ready.

DON'T miss this

Have another member of the organization initiate emergency drills— not the emergency response team. You'll want to test the team's readiness too, so the team shouldn't have advance warning.

Other emergency readiness measures

In addition to preparing your written crisis management plan, you'll need to take other important steps toward implementing your emergency readiness goals:

◆ Train HR staff and several employees in various work areas in CPR and other emergency medical procedures.
◆ Conduct periodic emergency drills to maintain employees' readiness, at least one a year. Evaluate each practice run. How did it work? How did the response team do? Was there anything that was overlooked?

◆ Clearly mark evacuation routes. Ensure that the routes are sufficiently lit with emergency lighting. Enforce a policy restricting the blocking of emergency exits. Emergency exits should not be used as storage. Make sure they are open and accessible, and wide enough to accommodate your employee population and a typical number of onsite visitors.

Again, as you do your risk assessment and construct your crisis management plan, you will identify many other tasks that must be completed to prepare your organization as well as possible for emergencies that can arise. Now is the time to complete these tasks—not when disaster hits!

Managing the crisis

If a crisis hits your organization, your management plan can serve as a blueprint for taking control of the situation. Of course, there's no way to predict every decision you'll need to make, and every action you'll need to take on the spot. There's also no way to predict how employees will behave in an emergency.

But several key functions will need to be performed:

Take control

Your emergency response team must take immediate control of the situation. A team member should be designated to serve as the lead, who will make final judgments at crucial decision-making times in an emergency. If evacuation will be necessary, the lead member should be the first to make the call.

Set up an operations center

Establish a centralized management location where information can be gathered and decisions made. "Regardless of size or process," Engelmeier, Fischer, and Jaeb advised, "every facility should designate an area where decision makers can gather during an emergency." They also recommend identifying an alternate emergency center in case the intended location is unsafe or otherwise unfeasible for use.

Accounting for employees

Assuming evacuation is necessary, how will you make sure that all of your employees have successfully left the building? How will you know they are safe and out of danger? A predetermined plan is important here too. In advance of such an incident, you should:

◆ Designate assembly areas where employees should gather after evacuating.

◆ Take a head count.

◆ Identify the name and last known locations of anyone not accounted for. Pass the list to an official in charge of the situation.

Workplace violence

Of the many potential crises that can arise in the workplace, the possibility of an incident of workplace violence is foremost on the minds of many HR professionals.

The substantial majority of incidents of workplace violence occur at the hands of outsiders—customers, clients, or criminals. According to the National Institute of Occupational Safety and Health (NIOSH), for example, most incidents of workplace homicide are primarily robbery-related. And like terrorism, or natural disasters, HR professionals have little control over these actions. You can only try to erect some physical barriers to the danger, and educate and prepare employees as best as you can.

But there is more you can do to prevent and avert workplace violence perpetrated from within:

◆ Adopt careful recruiting strategies, as discussed in Chapter 2, to screen out potentially violent individuals from your workforce.

◆ Implement violence-free workplace provisions, and use performance management strategies to address even slight altercations so that they don't boil over into more dangerous confrontations.

◆ Utilize an Employee Assistance Program to help alleviate employee stress (a factor in escalating violence) and screen potentially violent employees.

◆ Train employees to recognize warning signs of violence, to appreciate the danger posed, and to report violent behaviors or other concerns according to your organization's reporting procedures.

Let's look more closely at other prevention measures:

Root out the systemic factors

Earlier in the book, we discussed an important safety principle: the first, best measure to take for safety purposes is to implement engineering or administrative controls to minimize safety hazards. That principle can apply to workplace violence too. That is, we need to minimize the *systemic* factors that can cause potentially violent employees to react. Certain practices that occur in the workplace are believed to lead to higher incidents of violence. These include:

- ◆ Poor grievance procedures
- ◆ Poor employee relations
- ◆ Harassment, threats, and intimidation
- ◆ High levels of stress.

HR professionals have considerable power over these practices. Step back and make an honest assessment of your workplace. Evaluate whether systemic improvements must be made. This isn't to say that we "blame the victim" when violence is perpetrated against an organization or its members. It simply means we correct those hazards over which we have direct control. Consider this step part of your broader safety goal of eliminating known hazards.

Think about how your line managers carry out their performance management role. Have they been sufficiently trained to minimize conflict, handle confrontation, treat employees with dignity and respect—even when terminating them? Clearly these skills are even more critical when confronting an employee whom you fear may be troubled. Are your supervisors prepared to identify which employees might need intervention?

Human resources professionals, and the HR systems in place, are critical to workplace violence prevention and response. HR's contributions to these functions are outlined below:

- ◆ Effective applicant screening
- ◆ Training supervisors and managers to interview effectively
- ◆ Following up on probationary or introductory period employment decisions
- ◆ Identifying violence prevention training needs and delivering training
- ◆ Providing EAP services, wellness benefits, and internal support systems
- ◆ Ensuring a fair performance review system and reviews that are timely, accurate, and consistent

- ◆ Ensuring a fair progressive discipline system and strenuously enforcing the system
- ◆ Ensuring legal compliance, consistency and fairness
- ◆ Conducting periodic employee surveys and encouraging feedback.
- ◆ Monitoring grievances
- ◆ Communicating lingering issues to management
- ◆ Exit interviewing to identify patterns or trends in employee concerns or grievances
- ◆ Aiding survivors of violence, including coworkers and the victim's family
- ◆ Helping survivors to heal and regain productivity.

The list below of systemic factors is by no means exhaustive. But it should illustrate the variety of indicators you might consider when assessing your organizational climate and the level of hazard it might face at a given time.

✓ Checklist

Situational factors

To gauge the possibility of violence within your organization, consider whether:

- ☐ certain supervisors or managers are viewed as difficult or abusive toward employees
- ☐ new issues affecting employees are causing concern or frustration
- ☐ unresolved grievances remain that should have been resolved by now
- ☐ there are signs of animosity from employees who have been recently discharged or laid off
- ☐ the organization recently had bad press that might cause former employees or customers to be reminded of past difficult experiences.

Heed the warning signs

In many cases, there are early warning signs of a potentially violent employee. Train supervisors to recognize these signs. Also alert employees, in workplace violence prevention training, of behaviors that should raise concern. Stress to both supervisors and employees that they should honor feelings of uneasiness, if they are based upon identifiable behaviors or actions, and communicate their feelings or concerns to individuals who can take action.

✔ ✔ **Checklist**

Perpetrator profile

Here are some characteristics of a potential perpetrator of violence. The list is a composite from profiles developed by respected workplace violence experts:

☐ Lacks outlet for rage or anger
☐ Unstable family life; escalation of domestic problems
☐ Drug/alcohol abuser
☐ Male; 30 to 40 years old
☐ Migratory job history
☐ Excessive interest in media reports of violence
☐ Fascination with the military
☐ Gun or weapon collector, or recent acquisition of a weapon
☐ Depression/withdrawal
☐ Suicidal: Comments about "putting things in order" and the impact on others of his/her departure
☐ Unresolved physical/emotional injury claims
☐ Frequent, vague physical complaints
☐ Noticeably unstable emotional responses
☐ Behavior that suggests paranoia—"Everybody is against me"
☐ Increased mood swings
☐ Socially isolated, may be a loner
☐ Poor or low self-esteem
☐ Cries for help

DON'T
miss
this

Caution! Avoid using this profile to stereotype; many of these charac-teristics apply to nonviolent individuals as well. Use profile information with care, especially because they include "immutable" characteristics, and can raise ADA discrimination concerns as well.

✓ Checklist

Violence warning signs

Encourage your supervisors to consider these questions to gauge an employee's propensity for violence. The signs below are more concrete, observable predictors of potential danger.

☐ Has the employee had a particularly difficult personal experi-ence that has affected his/her work life?

☐ Is the employee leaving the workplace without authorization or having numerous excuses why the workday has been shortened?

☐ Does the employee demand more supervision, or more time and attention from the supervisor?

☐ Does the employee appear to be unable to concentrate?

☐ Has there been an increase in safety violations due especially to carelessness or stress?

☐ Was the employee previously productive but recently dropped off significantly in productivity?

☐ Does the employee stop talking when you approach?

☐ Is the employee unusually disgruntled about work, have chronic disputes with management, or continuing problems with working conditions?

☐ Does the employee complain excessively about stress at work?

☐ Does the employee strongly resist or overreact to changes in procedures and policies? Repeatedly and deliberately violate company policies?

☐ Does the employee talk about previous incidents of violence (child/spouse abuse, barroom fighting)?

☐ Has an employee made an increasing number of unsolicited comments about firearms and other dangerous weapons, vio-lent crimes, and empathy with individuals committing violence?

☐ Has there been an unexplained increase in absenteeism by the employee?

☐ Has the employee made a large withdrawal from (or closed) his/her account in the company's credit union?

☐ Has there been a noticeable decrease in attention to appearance and hygiene?

☐ Has the employee had an explosive outburst of anger or rage without provocation? Has the employee had difficulty controlling his/her temper?

☐ Does the employee make inappropriate comments to coworkers and supervisors about other employees or situations?

☐ Has the employee made threats?

☐ Is the employee receiving an abnormal amount of attention from his/her coworkers?

☐ Do employees seem to be talking about the individual in hushed or quiet tones, particularly when a supervisor is present?

☐ Have other employees expressed concern?

Adopt prevention strategies

The following measures should be an integral component of your violence prevention program:

◆ Assemble a workplace violence prevention team that will compose a workplace violence policy, assess current security and recommend added safety measures, assess reported threats, and respond to incidents.

◆ Assess external and internal security. Where appropriate, use a pass-card system and determine if more stringent security measures are necessary. Implement a system tailored to your organization's needs.

◆ Identify those members of top management who may be likely targets and make access to them difficult.

◆ Enlist employee involvement in reporting threats. Establish a policy calling for incidents of workplace violence to be reported to management within four hours.

◆ Consider adding a special telephone hotline number so employees can report suspicious activities or concerns of potential violence, sabotage or other acts of wrongdoing.

- Provide proper training for managers and supervisors. An organization's inability to address diversity issues is suggested as one significant cause of workplace violence. Also, supervisors need to know that domestic problems frequently create uncontrollable tension and potential workplace violence.
- Train employees and supervisors in conflict resolution.
- Provide safety/awareness training for employees. Expect employees inside the workplace to ask strangers to identify themselves.
- Develop a relationship with local law enforcement officials. The one hour of time it takes to "meet and greet" a local peace officer to develop a relationship, as well as to identify an officer with the ability to help diffuse stressful workplace violence issues, may become time very well spent on avoiding future violent situations.
- Provide outplacement assistance for employees who lose their jobs.
- Coordinate planning efforts with the employee assistance program. Identify a qualified psychologist through the EAP so that management concerns regarding a particular employee can be addressed quickly and constructively.
- Prohibit the possession of all weapons, either inside the workplace or transported in an employee's vehicle.
- Strive to develop a workplace environment that fosters trust among employees. That trust can become the buffer that prevents volatile situations from turning violent.
- Recognize that violence in the workplace involves much more than shootings and stabbings. Incivility and harassment are also episodes of violence, and can have a sharp impact on victims of such behavior. Tolerance of such conduct also fosters a culture of violence. Encourage a supportive, harmonious work environment. Develop effective policies against harassment and enforce them.

Workplace violence training for employees should include:
- ◆ personal safety measures
- ◆ the importance of the buddy system in the event of an incident of violence
- ◆ strategies for handling unsafe situations during off-hours.

The aftermath

Worst case scenario

A three-alarm fire rips through a food manufacturing plant and warehouse at 3:00 am on a Friday morning, destroying the building and its contents. Fortunately, only a skeleton crew was at work, and everyone evacuated safely. But as 8:00 am nears, employees start showing up for work. Some already learned of the fire on the morning news, but weren't sure whether to come in or stay home. Others found out upon seeing the rubble. But they were all equally bewildered. No one from human resources was present at the scene. And the supervisors who were there didn't know much either. To make matters worse, it was payday.

Several days later, employees were still unsure what would happen next. When would they get paid? Was the company going to relocate and reopen? Could they transfer to another facility? If so, would they retain their seniority? Were they losing their jobs? Do they still have health insurance? What's going on?

Many unanswered questions. Much fear and dismay. But still no word...

What happens after an incident of workplace violence, a disaster, or another emergency? You'll need to make immediate decisions, assist victims and "survivors," ensure prompt medical attention, and perhaps deal with the press. You'll still need to protect the physical safety and emotional well being of employees from aftershocks of the incident. And you need to minimize damage and disruption. By now you've summoned help from the authorities. Your crisis management team is handling the situation as well as can be expected. What happens next?

◆ **Communicate.** Family members and off-duty employees will be concerned. How will you communicate with them? If evacuation was necessary, how will you contact *all* of your employees once people have gone home? "When will the worksite be open again?" "Will it be safe?" "Will we be getting paid while we're out?" Your employees will already be uneasy and on edge. These questions, if unanswered, will add to the anxiety.

◆ **Respond quickly.** Within a fixed period of time (for example, 48 hours) schedule a group meeting to enable affected employees, their families, and interested parties such as customers to deal with their feelings about the incident. Have managers facilitate the meeting. The initial meeting should be held in a quiet, comfortable room. Consider a location away from the scene of the event.

◆ **Provide information and resources.** Disseminate accurate information about what has happened and explain what has been done and what the company will continue to do.

◆ **Manage the media.** Ensure that your media relations team responds proactively to inquiries from the media. Shield employees who are personally affected by the incident from the press and do not include media in your employee meetings. Consider distributing a fact sheet bulletin as necessary to curb the spread of misinformation.

◆ **Follow up.** Assign company representatives to visit the family of the victim(s). A member of the organization should stay in touch with the family for the time necessary to assist them in processing claims, for example, and to pass along needed information.

◆ **Learn from the crisis.** Prepare a plan for the future. Assess what was done well and what could have been done better. Take steps to ensure that the same mistakes and omissions will not occur again.

Healing your workforce

Perhaps the most critical role human resources will play is helping employees get through the crisis and get back to work. You'll need to assume the leadership role for your organization at this stage.

How will you get your employees back on track after trauma and tragedy? What tools and policies will guide you? How long of a "break" do you allow before making an effort to restore business as usual? Although you won't be able to predict the nature of the incident, and the extent of the pain your employees will face, you should be able to identify these questions in advance. What criteria will you use to assess the situation when the crisis hits, and afterward? Identify the criteria now.

It's helpful to keep in mind the stages through which your employees will pass as they gradually heal from the trauma.

Predictable stages of a crisis. A crisis is usually time-limited and progresses in predictable stages. In other words, employees may be expected to experience predictable reactions to the stress of a crisis, an accident or death on the job for approximately four to six weeks. Usually after that time, psychological balance returns. During this four-to-six week period, employees may experience various stages of crisis.

Those stages include:

◆ **Shock.** The initial stage, which usually lasts from several days to several weeks, is often characterized by shock and numbness. At this stage, employees may reject help from the company since this would force them to confront their feelings. However, continue to offer help to employees, since help may be accepted when employees move into the second stage of the crisis resolution.

◆ **Anxiety.** Guilt, depression and anxiety are usually associated with the second stage. This stage is characterized by obsessive thinking, sleep disturbances, and anxiety. For some individuals, these symptoms result in inertia and lethargy. During this stage, employees may have the greatest difficulty in dealing with their jobs. They may exhibit short attention spans, cry at inappropriate times, or may be disassociated from others. Employers should allow workers some time to resolve feelings and emotions associated with this stage.

Employees who receive appropriate help can work through this stage in several weeks.

◆ **Anger.** Strong, often irrational anger and defensiveness accompany the third stage of crisis. Employees in this stage often look for slights where none are intended. In this stage, employees are starting to fight back to cope with the crisis. They may overreact to criticism with defensiveness and anger.

◆ **Denial.** The fourth stage is usually one of denial. For example, if a worker created a hazard that led to a fire, he or she may blame the incident on the organization and accept no responsibility for his or her role. At this point, you may want to discuss culpability, if it exists, with employees. Help employees understand that the organization did whatever was possible to avoid the accident. Motivational or pep talks, on the other hand, may simply increase employee hostility.

◆ **Acceptance.** The final stage of the crisis is characterized by an uneasy acceptance of the crisis, death or accident and a desire to get on with normal life. Employees experience a sense of relief. Their periods of remorse or anxiety are brief. At this stage, initiate brief discussions with employees about anticipated work problems and provide concrete suggestions of ways they might handle on-the-job difficulties.

Helping your workforce cope.

◆ Educate your supervisors and managers. Inform supervisors about the signs of emotional distress, such as working slowly or overworking, irritability and anger, difficulty concentrating, and other indicators. Refresh their memory of policy changes being taken in response to the crisis.

◆ Facilitate communication among employees. Support among colleagues can help employees work through difficulties. Be flexible with work breaks. Provide gathering space.

◆ Consider loosening your time-off policies so that people who need time to recover can take extra hours or days off even if they have no time available.

◆ Hold a memorial service for a fallen employee or for employees' loved ones.

◆ Urge them that life—and business—must go on. Getting back to full productivity, at an appropriate juncture, is a healthy part of the healing process. Ultimately, it's the best sense of closure for employees, and of course, it's essential to the organization's long-term well being.

?The Quiz

1. Since, 9/11, most employers have put extensive crisis management systems in place. ❑ True ❑ False

2. Because you don't know which employees will be the most level-headed in a crisis, it's best to set up the crisis management team when the emergency unfolds. ❑ True ❑ False

3. A list of employees with disabilities should be distributed throughout the workplace so coworkers will know who needs special help in an emergency. ❑ True ❑ False

4. Systemic factors within an organization can make a potentially violent employee more likely to carry out a violent act. ❑ True ❑ False

5. Holding pep talks can be counterproductive during the healing stages following a crisis. ❑ True ❑ False

Answer key: 1. F; 2. F; 3. F; 4. T; 5. T

Workers' compensation

Jacob went immediately to Sam, his foreman, after he was burned slightly on the face by some sparks. "I've gotta get this checked out, boss," and he showed Sam the injury. "Weren't you wearing your mask? How did this happen?!" Sam reacted angrily. "Yes, I was wearing it," Jacob answered, his voice rising. "I just lifted it for a second because I was coughing!" "Well, you violated safety rules," Sam responded. "You're off the clock. Go get it looked at, but the company's not paying."

Sam came to you the following afternoon, clearly troubled that Jacob wasn't back at work. "I was way out of line," he told you. His crew was missing its production quota, he was upset that his worker got injured, he didn't think it was that serious—he was having a bad day. Of course, it was all a bit too late for contrition. You had already received a call from Jacob's lawyer...

Introduction

No matter how effective your efforts are to provide a safe and healthy workplace, the reality is that injuries sometimes will happen. That's why a post-accident action plan is essential.

Educate your employees about their workers' compensation benefits. Take their injuries seriously. See that they get the best possible healthcare. Actively encourage and facilitate their return to work. All of these measures will reduce your workers' compensation costs and increase the likelihood that your valued employees will return to the team—and will want to stick around. Taking good care of your injured workers pays off.

Like all healthcare costs, workers' compensation expenses are steadily increasing. In fact, these costs are rising more sharply than other healthcare expenditures. There is a growing cost burden on employers from workplace injuries.

Your manager, Sam, didn't help matters, either. When he got hot under the collar, he virtually assured an adversarial relationship between Jacob and the company. Maybe if Sam had come to you yesterday, you could have called Jacob, inquired about his injury and doctor's visit, and tried to smooth things over. Sam needs to be trained on accident response—the importance of treating employees compassionately and reporting injuries promptly.

By knowing how to administer workers' compensation claims and working with your injured employees, you can help injured workers get the benefits they deserve, avoid paying out unwarranted expenditures, and return injured workers to their jobs more quickly. Effective handling of claims and caring human resources policies can also help your organization avoid litigation and control the costs of regrettable lapses in workplace safety.

What is workers' compensation?

Workers' compensation is payment to employees for personal injuries or illness that occurred in the course of their employment. Unlike employee benefits for disability income and sick pay, workers' compensation payments are made only for on-the-job injuries or occupational illness.

The workers' compensation system emerged at the state level as a way to compensate injured workers while controlling the costs of liability to employers. Workers' compensation is still defined by state law and administered by the states. Legislation is in effect in all 50 states, the District of Columbia, and Puerto Rico. (Separate federal workers' compensation laws exist for federal employees and certain private employees such as railroad workers, longshoremen and shipyard workers.)

The workers' compensation facts below explain some of the legal provisions that all state laws have in common. But for a fuller understanding of the specific legislation that applies to your organization, you will need to consult your state statute.

Workers' comp: fast facts

Coverage is mandatory. Employers must be covered; it is mandatory that they carry liability insurance.

Employers fund benefits in one of three ways. They make premium payments into state insurance funds. (The employer's premium rate depends upon the risk involved—the degree of hazard its employees face, and the company's accident history.) The employers can "self-insure." (Large employers sometimes find this method more cost-effective.) Or they can contract with an approved private insurance company.

"Employees" are covered. Only those workers who are defined by law as "employees" are covered by workers' compensation. This means that independent contractors, for example, are not entitled to workers' comp benefits. Employers *have* defended against workers' compensation claims by showing that the injured worker was not an "employee" at the time of the accident.

Does your organizations "lease" employees? In the typical leasing situation, an employer shifts its employees to a payroll company and then leases the same employees back again.

Don't assume a leasing arrangment will automatically free your company of liability. It's quite likely that your organization will still be the "legal" employer for purposes of employee lawsuits and workers' compensation claims, depending on the level of supervision you exert and other factors.

WHAT you need to know

Employees must give notice of injury. An employee must notify the employer of an injury within a certain time period after the accident or injury occurs. Even if an employee doesn't directly report an injury, if the employer actually knows about the injury, that's enough to satisfy the notice requirement.

The injured worker or "claimant" must also file an application for benefits within a set period of time. (Some states provide specific notice of injury forms.) If an employee dies after a workplace accident or injury, there is an added requirement to claim death benefits: the family or dependents must give notice of death within a certain time period.

Notice must be timely. The employee must notify the employer or insurer of the injury as soon as possible. This way the employer can investigate the accident and ensure that the injured employee gets prompt medical treatment. In most states, the notice period begins to "run" once the employee knows (or *should* have known) about the injury and how serious it is.

DON'T miss this

Is late notice ever excused? *Most states will excuse an employee's late notice of an injury for a variety of reasons, including:*

◆ *A medical provider indicated that the injury was not serious or compensable.*

◆ *The employer paid benefits voluntarily before notice was provided.*

◆ *Mental or physical incapacity prevented the employee from providing notice.*

◆ *The employee had no way of knowing that an apparently minor injury would eventually develop into a compensable injury. (This exception usually applies to occupational diseases that may not become apparent until years after the hazardous exposure, or latent injuries that don't manifest immediately.)*

Minors. *Some state laws also provide that minors without guardians should not be restricted by notice requirement deadlines.*

Employers must file reports. States also require employers to file accident reports with the state agency. An employer that fails to file the required report may be penalized.

Injured employees receive "wage-loss" and medical benefits.
Workers' compensation pays hospital and medical expenses as well
as wage-loss benefits that are usually one-half to two-thirds of an
employee's average weekly wage. If an employee's average salary
includes regular overtime pay, then those earnings are factored into
the benefit award as well.

Benefits are classified as:

- temporary partial disability (when workers can't do
  customary work for a limited period)
- temporary total disability (the majority of cases—workers
  can't do any work for a limited time)
- permanent partial disability (when a worker can no longer
  perform his or her particular occupation)
- permanent total disability (where a worker is completely
  incapacitated to work for life).

Death benefits are also compensable. When a worker dies following a workplace accident, the family or dependents receive
death benefits.

No income taxes on benefits. Workers' compensation benefits can
be excluded from an employee's gross income, so the employee
doesn't pay income taxes on these funds. That means the employer
also doesn't have to withhold income tax or pay payroll or unemployment taxes on these benefits. (However, payments for certain
non-occupational injuries under state law are subject to taxation
and do require the appropriate withholding.)

A waiting period applies. There is a gap between the time a work-
related injury or accident occurs and the time benefits begin. There
is no delay, however, for payments of medical or hospital care, which
is paid from the time of injury. In some states the waiting period
only applies to temporary disabilities. Some states waive the waiting
period altogether if the injured employee is hospitalized.

The waiting period usually runs from three to seven days. It
may be covered by paid sick days provided by the employer's paid
time off policy (so the employee isn't completely without income
for the first days of a disability). Also, in most states, the waiting
period is paid retroactively if the disability lasts a certain length of
time—anywhere from 5 to 42 days.

Which injuries are covered?

An employee is entitled to benefits from the employer when he or she suffers an injury "arising out of and in the course of employment." That seems fairly straightforward, but it can get complicated.

Employer's premises

Consider these scenarios:

> ***Example 1:*** *A Kmart cashier was on her lunch break in the store's (public) cafeteria. One of her coworkers, also on lunch and seated at the next table, was suddenly attacked by her husband with a knife. The employee rushed to her coworker's defense, and was stabbed in the arm.*
>
> *The employee was not acting in the course of her employment and therefore was not covered by workers' compensation for her injury. She was at lunch, and rescue efforts aren't a normal part of her job.*
>
> ***Example 2:*** *A machinist was blinded in one eye by flying glass from a cola bottle while on his lunch break. The bottle had exploded as he placed it in the cooler.*
>
> *The employee was acting in the course of his employment, and his injury was covered. He was required to stay on the premises during his lunch break, and he was paid for his lunch hour, so the injury was seen as work-related.*

Are these two results at odds? Well, there is an important difference that can explain the disparate results: one employee (the exploding bottle victim) was still on the clock, while the other was on an unpaid break (our Kmart heroine). The Kmart employee wasn't required to be on the employer's premises during her break, but the machinist was.

Let's try a few more. An injury that happens "in the course of one's employment" doesn't typically include injuries suffered coming and going from work. But there are exceptions. Look at these examples:

> **Example 1:** *A customer service rep tripped on an open sewer grate on her way from the train and broke her ankle. Her injury is not covered; she wasn't at work—just getting to work.*
>
> **Example 2:** *A purchasing assistant tripped on an open sewer grate in the employee parking lot at work. Her injury is probably covered; she was at work—at least on the employer's premises.*

Why the distinction? While the purchasing assistant wasn't yet acting in the course of her employment, her injury arguably "arose out of her employment." That is, if she weren't going to work for the employer, she would not have been in the company parking lot, and would not have been injured. On the other hand, her injury getting off the train was a bit too far removed from the office—she might just as well have been off to the gym when it happened.

Telecommuters are covered by workers' compensation protections if they are injured while performing their job—even if it's in their own home. The trick is to identify exactly when they are "in the course of employment" and when they're off the clock—especially for those workers who don't have defined work hours. It's important to hammer out the details and reach a clear understanding between the employer and the telecommuter. And be sure to enforce the same workplace safety rules for your off-site employees as you do for those physically on the employer's premises.

Course of employment

So what if a programmer suffers a back injury while helping the building crew situate his new office furniture? Was his injury "in the course of" employment? The programmer's job isn't to move furniture, after all. What if the programmer was injured by the loading dock instead, assisting the dock crew in unloading his new motorcycle that he had delivered to his work address?

Company-sponsored or even loosely related recreational and social events, particularly sporting events, can increase your exposure to workers' compensation liability. Many courts find injuries that occur at these gatherings to be covered. So when you sponsor a sports team, host a company picnic, or put a ping-pong table in the employee lounge, know what you're getting into!

There are some general principles that define what injuries occur "in the course of employment" and "arise out of" employment. There are some general exceptions to those principles, too. But how they apply in particular situations can sometimes be up for grabs. Some of the variations in how the cases turn out are simply a result of different courts in different states. More often, the results turn on the very unique facts that arise in each individual workplace injury scenario.

What's the moral of these stories? When an accident happens, you don't always know whether the injury will be covered. Don't let that change your initial response when an employee is injured. Treat every injury seriously and as potentially covered by workers' compensation. Provide the standard benefits information and the ongoing support. You don't need to make an immediate judgment call on whether the injury will be covered.

Further down the line, a more accurate assessment is important, though, so that the organization doesn't waste money fighting a legitimate claim—or paying out noncompensable claims. The checklist below can offer some guidance in determining whether an injury is covered.

✓ Checklist

Evaluating injuries

Will an employee's injury be covered by workers' comp? Consider these factors:

☐ Was the injury caused by an *increased* risk from the job that is greater than the risk held by the general public?

☐ Would the injury not have occurred *but for* the fact that work obligations placed the employee in a position where he was injured?

☐ Could the injury be characterized as *purely personal,* unconnected in any way to the employment? Did the injury occur at the workplace, even if the circumstances were purely personal?

☐ If the injury results from a dispute in the workplace, was the dispute over a private and personal matter? Whether an injury is covered may depend on whether workers were fighting about an overtime shift, or over an insult hurled at a bar over the weekend.

☐ If your employee is assaulted at work by a member of the general public, was the danger greater due to the nature or setting of the work (security guards, police officers, convenience store clerks, and bartenders)?

Disqualification from coverage. A few states allow employers to defend against workers' compensation claims by showing that the injured employee was guilty of willful misconduct, such as an intentional violation of a safety regulation. This disqualification rule is very narrowly applied, however.

A growing number of states limit benefits, either entirely or in part, when the employee has an accident due to drug or alcohol use on the job. But some states add that if the employer knew of the worker's drug or alcohol use and didn't try to address it, the injury is still compensable.

Further, disqualification for alcohol or drug use has a "causation" element attached. While the extent of causation that you need to show varies by state, the essential question is the same: Would the employee have been injured even if he or she were not intoxicated? The answer determines whether the injured worker is disqualified from receiving workers' compensation benefits.

The injury aftermath

Employees need to feel they are cared for and valued. You can ensure that they do by making sure that all managers and supervisors, as well as the HR staff:

◆ express concern for the injured worker and the family;

◆ seek to relieve the worker's anxieties over health and income; and

◆ encourage the earliest possible return to work.

Consider every injury legitimate

Avoid an adversarial relationship. This means trusting your employees. Assume that every reported injury is legitimate until proven otherwise.

An attitude that conveys to employees your belief that they are exaggerating—or even faking—their injuries will do far more harm than good. People tend to respond to what is expected of them, and injured employees are no exception. An atmosphere of distrust and suspicion breeds fraudulent claims. An environment of trust fosters open and honest communication and reduces the likelihood of fraud.

Combating fraud. Is the injury fake or real? Whatever it may appear to be up-front, rule number one is this: *Never accuse a worker of faking an injury.*

Why? First of all, "hard-core" fraud like faking injuries is relatively rare. A survey conducted for the American Management Association by William M. Mercer, Incorporated, found that only 10 percent of workers' compensation claims were deemed fraudulent by participants. (However, that small percentage of fraudulent claims generated more than 50 percent of the employer's workers' compensation medical costs!)

Having said this, there are, of course, occasional instances of fraud, and you need to identify them in the course of managing the claim. There are certain things to look out for to spot *possible* fraud. Here are just a few:

◆ The employee had the accident at an odd time, such as at lunch hour; there were no witnesses present at the time.

◆ The details of the accident are vague or contradictory.

◆ The employee does not promptly report the injury to a supervisor.

◆ The claimant moves out of state soon after the injury.

◆ The claimant frequently changes physicians or medical providers.

◆ Medical report descriptions of the claimant are inconsistent with his or her actual appearance, for example: a rehabilitation report describes the small-framed, fastidious claimant as being muscular, with callused hands and grease under the fingernails.

◆ The claimant is unusually familiar with workers' compensation claims-handling procedures and laws.

◆ Tips from fellow employees, friends, or relatives suggest that the injured worker is either working or is active in sports.

◆ The injured worker leaves different daytime and evening telephone numbers.

If you explain workers' compensation to your employees, work with employees to make the job safer, line up the best medical care available, reassure employees of their value to the organization, and pay benefits that are due, employees are highly unlikely to abuse that trust.

Support the injured worker

Counsel managers and supervisors to support injured workers and assure them they will be cared for if they are injured. Nothing causes lower morale and discontent than uncaring bosses. While injuries in the workplace are often avoidable, employees are *human*, and it's inevitable that some accidents will happen.

Workers' compensation expert Edward M. Welch uses the example of a sports injury. What happens when a football player is injured on the job? All action stops and attention is focused on the injured player, who is assured "you'll be all right; we'll take care of you." Applause greets him as he is carried from the field.

In football, injuries are a cost of doing business. You should look at workplace injuries the same way.

So many unanswered questions... What must be going through your injured worker's mind? Well, for starters:

◆ Where should I go for medical care?

◆ Will I get paid?

- Will I get my job back?
- Will I be able to do my job?
- Will I have a job to go to while I recuperate, if I can't do my old job?
- How do I get benefits?
- Who is this "claims adjuster" that is calling?
- Does anybody care? Is anybody on my side?
- *Do I need an attorney?*

Report promptly

Reporting relevant information to the claims personnel and the insurance carrier does not have to be a complicated process. In fact, the easier the procedure, the more likely that people will use it. If your organization's reporting procedures are difficult or complicated, streamline them!

Prompt investigation is important too. The insurance carrier should be notified and be able to contact the injured worker's treating physician within the first 24 hours. According to ManagedComp, a private workers' compensation insurer, claims that are reported within 24 hours lead to better treatment, reduced attorney involvement, and a significant reduction in average costs than claims reported after 24 hours.

Information to report. In addition to reporting the vital statistics on the employee—personal data and employment history at your organization, you'll want to compile information on the specific injury and the accident that caused it. Information on the claim itself will also be essential. The list below is a good place to start for gathering the claim information you'll need:

✓ *Checklist*

Claim information.
- ☐ Time and date the injury was reported
- ☐ To whom the injury was reported
- ☐ Who filled out the first report of injury
- ☐ Date employer was first notified
- ☐ Who was notified, by whom?

- ☐ Date employer's workers' compensation claims department was notified
- ☐ Date insurance organization or service organization was notified
- ☐ Date state agency was notified
- ☐ State case number
- ☐ Average weekly wage
- ☐ Benefit rate
- ☐ Healthcare providers
- ☐ Healthcare costs
- ☐ Other benefits lost (Did the employer stop paying vacation, health benefits, etc.?)
- ☐ Other benefits received
- ☐ Offset for other benefits
- ☐ Date disability started
- ☐ Date of first payment
- ☐ Projected return-to-work date
- ☐ Date case closed
- ☐ Date of maximum medical improvement
- ☐ Impairment rating
- ☐ Lost days
- ☐ Total benefits paid
- ☐ Reserves
- ☐ Vocational rehabilitation activity
- ☐ Subrogation (Is a third party responsible?)
- ☐ Second injury fund potential

While out of work...

So your employee has been injured and will be out on disability for a short term. Can human resource policies make a difference in workers' compensation costs? Research has found that, in addition to the safety measures aimed at reducing injury and illness, proper disability management can significantly reduce costs as well.

Consider the HR skills entailed in the functions below. While the HR team will be key players in managing an injured employee's workers' compensation claim, supervisors will be the primary points of contact. Are your front-line managers up to the task? Remember Sam? Is he ready to reach out effectively to Jacob—or another member of his crew who becomes laid up?

Tell employees how the system works

Many employees don't understand workers' compensation. In fact, a surprising number think they cannot receive workers' compensation for accidents that were their fault. What's the downside to your organization? Wouldn't it be better to have employees stay "in the dark" so they're less likely to try to work the system to their own advantage? Not really—uninformed employees are more apt to have problem claims than those in the know. Employees who think they have to prove an accident wasn't their fault are more likely to hire lawyers than those who understand workers' compensation is a no-fault system. If you explain workers' compensation to your employees, they won't need outside "help."

Here's what your workers' compensation "curriculum" should entail:

- ◆ Instruct employees about what to do if they have an on-the-job injury or illness.
- ◆ Urge them to go to human resources if their immediate supervisor discounts their injury.
- ◆ Explain what benefits they can expect under workers' compensation.
- ◆ Identify their contacts in human resources who will assist them with claims and benefits in the event they are injured.
- ◆ Provide a full explanation of your return-to-work policy and procedures. Direct them to your employee handbook, which discusses your organization's commitment to return-to-work.
- ◆ Communicate that every employee makes a valuable contribution to the workforce—and that contribution must not be lost to injury or illness.

It's equally important for you to train your managers and supervisors. If they know how your workers' compensation procedure works, they can help lead their employees through the system quickly, without unnecessary costs or delay.

Best Practices

One large food service provider with more than 90,000 domestic employees candidly tells its workers that if they are injured on the job, the company will pay their medical bills and may even replace their wages. "Don't make it a mystery as to how the workers' comp program works," the company's risk manager urged. "If the employer doesn't tell employees up front where their benefits are coming from, the employee will get the information from someone else—most likely an attorney."

Reflect the company's concern

Show your sincere interest in the employee's well being when an injury does occur. Have a member of the HR team contact each injured or ill employee who is out on disability to convey the company's concern and its commitment to the employee's eventual return to work. See that employees receive the benefits they are entitled to in a timely manner. After all, behind every workers' compensation claim is an individual who has the same needs to feed the family, pay the rent or mortgage, and make car payments as you do.

Partner with the injured employee

He may be out on disability, but he's still your employee! Keep in regular contact with your injured worker, and demonstrate the organization's continued interest in his health and healing. Talk about the workers' compensation process and the status of the employee's injury and job. Share resources that might assist him. Most important, don't make your employee have to look elsewhere for answers to his questions.

Keeping in touch with employees serves another purpose of keeping them a part of your organization's community. You want them to feel they are still part of the team. Send employee newsletters and keep their email account active if possible.

Remind the injured worker that he has a responsibility, too, to keep you informed of the progress of his recovery. Tell the employee to call after each doctor appointment to give an update. Urge him to follow the physician's treatment orders. If the employee wants to see his own physician, he should still keep the company informed.

Best Practices

A caring attitude on the part of employers can shorten an injured worker's time away from work and decrease workers' compensation costs. Minnesota Power Co. serves as an example. At Minnesota Power, supervisors are responsible for taking their injured workers for medical treatment and for maintaining regular contact with them and their families if the injury requires lost time from work.

The company has experienced reduced costs as a result. In fact, its workers' compensation costs are significantly lower than the national average.

Partner with the medical care provider

Know the medical provider. After the injury is *not* the time to locate a good physician. Your organization should have prearranged preferred providers so that injured employees can get immediate medical attention. Use doctors and clinics familiar with your worksite. Have your prearranged physician review your facilities ahead of time. A full knowledge of the worksite will enable the doctor to be more effective when suggesting light-duty work for an employee returning from injury.

DON'T miss this

Who selects the initial treating physician? Some states specify who chooses the medical care provider. In some states, a state agency provides a list of doctors from which the employee makes a selection. Other states allow the employer to select the initial health care provider, but the employee can make at least one change. Some states do not allow employers to select the physician, but they can suggest (not coerce!) a healthcare provider.

An employee who is treated by the organization's designated provider but wants an opinion from his or her family physician should be encouraged to get one.

Play an active role in the employee's medical care. If possible, have a member of the organization take the injured worker to the provider for treatment. Explain your return-to-work program to the provider; don't leave it up to the injured worker to do so. Educate the treating physician about the workplace as a whole. By cultivating a relationship with the injured worker's physician, you'll get full reports immediately following diagnosis, information on the course of recovery, and an estimated return-to-work date.

Ideally, getting the employee back to work becomes a cooperative venture between the employee, the physician, and the employer. The physician, physical therapist, supervisor, human resources contact, insurance company, and employee should be a part of a team to develop a realistic back-to-work plan.

Partner with coworkers

Encourage the employee's manager and coworkers to maintain regular communication too. Have them call or write, tell their injured colleague that her presence is missed, that her coworkers are concerned about her, that they look forward to the day she comes back. Suggest they invite her to a department meeting, or even an after-work gathering, if it's cleared with the physician and claims manager. In short, keep the employee immersed in the social life of the work team.

After the recovery period starts to drag on, coworkers can develop a negative attitude toward injured workers. They can become suspicious after an extended absence and even resentful if an injured worker is assigned light duty. Address this potential problem head-on. Take a positive attitude overall. Let the employees know that you understand the stress they're under as well. Acknowledge their added workload, the uncertainty of the situation, and the potential effect it may have had on their morale. Show a positive attitude about the employee's impending return, and his coworkers may become more positive too. The injured employee's return-to-work transition will be greatly eased.

Consider assigning a mentor or "return-to-work advocate" to assist the employee with unforeseen problems when they return to work. The employee will be pleased to know you've thought in advance of their needs, and reassured that a strong support system is in place.

Plan ahead for return to work

Set a target date for a return to work with the employee and the employee's medical care provider. Set the expectation of return to work immediately, and continue to reinforce this goal at each possible opportunity.

Have a job ready for the injured worker. Develop a series of transitional or modified jobs in which to place the recovering employee temporarily, or try to restructure or redesign the injured worker's existing job to get as quick a return to work as possible.

Implement your return-to-work program. Employers who have light-duty work programs are more likely to provide a successful return-to-work transition for their employees. Does your policy provide that workers can't return to duty until they are at 100 percent? Trash it. It undermines your goal of getting them back to work as soon as possible. Leaving your workers on the couch watching soap operas is of no benefit to you or to your employees.

✔
✔ *Checklist*

Handling claims.

Immediately:
☐ Assign case manager or other responsible person to follow claim.

First day:
☐ Report injury to your outside claims handler (insurance organization or third-party administrator).
☐ Determine, on a preliminary basis, whether the injury is covered by workers' compensation.
☐ Contact the injured worker's union, if applicable.
☐ Counsel employee and/or family on claims procedures, available benefits.
☐ Remind the employee of the organization's continuing interest in the employee's welfare.
☐ Follow up with the employee or family.

First week:
- ☐ Coordinate payment of initial benefits.
- ☐ Advise employee generally of when workers' compensation payments will be made. (Most injured workers get little if any information about the benefits to which they are entitled until almost a month after the accident!)
- ☐ Talk to the treating physician to learn the diagnosis and treatment plan.
- ☐ Evaluate whether medical rehabilitation is necessary or appropriate.
- ☐ Develop a return-to-work plan.
- ☐ Forward the employee's mail.
- ☐ Contact the injured employee and/or the family.

First month:
- ☐ Use a "wellness" approach (cards, phone calls, visits) to continue to reinforce your organization's concern.
- ☐ Consider medical examination by independent physician, if warranted.
- ☐ Reevaluate treatment plan based on new medical information.
- ☐ Update the return-to-work plan.
- ☐ Check for third-party involvement (for possible recovery).
- ☐ Contact the injured employee and/or the family.

Ongoing:
- ☐ Continually reevaluate the injured employee's treatment plan.
- ☐ Update the return-to-work plan.
- ☐ Refer for vocational rehabilitation, if appropriate.
- ☐ Refer for pain management evaluation of chronic pain, if appropriate.
- ☐ Maintain contact with the injured employee and/or the family.

✓ Checklist

Out-of-work practices

Take a quick assessment of your current practices:

☐ Are your workers' compensation policies aimed at getting injured employees back to work—not denying benefits?

☐ Are return-to-work goals set and regularly updated on every claim?

☐ Are injured workers kept on the job site if at all possible, even if their jobs are modified?

☐ Does the immediate supervisor visit the injured worker who is out on disability?

☐ Are supervisors (and other relevant members of the organization) instructed on how best to communicate with injured workers?

☐ May supervisors or other employer representatives visit injured workers on company time?

Return to work

John was cleared to return to light-duty work in Bruce's department where he had worked for four years. Bruce can't seem to find light-duty work for him, though. The operations manager thought John would be able to salvage manufacturing parts that were wrongly discarded, and that this task was consistent with the work restrictions provided by John's physicians. Bruce dismissed this idea as "a waste of time," and said John would just get in the way if he couldn't come back full-speed.

It's no secret that John was a difficult employee. But he had never received any formal discipline, and his reviews were always "good." Still, you sense that Bruce is looking for reasons to prevent John's return.

Return to work should be the goal from the day your employee suffers an injury. Why? Because return-to-work programs allow employers to retain experienced employees. And organizations gain a lot in employee goodwill when employees return to work faster at their full salaries. What's more, you reduce the cost of wage-loss benefits, and eliminate the possibility of unemployment payouts.

To this end, rehabilitation and return-to-work programs make good sense.

The unmotivated employee

Sure, you've heard the stories of employees on disability trying to stretch out their benefits and avoid the "9-to-5" as long as possible. "*Malingerers*," we call them. But it's more productive to try to understand what is keeping your employee from wanting to return.

Try to engage the employee in a candid discussion of her concerns. Is the employee worried about her skills, and whether she'll really be able to perform? Perhaps she fears that her coworkers will resent or ridicule her if she needs them to cut her some slack while she gets back on her feet. Or maybe she's depressed—it's a frequent outgrowth of disability leave, and a condition that's often mistaken as malingering.

Don't give up on this employee too fast. You can probably resolve her concerns about her coworkers on your end, either through your direct intervention or by appointing a return-to-work advocate. Then set her up with the services of a top-notch EAP professional, and it's quite possible that she'll soon be ready and enthusiastic about coming back.

Employee stress and psychiatric conditions are a rapidly growing health challenge for employers, and one that your disability management program should be prepared to address. Employees who are on disability for mental health conditions can benefit from the same strategies and return-to-work commitment as their coworkers with physical injuries.

WHAT you need to know

The unmotivated employer

How to handle the problem when it's *yours*, though? What do you do when your supervisors and managers lack the motivation to bring the worker back?

Quite often, when you delve more deeply, you'll find that difficult return-to-work scenarios are really unmanaged performance problems. A less-than-stellar employee gets injured, she goes out on disability, and the manager is in no rush to get her back. Maybe this is what's happening in Bruce's case. On the other hand, maybe Bruce just truly can't envision how this light duty set-up can work. And he resents being asked to arrange it.

Like so many of your front-line supervisors, Bruce struggles with performance management issues. No doubt John needed some discipline and direction, which he never received. In addition to brushing up on those managerial skills, though, Bruce (and all of your managers) needs instruction and information on return-to-work. Training your managers on this topic will smooth the transition for returning employees. Reward them for good return-to-work records.

Another important step: Require your managers to come up with some productive, useful light-duty assignments in their department *before* one of their employees goes out on leave. (If you suspect a manager is simply trying to avoid a particular returning employee, this exercise will control for that variable.)

In the meantime, consider placing John elsewhere in the unit. Of course, it's not the ideal situation—you want him back in his regular department as soon as possible—but it's a matter of weighing which environment will be the most comfortable and productive for John as he works his way back to health. Besides, maybe John would be a better fit, and could benefit from a new start, under a different manager.

DON'T miss this

In most states, the employee need not be returned to the same job the employee had at the time of injury. However, the job he returns to must be within his vocational and physical abilities.

Return-to-work program options

Rehabilitation and "work hardening." Your employee might need rehabilitation prior to returning to work even on light-duty assignment. It should begin as soon as possible after the injury to be most effective. One trend in rehabilitation is "work hardening," an individualized program of physical therapy involving simulated or real work tasks. By duplicating the conditions of actual jobs, therapists claim they can better prepare an injured person to return to work. In order to make the experience as much like a job as possible, the injured employee may actually punch in and work up to an eight-hour day.

Job modifications. Job modifications are changes in the employee's pre-injury job to match it to the worker's physical capabilities. For example, the employee's production quota might be cut down to reduce the number of repetitive motions a worker must make. Or you may alter work structures or install labor-saving equipment, machinery, tools, or furnishings.

Light-duty work. Letting workers stay out on disability is so costly that it would be foolish to keep them home if they could make *any* contribution to the company. If just to improve an employee's mental state, light-duty work should always be offered. Unlike job modifications, light-duty work usually entails tasks entirely different from the pre-injury job. Light duty can be performed in the returning employee's regular department, or in another department that has light-duty opportunities more readily available. If an employee can only work part-time or half days at first, that's ok. At least it will get him out of the house and will convince him that return to work is possible.

ADA issues. The Americans with Disabilities Act prohibits an employer from discriminating against a person with a disability, as defined by the Act, who is "qualified" for a desired job. That means you cannot refuse to let an individual with a disability return to work because the worker is not fully recovered from injury.

You may need to provide a reasonable accommodation to an injured worker in a light-duty position to enable the worker to perform the essential functions of that position.

Suppose a telephone line repair worker broke both legs and fractured both knee joints in a fall. She will have to use a wheelchair for nine months. Unable to do her previous job, she is placed in a light-duty position processing paperwork. If the office to which she is assigned is not wheelchair-accessible, she may have to be given a different office. Or the office could be made accessible by widening the door, if this would not be an undue hardship. Her work schedule also might have to be modified if she needs to attend weekly physical therapy sessions.

Tips for easing the transition

"Welcome back." If the worker has been out for a while, the manager needs to make sure the transition back to the workplace takes place with as little trauma as possible. Encourage the line manager to invite the worker back for coffee or lunch before the day the employee officially is supposed to return to the job. Review the comments from the doctor about what the employee can and cannot do, and discuss how the job is within the worker's capabilities. The supervisor should let the employee know that he or she has the employee's best interests at heart.

Make it a team effort. A return-to-work coordinator should oversee the program. The coordinator's responsibilities may include maintaining records, communicating with the insurance claims person, preparing forms, overseeing claims management activities (e.g. investigation, light duty, drug testing), obtaining job descriptions for the treating physician, and conducting progress reviews. The coordinator should work with the support of a return-to-work team made up of the injured employee, physician, supervisor, union representative, human resources contact, and safety officer.

Work with the medical provider. Review any physical restrictions cited by the medical provider. If you fully understand the most demanding aspects of each job, you can match up job functions to the restrictions. Continue to monitor the restrictions as the employee recuperates and adjust the job accordingly. Partnering with physicians can help the employee reduce lost workdays.

Physician's release. Make sure the returning employee has a written release from the doctor. Any work restrictions should be noted on the release. Inform the physician beforehand exactly what the job requires in order to determine whether the employee is capable of performing it.

Medical exams. In some instances, you might require a medical exam to ensure the worker is able to perform the functions of a light-duty job, or the job held before the injury or illness. You may want the physical exam in order to identify an accommodation that may be needed in order to enable the person to perform the essential functions of an available job. If so, note that the employee can only be required to have a "job-related" medical examination, not a full physical exam, as a condition of returning to work.

Set a time limit on light duty. In your consultation with the employee's doctor, find out how long the employee needs to stay in a light-duty job. As soon as possible after the injury, the type of light-duty job and the length of time it will last should be settled with the employee. As the worker's condition improves, the light-duty job should be modified.

A 60-day target for light duty is usually a good one. If the worker is unable to return to full employment after that time, then HR should again consider ADA issues and ensure compliance with the disability law.

Use a written agreement. Have your employee, his or her supervisor, and the return-to-work coordinator sign an agreement that identifies the nature of the work the employee will perform and expectations about how long the light-duty arrangement will last.

Monitor the employee's progress. Establish regular intervals for reviewing the employee's progress; not just in his or her physical recovery, but with other transitional issues as well. This is a good opportunity to remind the worker and supervisor of the work restrictions imposed on the employee, in order to avoid reinjury.

Evaluate the program results. Once an employee completes the return-to-work program, sit down with the employee to find out how the program worked and note areas for improvement. Track program indicators such as days away from work, medical costs of disability, length of transitional duty, etc. These benchmarks will help you measure the success of the program and make improvements.

What not to do

Avoid these return-to-work pitfalls:

◆ **Don't apply the program inconsistently.** Return to work options should be available for your popular employees as well as your less favored workers. Include your workers who were injured off-the-job in your return-to-work program too.

- ◆ **Don't assign sedentary work** (unless the doctor prescribes it). Keep the job as physically challenging as the doctor will allow. Focus on assigning active work, on getting workers back into their departments, into their regular workflow, and engaged with their usual coworkers.
- ◆ **Don't fail to update the doctor's restrictions.** The employee shouldn't go more than two weeks without seeing the doctor again to update the work restrictions.
- ◆ **Don't make light-duty work punitive.** This accomplishes nothing and only hurts the employer.

Worst case scenario

One company required employees on light duty to paint a waist-high line around the facility. When the task was finished, the worker had to do it over again. This chore was repeated over and over until the worker was able to return to full duty.

Solution. Let your light-duty workers make a meaningful contribution. If you set your mind to it, there are probably countless valuable light-duty functions to be done. In fact, some workers returning to their old departments can probably tell *you* several light-duty but useful tasks that would really be worth doing.

A last thought: retaliatory discharge

Firing an employee because he or she has filed a workers' compensation claim is prohibited as "retaliatory discharge" in the vast majority of states.

Does that mean you have to hang onto an unproductive or insubordinate worker? No. It just means you can't use one of those rationales as an excuse to fire an employee for filing a workers' comp claim. Ask yourself whether you would have discharged the employee even if a workers' compensation claim had not been filed. If so, then discharge is not illegal. (But be prepared to back up your action with evidence of the employee's insubordination or lack of productivity.)

Here's a trickier scenario: What if you want to discharge for excessive absence an employee who has filed a workers' compensation claim? Tread carefully. But if you have a uniformly applied nondiscriminatory absence policy that provides for termination, you may be able to terminate an employee for excessive absenteeism regardless of whether a workers' compensation claim is involved.

The Quiz

1. Workers' compensation is a program enacted by the federal government.   ❏ True   ❏ False

2. Employees who are injured in the course of their employment are entitled to wage-loss benefits and medical care costs.   ❏ True   ❏ False

3. The injured employee's coworkers should have no contact with the employee while he or she is on disability leave.   ❏ True   ❏ False

4. The best practice for employers trying to ensure the speedy recovery of their workers is to keep them at home until they're at 100 percent.   ❏ True   ❏ False

5. There should be a clearly established time limit on light-duty work.   ❏ True   ❏ False

Answer key, 1. F; 2. T; 3. F; 4. F; 5. T

OSHA compliance

Your HR director calls you into his office. He is really pleased at how quickly you got up to speed with your organization's health and safety issues. The safety program and policies you shepherded to implementation were well received. After congratulating you on your achievements, he hands you a thick file. "I should have given this to you before. It's the OSHA paperwork. It hasn't been looked at in three months. Can you see what needs to be done with it?"

Introduction

If your HR department plays a direct role in compliance with health and safety laws, then knowledge of OSHA standards and requirements is essential. Even if you have a safety officer in your organization, though, you need a general understanding of the agency and its compliance directives as you craft your workplace safety initiatives.

Federal workplace safety laws are enforced by the Occupational Safety and Health Administration, or OSHA. The agency issues standards to ensure the safest environment for U.S. workers. To enforce its standards, OSHA conducts inspections at worksites to make sure employers follow the health and safety guidelines. It also provides assistance to help employers comply with the law and reduce injuries and illness.

OSHA encourages states to develop their own workplace safety programs, and OSHA reviews the state program for approval. To be approved, the state's regulation of employee health and safety must be "at least as effective" as the federal program. That means that state programs might be even more stringent than OSHA's compliance requirements. If a state's program is OSHA-approved, then it operates in place of the federal agency's program. The map below shows those states with OSHA-approved programs:

States with OSHA-approved plans

■ OSHA-approved plans
□ plans cover public sector employees only

Are you covered?

Is your organization covered under the Occupational Safety and Health Act? The federal statute is very comprehensive, and it covers most private employers. Perhaps the more instructive question is: which employers *doesn't* OSHA cover?

- ◆ Churches and nonsecular church activities
- ◆ Domestic home workers
- ◆ Immediate family employed as agricultural workers
- ◆ Organizations whose safety and health is regulated by another federal agency
- ◆ States and political subdivisions
- ◆ Employers not engaged in interstate commerce.

Small businesses are exempt from OSHA enforcement actions if they have ten or fewer employees—unless there is a hazard or another compelling inspection reason to enforce the law in this circumstance.

Employer obligations under OSHA

The federal government (and most individual states) expects employers to keep their employees free from exposure to excess danger in the workplace. While it's impossible to eliminate all the hazards that employees face in the workplace—especially when the work is by its very nature dangerous—going to work should be as safe as reasonably possible.

To this end, the law imposes certain requirements upon private employers. Most employers are mandated to "provide a workplace free from known hazards that are causing, or are likely to cause, death or serious physical harm to employees." This obligation is set forth in the "general duty clause" of the federal Occupational Safety and Health Act.

Encompassed within this "general duty" are several basic obligations that employers have under the law:

- ◆ Establish and maintain safety and health programs (an implied obligation);
- ◆ Comply with published safety and health standards;
- ◆ Maintain a workplace free from known hazards when there are no published standards;
- ◆ Maintain records of accidents and illnesses in the workplace;
- ◆ Report certain accidents and illnesses that occur;

◆ Cooperate with workplace inspections; and
◆ Post certain information in the workplace.

✔ *Checklist*

Employer OSHA responsibilities

Adhering to OSHA standards requires a number of specific actions, too. This checklist identifies your organization's responsibilities.

☐ Know mandatory OSHA standards that apply to your worksite(s).
☐ Examine workplace conditions to make sure they conform to applicable standards.
☐ Provide a workplace free from known hazards, and examine for unknown hazards.
☐ Adopt work practices and other "controls" to reduce or eliminate hazards.
☐ Provide personal protective equipment to employees whose jobs require them.
☐ Make sure employees have tools and equipment that are safe and properly maintained.
☐ Warn employees of potential hazards through posters, labels, signs or codes.
☐ Train employees in health and safety hazards and practices.
☐ Train employees in the proper use of equipment, including personal protective equipment.
☐ Inform employees how to report an injury or illness.
☐ Post information about employee rights and responsibilities under the OSH Act.
☐ Make copies of applicable OSHA standards available to employees.
☐ Keep various logs and records of work-related injuries and illnesses.
☐ Post an annual summary of injuries and illness.
☐ Make copies of OSHA logs and injury/illness summaries available to employees.
☐ Keep records of exposures, tests, inspections, and training.
☐ Conduct medical surveillance of the health of affected workers.

☐ Provide medical examinations when required by OSHA standards.
☐ Provide employees access to their employee medical records and exposure records.
☐ Report fatal accidents, or an accident resulting in the hospitalization of five or more employees, to the nearest OSHA office.
☐ Cooperate with OSHA inspectors at your worksite.
☐ Post OSHA citations at or near the work area involved.
☐ Correct cited violations and provide documentation of hazard abatement.

Employee rights under OSHA

Your employees have particular rights under the OSH Act. One of your OSHA responsibilities, especially in your employee advocate role, is to ensure that your organization doesn't interfere with these rights. The list is a long one.

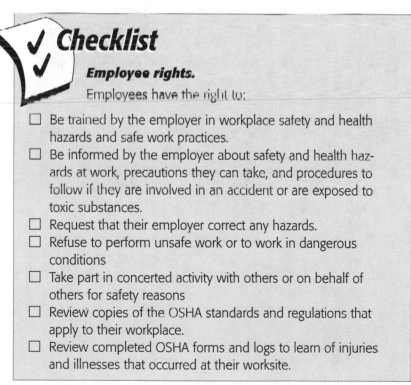

✓ *Checklist*

Employee rights.

Employees have the right to:

☐ Be trained by the employer in workplace safety and health hazards and safe work practices.
☐ Be informed by the employer about safety and health hazards at work, precautions they can take, and procedures to follow if they are involved in an accident or are exposed to toxic substances.
☐ Request that their employer correct any hazards.
☐ Refuse to perform unsafe work or to work in dangerous conditions
☐ Take part in concerted activity with others or on behalf of others for safety reasons
☐ Review copies of the OSHA standards and regulations that apply to their workplace.
☐ Review completed OSHA forms and logs to learn of injuries and illnesses that occurred at their worksite.

☐ Receive a copy of the incident report for any accident or incident they were involved in.

☐ Consult with an OSHA representative in person or on the phone at the local OSHA site.

☐ Ask OSHA to conduct an inspection, if they believe there are hazardous conditions or violations in their workplace.

☐ File a complaint with OSHA or any other applicable work-place safety regulatory agency, and have their name withheld from the employer after filing the complaint, upon request.

☐ Be advised of OSHA actions regarding their complaint, and have an informal review, if requested, of any decision not to inspect or issue a citation.

☐ Sue in court if danger is imminent and OSHA does not take action.

☐ Have an authorized employee representative (usually a union rep) accompany the OSHA inspector during the in-spection tour.

☐ Respond to questions from the OSHA inspector, particularly if there is no authorized employee representative accompany-ing the inspector.

☐ Be paid for any time they spend on OSHA inspection activity.

☐ Request a closing discussion with the inspector following an inspection.

☐ Know the results of an OSHA inspection.

☐ Observe any monitoring or measuring of hazardous materials and have the right to see these records.

☐ Request an investigation of possible health hazards at work by the National Institute for Occupational Safety and Health (NIOSH), and have their name withheld from the employer upon request.

☐ Receive copies of their own exposure and medical records

☐ Request and receive notice of citations and penalties.

☐ Object to the abatement period set forth in the citation issued to the employer.

☐ Request and receive notice of all contested actions and proceedings.

☐ Be notified by the employer if it applies for a variance from an OSHA standard, testifies at a variance hearing, and ap-peals the final decision.

☐ Testify during an OSHA proceeding
☐ Submit information or comment to OSHA on the issuance, modification, or revocation of OSHA standards and request a public hearing.
☐ Be protected against punishment or discrimination for complaining about job safety and health, filing safety and health grievances, participating in job safety and health committees, involvement in union activities regarding job safety and health, or participating in OSHA inspections or other OSHA activities.

Overwhelming, isn't it? Many of these rights, particularly those related to OSHA investigations, will fall under the purview of your safety officer, or your organization's legal staff. If you're faced with administering rights you are unfamiliar with, confer with a safety consultant.

Don't even ask about waivers! If an employee waives her right to know about workplace hazards, even in writing, it's almost certainly inapplicable. Employees can't waive this right, and even asking a job applicant to do so can be considered unlawful under OSHA.

OSHA standards

General duty. The employer has a basic responsibility to protect workers from recognized hazards that could cause death or serious injury, as we discussed. This general duty clause covers hazardous workplace conditions that aren't covered by a specific OSHA standard. The general duty clause is sometimes called the "catch-all" standard.

Specific OSHA standards. Specific OSHA standards are divided into four groups:
◆ General Industry
◆ Maritime
◆ Construction
◆ Agriculture

As you can see, they are generally geared toward industries that are inherently more dangerous, like construction or manufacturing. You won't find specific standards regulating safety in the financial or public relations industry, for example. Note that OSHA briefly visited the idea of adopting specific ergonomics standards—which would have been more applicable to these types of office-setting worksites—but the agency implemented voluntary guidelines instead.

Here are a few examples of the specific standards that OSHA enforces:

◆ Hazard communication standard (in worksites where hazardous chemicals or other substances are present)
◆ Fall protections (a construction industry standard)
◆ Bloodborne pathogens standard

WHAT you need to know

Sometimes meeting these standards can be a real challenge! An employer may be able to obtain a temporary "variance" from a standard if compliance isn't possible because it doesn't have the personnel, materials, or equipment needed. For example, if construction were needed to comply with a standard, but the construction would not be completed by the effective date of the standard, this may constitute grounds for a temporary variance.

OSHA may grant a permanent variance if an employer's practices don't adhere to "the letter" of the standard, but they provide equal or better safety protection than would be provided by the OSHA standard.

"Guidelines" vs. "standards": the ergonomics example. In 2001, OSHA shelved a standard it had developed on ergonomics. Instead, the agency issued "guidelines" to assist employers in creating a more ergonomic and healthy workplace.

OSHA defines a "guideline" as "a tool to assist employers in recognizing and controlling hazards." A guideline differs from a standard in that it is voluntary, not federally mandated. Therefore, it's not in itself a violation of OSHA if an employer does not implement the ergonomics guidelines.

On the other hand, if an employer has a workplace that is teeming with ergonomic hazards, it can still be cited for violating the general duty clause, since it failed to provide a workplace free of recognized hazards.

Posting requirements

Several provisions of the OSH Act require that employers post notices for the benefit of their employees. Posting requirements include:

◆ **OSHA "Job Safety and Health" poster.** The poster outlines obligations of the Occupational Safety and Health Act in each worksite. The notice must be placed in a conspicuous location—usually where you'd post any other employee notices that you want to make sure they see. The poster must:

  ◆ Inform employees of their rights and duties under the law;

  ◆ Advise employees to contact their employer or the nearest OSHA regional office for additional information; and

  ◆ Contain information from the Act regarding specific safety and health standards and other applicable regulations.

If your organization operates in a state that has an OSHA-approved regulatory plan, then you should post the state-supplied version. However, if your activities aren't covered by the state's approved safety plan, post the federal poster instead.

DON'T
miss
this

Your organization must post the notice for as long as it remains in operation. You may order a printed copy from OSHA Publications at 1-800-321-OSHA or download and print one from its website in English or Spanish.

Make sure the poster is kept in good order and remains uncovered by other items; OSHA says it may not be altered, defaced or covered over. If you display a reproduction or facsimile of the poster, it must be at least 8 ½ inches by 14 inches in size, printed in at least 10-point type, with its heading in large type, generally not less than 36-point type.

◆ **Annual Summary of Occupational Injuries and Illnesses (OSHA Form 300A).** The annual summary is a list of injuries and illnesses that took place at your worksite in the prior year. A summary must be posted at each of your worksites, and summarize the incidents that took place at the specific site. The annual summary must be posted conspicuously from February 1 to April 30 of each year.

Information in the summary is taken from the compilation of injuries and illnesses recorded on an employer's OSHA log for a given worksite. Review the entries on your OSHA 300 log to verify that they are complete and accurate. Then an executive member of your organization must verify the summary. One of the following individuals can sign off on the document:

◆ Owner of the company (only if the company is a sole proprietorship or partnership);

◆ Officer of the corporation;

◆ The highest ranking company official working in the establishment; or

◆ The immediate supervisor of the highest ranking company official working at the establishment.

If your organization had no injuries or illnesses during the year, give yourself and your safety officer a well-deserved pat on the back and a congratulatory note to your workforce. Then enter zeros on the "totals" line—the form must be posted anyhow.

WHAT you need to know

OSHA has prepared a worksheet to help employers fill out the summary. Find it on the agency's website at *http://www.OSHA.gov.*

◆ **Copies of OSHA citations.** If your organization is found to be in violation of an OSHA standard, you'll be required to post the OSHA citation at or near the work area where the incident took place. Each citation must remain posted until the violation has been corrected or for three working days, whichever is longer.

Training requirements

Under the OSH Act, employers have a legal duty to train their employees in safety and health in the workplace. Training is required in the following instances:

An OSHA standard requires specific training for certain employees. OSHA says every employee authorized to enter a regulated area where exposure to a carcinogen is possible must first be trained. Employees whose job requires them to use respirators must be thoroughly trained in their use. Only trained operators may drive powered industrial trucks.

Training can eliminate a "recognized hazard." No specific standard applies, but a workplace hazard is present, and training can eliminate the hazard. For example, an employer violated the general duty clause by failing to adequately train a new, inexperienced employee in the operation and dangers of a pressure vessel; the young employee was not informed there was a potential for explosion or that proper tools must be used.

Standards on work practice requirements can be satisfied only through employee training, supervision, and enforcement of safety rules. To comply with some OSHA standards, you need to purchase certain equipment or make engineering controls. But standards that address "the operation of" something or "work practices for" a job cannot be met without training.

Some of the standards don't have explicit training requirements, although they imply training is necessary because they require employers to use only "certified," "competent," or "qualified" employees to perform certain functions.

While not required, OSHA encourages organizations to develop an overall safety training program. Not a bad idea, just to keep the training requirements straight! There are literally hundreds of different training provisions scattered throughout OSHA's standards, requiring employers to train their workers in the safety and health aspects of their particular jobs. If a standard applies to your worksite, then the related training requirement applies, too.

Make the effort to carefully document your training program. Keep records of employee attendance. Document training content, duration of the sessions held, the instructor, and all the details that a training inspector might need to know how well you've met your obligation to educate your employees about job safety. Build a training schedule that provides for refresher courses at set times, or sooner as needed. Be prepared to show the schedule to an inspector, to demonstrate your commitment to ongoing safety training.

OSHA inspectors may ask whether employees received proper training when investigating workplace accidents. An employer that can quickly produce records of employee training will probably fare better during OSHA inspections. But records alone aren't usually enough. Inspectors will often question employees at random to determine whether the employees actually know about the subject in which they have been trained. This means just holding a training isn't enough. You need to show that employees have learned from your training!

There may come a time when you'll need to defend the effectiveness of your training program. This usually arises when your organization finds itself in the unenviable position of contesting an OSHA citation. Assume one of your employees violated an OSHA standard. When this happens, you'll need to show that the violation was a result of employee misconduct. (By the way, OSHA doesn't go after individual workers; they enforce standards and regulations solely against the employer.) Your challenge will be to demonstrate that the violation was a departure from a work rule that you enforce uniformly, and that the employee *knew* of the work rule. OSHA will want to know whether you took reasonable steps to educate and inform the employee. That means showing that you trained the employee appropriately—that your training program measures up.

"I only use union workers, and they're already fully trained." Tell it to the judge! One manufacturer did, after it was found to be in serious violation for failing to provide employees with training in unsafe conditions. The employer didn't provide training in fall protection, saying its employees had already been trained through a union-sponsored apprenticeship program.

But some of the employees took the training so long ago they didn't even remember having received it. And when they were hired out of the union hall, the employer didn't even inquire about the extent of the apprenticeship training.

Remember, the union isn't responsible under OSHA for training your workers—you are.

Training requirements and non-English speaking employees

What about training for your employees who are non-English speaking? The number of workers who are not fluent in English is growing rapidly in many industries—especially in some more hazardous occupations.

DON'T miss this

Spanish-speaking workers, in particular, are concentrated in high-risk jobs, and Labor Department statistics reflect that Hispanic workers are dying on the job at a much higher rate than their English-speaking coworkers. It would be hard to argue that you've met your OSHA training requirements, especially in these industries, if your workers can't understand the language in which the training is conducted.

OSHA has stepped up its training initiatives for Spanish language training. Labor unions with a heavy safety emphasis provide train-the-trainer sessions geared toward trainers of Spanish-speaking workers. Do you need to do so too?

OSHA has issued voluntary training guidelines that provide employers with a model for designing, conducting, evaluating, and revising their training programs. (These guidelines are discussed in Chapter 4.) The agency encourages employers to develop customized approaches to training programs at individual worksites. This will ensure that employers provide the training that is most relevant to local working conditions.

Recordkeeping and reporting requirements

Almost all employers are governed by OSHA's general recordkeeping rules. These rules require organizations to keep careful track of their work-related injuries and illness. The recordkeeping requirements apply to employers with 11 or more employees. Employers in certain "low-hazard" retail, service, finance, insurance, and real estate industries are exempt from the recordkeeping requirements. However, all employers have a duty to report work-related deaths or hospitalizations of three or more employees.

OSHA implemented some major changes to the recordkeeping requirements in 2001. Most obvious was its change to the standard recordkeeping forms that the agency asks employers to complete. Here's what OSHA requires now:

- ◆ **OSHA 300, Log of Work-Related Injuries and Illnesses.** This form is known as the OSHA log. You must maintain separate records for each "establishment" you operate— that is, each separate physical location where business is conducted or where services or industrial operations are performed. Special provisions exist for employers engaged in physically dispersed activities. The employer must add each "recordable" injury to the log within six working days from the time it knew of the injury or illness.
- ◆ **OSHA 300A, Annual Summary of Work-Related Injuries and Illnesses.** This form, as we discussed above, must also be posted in the workplace.
- ◆ **OSHA 301, Injury and Illness Incident Report.** This form must be completed for each recordable injury or illness that was entered on the OSHA log. It asks for more detailed information about individual incidents.

DON'T miss this

Employers don't automatically have to send the completed forms to OSHA, but the agency might make a specific request that you send them.

If such a request is made, you must provide the forms within four business hours! Be sure your recordkeeping is current, and keep those forms within easy reach.

In addition to these general recordkeeping requirements, some OSHA standards that address specific hazards require employers to maintain records of employee exposures to potentially toxic materials.

Organizations that follow OSHA-approved state regulations must comply with the state's particular recordkeeping requirements, which are sometimes more stringent than the federal rules.

What work-related injuries and illnesses are recordable?

Not every injury or illness that happens at work will need to be included on your OSHA log. First, the incident must be "work-related." Also, the injury has to be serious enough according to the agency's recording criteria, and it must be a new case. A new case is one in which the employee with the injury or illness has not previously experienced a recorded injury or illness of the same type that affects the same part of the body.

When is an injury work-related? When it took place in the "work environment." If so, there's a *presumption* that the injury is work-related. But there are a few exceptions to this principle. There's no presumption that an injury is work-related in the following instances:

◆ The injured employee was present in the workplace as a member of the general public rather than as an employee.

◆ The injury or illness involves signs or symptoms that surface at work but result from a non-work-related event.

◆ The injury or illness results solely from voluntary participation in a wellness program, blood donation, exercise class, or similar event.

◆ The injury or illness results solely from eating, drinking, or preparing food brought to the worksite.

◆ The injury or illness results solely from an employee doing personal tasks unrelated to his or her employment while at the worksite, but outside of assigned working hours.

◆ The injury or illness is the result of personal grooming or self-medication for a non-work-related condition.

◆ The injury or illness is caused by a motor vehicle accident and occurs on a company parking lot or access road while commuting to or from work.

◆ The illness is the common cold or flu.

◆ The illness is mental illness (unless the employee provides an opinion of a physician or another licensed healthcare professional that the mental illness is work-related).

Injuries and illness that occur while an employee is working at home, including work in a home office, are work-related if they occur while the employee is performing work for compensation in the home, and the injury or illness is directly related to the performance of work rather than to the general home environment or setting.

What are the OSHA criteria? OSHA's recording criteria provide that only incidents that result in one of the following outcomes are to be added to the OSHA log:

- ◆ death
- ◆ illness
- ◆ days away from work
- ◆ injury requiring medical treatment other than first aid
- ◆ injury involving loss of consciousness
- ◆ injury causing restriction of work or motion
- ◆ injury that compels transfer to another job

Employers must record fatalities that result from motor vehicle accidents that occur in construction zones. (Other motor vehicle fatalities don't need to be recorded, though.)

Reporting requirements

In addition to its recordkeeping requirements, OSHA requires employers to report certain information to the agency.

An organization is required to report to OSHA within eight hours of learning of the death of any employee or the inpatient hospitalization of three or more employees from a work-related incident. This includes fatalities at work caused by work-related heart attacks. You must report such incidents by telephone or in person to the OSHA area office nearest to the site of the incident. OSHA's toll-free telephone number may be used: 1-800-321-OSHA (1-800-321-6742).

What do you need to report?
- employer's name, contact person, and phone number
- location, time, and date of the incident
- number of fatalities or hospitalizations
- names of injured employees
- location and time/date of the incident
- brief description of the incident (type of injury, nature of the accident, equipment involved, etc.)

Access to records

Injury and illness logs must be made available for inspection and copying by employees, their representatives and OSHA inspectors. Employee exposure and medical records that have been voluntarily maintained by an employer must also be made available to employees and OSHA.

Failure to provide access can cost your organization. If an employer fails to provide requested copies of required injury and illness records to an employee, former employee, personal representative, or authorized employee representative by the end of the next business day, a citation will normally be issued. The penalty is $1,000 for each form not made available.

Retaining records

The law requires your organization to keep records of occupational injuries and illnesses on a calendar-year basis, and to retain these records for five years. Employers are also required to keep medical records and records of employee exposure to toxic substances for the affected employee's entire period of employment, plus 30 years. A few substances require a 40-year retention period. The rule covers workers exposed to toxic substances or harmful physical agents who have worked for more than one year.

In addition, the law requires employers to provide access to these records for OSHA and to employees or their representatives, if they can show their need for such access, within 15 days of a request to review the materials.

Enforcement and inspections

The front-desk receptionist peeks his head in your door. "There's some man out there who says he's with the government. He wants to inspect the plant because they received a complaint. What do you want me to tell him?"

Do you:

A) March right out there and demand to know who filed the complaint.

B) Have your guest sign in, hand him a visitor's pass, and tell him you'll be in your office if he needs you.

C) Tell the inspector he can't come in without a warrant and have security remove him.

D) Tell the inspector to have a seat, offer him a cup of coffee, and assure him you'll return shortly with your safety director, who will be able to assist him.

That was probably an easy one for you. The correct answer is D. (Were you secretly hoping it was B? Wouldn't that have made life a lot easier?)

But the correct answer in the scenario above presumes you have a safety director—and that she's not out sick that day or out of town at a conference. *Then* what? Knowing what you can expect if an OSHA inspector shows up at your workplace can help you prepare your organization's inspection policy and procedures before the agency arrives at your doorstep.

Hardly any employer is pleased to see the OSHA inspector. First, you're given no advance warning, no time to prepare. That's the point. The inspector wants to observe your workplace as it is every day—not sugarcoated for his or her benefit. The agency's efforts of late have been highly focused on providing compliance assistance, rather than punitive measures. Nonetheless, in 2002, OSHA conducted 37,500 inspections. (State "OSHA" agencies typically conduct an additional 50,000-60,000 inspections.)

OSHA inspectors have fairly broad enforcement authority. They can conduct inspections and investigations, issue citations, seek a restraining order where conditions place employees in imminent danger, subpoena witnesses and evidence, propose penalties for violations of the Act, and set time limits for abating hazards.

OSHA inspection targets

Could your organization be a target? There's a greater chance if you operate what's considered a high-hazard workplace. But OSHA also gives priority to inspecting workplaces from which they've received employee complaints. OSHA will also come out if there's been an accident at your worksite where three or more employees were hospitalized—or where an employee has died.

The agency's inspection priorities are ordered as follows:

First are the "unprogrammed," or unplanned inspections.

- ◆ **Imminent danger.** These situations have top OSHA priority. An accident is about to happen—there is a condition in which there is reasonable certainty a death or serious harm could immediately result. (This is an "unprogrammed" inspection.)
- ◆ **Fatality and catastrophic incidents.** These are second in OSHA's priorities—incidents where a fatality occurs, or three or more employees are hospitalized.
- ◆ **Other unprogrammed inspections.** OSHA places third priority on inspecting workplaces from which employee complaints of OSHA violations or unsafe/unhealthy conditions have arisen.
- ◆ **Programmed inspections.** These are primarily inspections of high-hazard industries, or those with the highest lost workday injury and illness rates. In the "General Industry" category of employers, sampling techniques are used to insure that those worksites with the highest number of citations are twice as likely to be selected for an inspection. Inspections of randomly selected workplaces in low-hazard industries represent only five percent of programmed inspections.
- ◆ **Follow-up inspections** have lowest OSHA priority.

The inspection

Here's what you can anticipate if your organization is targeted for an inspection:

Step 1. The inspector appears at the worksite and presents his or her credentials to the employer's representative.

Step 2. If the employer refuses to admit the inspector, the inspector must obtain an inspection warrant. The inspector will return within 1-2 days with the warrant.

Step 3. The inspector will usually delay an inspection for up to an hour to give a management representative time to get to the site.

Step 4. The inspector meets with the safety officer or other representative in an **opening conference**. Here the inspector will explain why the employer was selected for inspection, and what OSHA standards apply to its worksite. The inspector explains the methods to be used in the inspection and the areas of the workplace and records to be inspected.

Step 5. At this juncture, the employer will designate areas in which **trade secrets** are located. Inspectors are bound by OSHA regulations to protect any trade secret information they acquire during an inspection. (Your organization can designate that only employees who are permitted access to trade secret areas be allowed to accompany the inspector in those areas.)

Step 6. If the inspection was initiated by an employee complaint, the inspector will provide a copy of the complaint. If the complaining employee requested anonymity, his or her name will be deleted.

Step 7. The inspector will conduct a **walk-around** of the worksite. Employer representatives, employees, and union reps are permitted to accompany the inspector during the walk-around.

Step 8. During the walk-around, the inspector may offer suggestions for the abatement of violations that are found, but the employer is not bound to accept the suggestions.

Step 9. The inspector holds a **closing conference** with the employer and the employees' representatives (the union rep, for instance). The inspector advises the employer of any apparent violations for which a citation may be issued and suggests abatement methods.

Step 10. At the closing conference, the employer can offer explanations or share relevant information with the inspector.

Step 11. The inspector explains the citation procedures and how to contest citations.

What else happens at the walk-around? The inspector also might:
- *take photos and instrument readings;*
- *examine records (OSHA-required records and other employer safety records);*
- *collect air samples;*
- *measure noise levels;*
- *survey engineering controls;*
- *measure employee exposure to toxic fumes, gases, and dusts;*
- *review your written hazard communication program; and*
- *talk to employees to confirm that they have been trained on the hazard communication standard.*

Inspection tips

Before
- Prepare an inspection policy in advance, and communicate the policy and procedures to members of the organization who might have contact with an inspector.
- Your policy should dictate that the receptionist is to have a list of people to notify when an OSHA inspector arrives, but that the inspection should not be announced over a loudspeaker.
- Your policy should dictate which member(s) of your organization are authorized to give consent to an inspection. Relevant employees should be trained in advance to say "I am not authorized to give consent to an inspection" as well as the name of the person who is authorized.
- Set up an "OSHA inspection team" that will accompany an inspector during a walk-around, and conduct periodic mock inspections.
- If you're in an industry with a higher probability of inspection, prepare employees in advance. At your general safety orientation, discuss what they might expect, how to handle questions, and what rights they have as employees when OSHA knocks on your door.
- Make sure you've posted the OSHA poster in a prominent place, as well as the OSHA recordkeeping log totals.

During

◆ Check the inspector's credentials and record the inspector's name, address, and phone number.

◆ Treat the inspector will respect at all times. Your organization's representative should act as a well-informed tour guide of your facility, making the inspector feel comfortable. Look at the event as an opportunity to impress the inspector will all of your company's safety and health programs and initiatives.

◆ Ask the inspector at the outset the reason for the inspection, and whether the inspection will be limited to one area or if it will be a "wall-to-wall" comprehensive inspection. (The less the inspector observes, the better. One employer used a golf cart to drive an inspector to a door nearest the area to be inspected. When the inspector questioned why he was being driven outside the facility, the employer told him the plant was so large that using the cart would save him valuable time.)

◆ Ask the inspector if evidence will be collected, and what procedures will be used for doing so. Take "comparison" samples or photographs of any items of evidence the inspector collects, for later comparison with OSHA results, if necessary.

◆ Provide a copy of your written safety program, and review it with the inspector before the actual inspection begins.

◆ Have two representatives of your organization accompany the inspector on the walk-around—one to respond to questions and direct the inspector, and another to take detailed notes of all comments or questions raised.

◆ You may want to designate a special time and place for employee interviews to be conducted by the inspector in order to minimize disruption of work or production schedules.

◆ If the inspector spots a clear violation during the walk-around, take steps to abate it immediately. You're not required to following the inspector's abatement suggestions, but doing so could result in a reduced penalty. Ensure that a member of your maintenance staff is available to make necessary repairs on the spot. *However*, don't say anything that might be construed as an admission of an OSHA violation!

◆ Privacy is still priority. Inspectors cannot review employee medical records without a "medical access order." Don't turn the records over without one.

◆ Even if you allowed the inspection, you may withdraw your consent later, and the inspector will need to leave. Or you might object to certain aspects of an inspection, or inspection of certain portions of your workplace. Keep in mind, though, that OSHA will probably return with a warrant for the remainder of the inspection, and a subpoena for records that you did not provide voluntarily.

And after

◆ Immediately after the inspector has interviewed them, schedule an "exit interview" with employees. The law does not prevent you from doing this. But avoid the appearance that you're forcing your presence or making employees feel uncomfortable.

WHAT you need to know

Encourage your employees to cooperate during an inspection, and to answer general questions. But warn employees that only the safety officer or other safety representative can speak for the organization. That means the employee shouldn't respond to questions about the safety program or policies if it would mean he or she would be answering on behalf of the organization. In this case, tell the employee to politely suggest the inspector contact the safety officer, who is more qualified to answer the question.

Quandary

Warrant or no?

You may insist that OSHA obtain a warrant before entering the workplace. The inspector will usually be able to quickly get a warrant anyhow, usually within a day or two so that your advance notice is limited. The better strategy is to attempt to establish a cooperative rapport with the inspector. One study showed that employers who deny OSHA inspectors entry are charged with almost twice as many violations per inspection, and are assessed nearly double the total penalties assessed employers who cooperate with the inspector!

On the other hand, if someone from your organization with real safety knowledge is not available when the inspector shows up, or if you think a small bit of time will help you prepare for the inspection, it might be preferable to require the warrant. That's what attorneys at the California firm of Curiale Dellaverson Hirschfeld Kraemer & Sloan have advised.

Sometimes it's a tough call. One strategy to consider is to consent to an inspection based upon a complaint, which will usually mean a limited inspection of a particular area, but require a warrant if a broad inspection of the entire facility will be conducted.

Even without a warrant, an inspector may issue citations for any violations that are in his "plain view" while he is on or off the premises. He can also use those "plain view" violations as a basis for obtaining a warrant.

DON'T miss this

If OSHA inspects your workplace and the organization does not agree with the findings, you have the right to contest. OSHA citations and penalties can be appealed before the independent Occupational Safety and Health Review Commission. You must file a notice that you are contesting the OSHA action within 15 working days following the issuance of citations.

Violations and penalties

OSHA penalties can vary widely, depending upon a variety of factors. The agency considers the "gravity" of the violation based upon a severity assessment (high severity, medium severity, low severity, and minimal severity). OSHA also considers the probability that an illness or injury could result (assessments are classified as either "greater" or "lesser" depending upon such factors as the number of workers in the situation and the proximity of employees to the hazard). Penalties may be discounted if an employer has a small number of employees, has demonstrated good faith, or has few or no previous violations.

The types of violations and the penalties are:

◆ **De minimus.** This violation does not directly affect employee safety and health. No penalties are incurred for these violations.

◆ **Nonserious violation.** This violation has adverse safety and health consequences that constitute a greater than negligible risk, but are less hazardous than "serious" violations. Penalty may be up to $7,000.

◆ **Serious violation.** This violation is issued for conditions in which there is a high probability that death or serious harm could occur. Penalty may be up to $7,000.

◆ **Willful violation.** This is a violation that is knowingly and intentionally committed by the employer. Penalties up to $70,000 may be imposed; the minimum penalty is $5,000 for each willful violation.

◆ **Repeated violation.** This is a repeated violation of the same standard. Penalties up to $70,000 may be imposed.

◆ **Failure to abate.** This is a separate violation issued for a failure to bring equipment or a condition into compliance. Penalties may be up to $7,000 for each day the condition is not corrected beyond the date that abatement was required.

◆ **Posting violation.** This is the failure to post the various requirements of the Occupational Safety and Health Act. Penalty may be up to $7,000.

An organization that fails to report fatalities and hospitalizations may be issued a nonserious violation. The penalty for such a violation is $5,000. However, if the OSHA area director finds it appropriate to adjust the penalty to achieve the necessary deterrent effect, the penalty may be $7,000.

Criminal penalties may also be imposed for certain violations.

WHAT you need to know

It's not just the penalty...

Your organization faces additional burdens in the event of an employee's death or serious injury resulting from a preventable situation in the workplace. Consider the adverse publicity, litigation, continuing community ill will, increased overhead costs (such as insurance), potential loss of business, and employee dissatisfaction.

Compliance assistance

OSHA offers assistance to employers in complying with safety and health regulations and establishing effective safety and health programs. Various partnership programs and other cooperative ventures are aimed at assisting and rewarding compliance:

OSHA's **Onsite Consultation Program** is geared primarily toward small businesses, particularly those in high-hazard industries. The free consultations are similar to inspections, with an opening conference, walk-around, and closing conference that will help the employer identify hazards and possible violations. The critical difference, of course, is that the consultants advise, they don't issue citations.

The **Voluntary Protection Program** (VPP) is the agency's premier partnership program designed to recognize workplaces with exemplary safety and health programs. VPP participants serve as models of excellence for others in their industries and communities and are exempt from routine OSHA inspections. VPP participants must meet an established set of stringent criteria and comply with all relevant OSHA standards and guidelines.

The **Strategic Partnership Program** (OSPP) is geared to employers with high-hazard worksites and varied backgrounds, experience, and compliance records in job safety and health. Participants do, however, share a common commitment to improving workplace safety and health. Employers in the program agree to develop safety and health programs following OSHA guidelines, and in return, OSHA inspects employers less often and on a more limited basis, and provides more technical advance and assistance instead of prosecution. OSPPs emphasize training and education in a voluntary, cooperative atmosphere. Key to the partnerships is tracking results. The agency's strategic partnership program covers more than 6,200 sites and 216,000 employees.

Finally, OSHA has various publications, technical assistance, and compliance tools to help you as well. These items and more are available at OSHA's website, *www.osha.gov.*

Why participate in OSHA partnerships? They can:

◆ indicate your organization's commitment and standing as a leader in workplace safety and health;

◆ serve as a useful means of building employer-employee cooperation;

◆ show a genuine concern for employee well being;

◆ reduce accidents and illness;

◆ save economic resources that would be otherwise spent on litigation or workers' compensation;

◆ demonstrate that safety and health is a top priority within your organizational culture.

Parting thoughts

Compliance with OSHA is important to your workplace safety efforts. However, some wonder if the challenge of adhering to OSHA standards is the best means of ensuring the safety and health of employees. Even if employers follow all the OSHA regulations, does it help make workers safe? "Instead of the difficult job of complying with all these standards, what we need is a proactive program where employers go out and look for problems and hazards, and where the organizing principle isn't 'is this something covered in the book?' But 'Is this safe or unsafe?,'" contends Michael Wright, Director of Health, Safety and Environment for the United Steelworkers.

The best human resources professionals know that ensuring a safe and healthy workplace has inherent advantages, OSHA enforcement aside. So top organizations go beyond the letter of the law. They understand that a safe workplace maximizes productivity, retention, and ultimately, the organization's bottom line.

> *You return to your boss' office, brimming with confidence. You've sorted through the OSHA file. "I completed the annual summary and sent it upstairs for review," you tell him. "Nothing to worry about. No injuries to report... I guess we're doing something right."*
>
> *Your phone is ringing as you return to your desk. It's Pete, the accounts receivable manager. "One of my employees says she refuses to work on her computer until we give her an antiglare screen. I'm ready to send her packing right now. What do you want me to do?"*
>
> *And yet another challenge awaits...*

?²The Quiz

1. State "OSHA" laws are as stringent—if not more so—than the federal health and safety standards.   ❑ True   ❑ False

2. OSHA requires you to discard all safety records after one year so as to reduce the risk of fire.   ❑ True   ❑ False

3. Only employers in construction, agriculture, and maritime are required to report workplace fatalities.   ❑ True   ❑ False

4. OSHA inspectors must give an employer 30 days' notice prior to an inspection.   ❑ True   ❑ False

5. OSHA offers numerous programs and compliance assistance initiatives to help employers conform to agency standards and the law.   ❑ True   ❑ False

Answer key: 1. T; 2. F; 3. F; 4. F; 5. T

Appendix

Appendix: Sample workplace safety policy

This sample safety policy can help you create a formal safety policy for your organization. It contains the essential elements of a safety policy and is broadly written to cover a variety of workplace environments that pose different hazards and degrees of danger.

Remember that there is no "one size fits all" safety policy. You'll need to customize and build upon this document to compose a policy that meets the unique needs of your organization.

SAFETY POLICY STATEMENT

Every employee is entitled to a safe and healthful place in which to work. To this end, [EMPLOYER] is committed to providing and maintaining a healthy and safe workplace. [EMPLOYER's] goal is to maintain a health and safety program that surpasses the best practices of our industry.

[EMPLOYER] intends to comply with all applicable laws and regulations, including the federal Occupational Safety and Health Act, rules and standards issued by the Occupational Safety and Health Administration, and state and local laws.

Beyond complying with the law, [EMPLOYER] will implement a safety and health program that strives to reduce or eliminate workplace injuries and illnesses. The personal health and safety of each employee is of primary importance. No employee is required to work at a job he/she knows is not safe or healthful. Prevention of workplace injuries and illnesses is of such consequence that it will be given precedence over operating productivity, whenever necessary.

[EMPLOYER] will make every reasonable effort to provide mechanical and physical hazard control, accident prevention, and health preservation in keeping with the highest safety standards.

[EMPLOYER's] objective is to reduce the incidence of injuries and illnesses to an absolute minimum. Our goal is zero accidents and injuries. To succeed, all employees of [EMPLOYER] must embody a commitment to health and safety. A successful program requires cooperation in all health and safety matters, not only between supervisors and employees, but between each employee and his/her coworkers. Only through such a joint effort can a health and safety program in the best interest of all employees be established and preserved.

Management, supervisors, and employees share responsibility for safety and health. Management accepts the responsibility for leadership of the safety and health program, for the program's effectiveness and improvement, and for providing safeguards to ensure safe working conditions. Supervisors must develop the proper attitudes toward safety and health in themselves and in the employees they supervise. They also must ensure that operations are performed with the highest regard for safety and health.

Employees are responsible for wholehearted, genuine cooperation with all aspects of the safety and health program. Employees should be alert to unsafe conditions. Your cooperation in detecting and reporting hazards and, in turn, controlling them, is a condition of your employment. Inform your supervisor immediately of any situation beyond your ability or authority to correct.

All employees of [EMPLOYER] are required to follow company safety and health rules. Employees who fail to comply are subject to disciplinary action, up to and including discharge.

[EMPLOYER's] safety and health program includes the following elements:

◆ conducting safety and health inspections to find and eliminate unsafe working conditions or practices, to control health hazards, and to comply fully with all applicable safety and health standards;

◆ training employees in good safety and health practices;

◆ encouraging employees to get involved in improving workplace safety;

◆ providing any necessary personal protective equipment and instructions for its use and care;

◆ developing and enforcing safety and health rules and requiring employees to comply with these rules as a condition of employment;

◆ investigating every accident to determine its cause and correct the problem;

◆ establishing a system of recognition and awards for outstanding safety performance.

(Source: excerpted in part from CCH Safety Management Handbook *by Barnett Lawrence, 1998; and* Guide to Developing Your Written Health and Safety Program, *State of Wisconsin, Department of Administration, Bureau of State Risk Management.)*

SAFETY PROGRAM

Your safety is [EMPLOYER's] constant concern. We have taken every precaution to provide a safe workplace. The safety policy and rules in this document are part of a larger initiative to reduce injuries and illness at work.

[NAME], Director of Safety, makes regular inspections and holds regular safety meetings. [He or she] also meets with management to plan and implement further improvements in our safety program. The executive team, human resources, and your immediate managers share the commitment to safety, and also have responsibility for executing the components of the safety program.

The list of rules below is not inclusive. Any clearly unsafe practices or actions, regardless of whether they are identified below, will be considered violations of the safety policy. Common sense and your personal interest in safety are still the greatest guarantees of your safety at work, on the road, and at home.

SAFETY EQUIPMENT

Your supervisor will see that you receive the protective clothing and equipment required for your job. Use them as instructed and take care of them. You will be charged for loss or destruction of these articles only when it occurs through negligence. You are required to wear these items if they have been provided to you. Failure to wear personal protective equipment is grounds for disciplinary action.

Safety shoes. The company will designate which jobs and work areas require safety shoes. Under no circumstances will an employee be permitted to work in sandals or open-toe shoes. A reliable safety shoe vendor will visit the company periodically. Notices will be posted prior to the visits.

Safety glasses. The wearing of safety glasses by all shop employees is mandatory. Strict adherence to this policy can significantly reduce the risk of eye injuries.

Seat belts. All employees must use seat belts and shoulder restraints (if available) whenever they operate a vehicle on company business. The driver is responsible for seeing that all passengers in front and rear seats are buckled up.

SAFETY RULES

To ensure your safety, and that of your coworkers, please observe and obey the following rules and guidelines:

+ Observe and practice the safety procedures established for your job
+ Don't distract another employee, as you might cause him or her to be injured. If you must get a coworker's attention, wait until you can do so safely.
+ Do not wear loose clothing or jewelry around machinery. It may catch on moving equipment and cause a serious injury.
+ Wear hard-sole shoes and appropriate clothing. Shorts or mini dresses are not permitted.
+ Where required, you must wear protective equipment, such as goggles, safety glasses, masks, gloves, hairnets, or any other gear provided for your safety.
+ Use designated passages when moving from one place to another; never take hazardous shortcuts.

- Do not tamper with electric controls or switches.
- Do not adjust, clean, or oil moving machinery.
- Keep machine guards in their intended place.
- Do not operate machines or equipment until you have been properly instructed and authorized to do so by your supervisor.
- Safety equipment such as restraints, pull-backs, and two-hand devices are designed for your protection. Be sure such equipment is adjusted for you.
- Shut down your machine before cleaning, repairing, or leaving.
- Tow motors and lift trucks will be operated only by authorized personnel. Walk-type lift trucks will not be ridden and no one but the operator is permitted to ride the tow motors. Do not exceed a speed that is safe for existing conditions.
- Use compressed air only for the job for which it is intended. Do not clean your clothes with it and do not fool with it.
- Smoking is not permitted anywhere on the premises.
- Lift properly–use your legs, not your back. For heavier loads, ask for assistance.
- Do not throw objects.
- Running and horseplay are strictly forbidden.
- Keep your work area clean.
- Do not block access to exits, fire equipment, lighting or power panels, or valves.
- Do not pile materials, skids, bins, boxes, or other equipment in aisles or stairways or in a manner that would block ingress or egress.
- Fire doors and aisles must be kept clear.
- Place trash and paper in proper containers.
- Clean up spills, drips, and leaks immediately.
- Report at once to your supervisor if you become injured or ill at work, no matter how slight the apparent injury or illness.
- Do not treat your own or another person's injuries. Never attempt to remove foreign particles from the eye.
- In case of injury resulting in possible fracture to legs, back, or neck, or any accident resulting in loss of consciousness or severe head injury, do not move the employee until medical attention has been given by authorized personnel.
- Report any unsafe condition or acts to your supervisor.
- Do not engage in such other practices as may be inconsistent with ordinary and reasonable common sense safety rules.

SAFETY CHECKLIST

Every employee is responsible to be on the lookout for possible hazards. If you spot one of the following conditions, or any other potential hazards, report it to your supervisor or safety officer immediately.

- ◆ Blocked aisles
- ◆ Blocked fire doors, extinguishers, hose sprinkler heads
- ◆ Dangerously piled supplies or equipment
- ◆ Directional or warning signs not in place
- ◆ Electrical equipment left operating
- ◆ Evidence of any equipment running hot or overheating
- ◆ Evidence of smoking in nonsmoking areas
- ◆ Leaks of steam, water, oil, etc.
- ◆ Loose handrails or guard rails
- ◆ Loose or broken windows
- ◆ Machine, power transmission, or drive guards missing, damaged, loose, or improperly placed
- ◆ Missing (or inoperative) entrance and exit signs and lighting
- ◆ Oily rags
- ◆ Open doors on electrical panels
- ◆ Poorly lighted stairs
- ◆ Roof leaks
- ◆ Safety devices not operating properly
- ◆ Slippery floors and walkways
- ◆ Tripping hazards, such as hose links, piping, etc.
- ◆ Unlocked doors and gates

REPORTING PROCEDURES

You are expected to report unsafe conditions or hazards immediately to your supervisor, safety officer, or member of the safety committee. This includes an obligation to report safety rule violations to your supervisor as well.

Any accident or incident, including a near miss, must be reported to your supervisor.

Any injury at work, no matter how minor it may appear, must be reported immediately to your supervisor and receive first aid attention.

DISCIPLINARY POLICY

[EMPLOYER] takes the safety of its employees seriously. You are expected to do the same. The cooperation of every employee is necessary to make this a safe place to work. While the standard progressive discipline policy may be used in the event of safety rule violations, management reserves the right to immediately discharge employees who jeopardize their own safety and the safety of their coworkers. Any willful or habitual violation of safety rules will be cause for dismissal.

FOR MORE INFORMATION

Questions about the safety policy in general should be directed to [NAME], [EMPLOYER'S] Director of Safety. Contact [NAME] in Human Resources if you have questions about workers' compensation, leave, or related issues.

If you are uncertain about how to adhere to specific safety rules in your operating area, consult with your immediate supervisor.

You are also encouraged to speak with members of the Safety Committee to discuss safety concerns or share your input regarding the safety program or ways to reduce injuries or illnesses in the workplace. Committee members are listed below.

Index